The Weary Boys

The Weary Boys

Colonel J. Warren Keifer and the 110th Ohio Volunteer Infantry

~♥ *Thomas E. Pope*

The Kent State University Press ⊠ Kent & London

©2002 by The Kent State University Press, Kent, Ohio 44242
All rights reserved
Library of Congress Catalog Card Number 2001003956
ISBN 0-87338-729-5
Manufactured in the United States of America

06 05 04 03 02   5 4 3 2 1

Library of Congress Cataloging-in-Publication Data
Pope, Thomas E., 1963–
    The Weary Boys : Colonel J. Warren Keifer and the 110th Ohio Volunteer Infantry /
Thomas E. Pope
        p. cm.
Includes bibliographical references and index.
ISBN 0-87338-729-5 (pbk. : alk. paper)
1. United States—Army—Ohio Infantry Regiment, 110th (1862–1865) 2. Ohio—History—
Civil War, 1861–1865—Regimental histories. 3. United States—History—Civil War, 1861–
1865—Regimental histories. 4. Keifer, Joseph Warren, 1836–1932. 5. Ohio—History—Civil
War, 1861–1865—Social aspects. 6. United States—History—Civil War, 1861–1865—Social
aspects. I. Title
    E525.5 110th .P66 2002
    973.7'4771—dc21

2001003956

British Library Cataloging-in-Publication data are available.

To my wife and sons—
Carolyn, Jonathan, Nicholas, and Evan.
And to my parents—
Bill and Sue.

Contents

Illustrations & Maps

Preface

As an adolescent, I visited my grandparents and looked through many of their prized possessions. Several items remain in the forefront of my memory: a diary, a captain's log, and a medal. During those visits, I spent many hours pouring over the diary and log, and I was thoroughly intrigued by the information contained in those treasured items. My ancestor, John McColley, faithfully recorded his business transactions and daily occurrences for many decades. It was this initial exposure to primary-source material that started my journey into historical research.

In a walnut display case handcrafted by my grandfather, my grandparents kept several items of sentimental value. I was always drawn to one in particular that was prominently displayed there, my great-great-grandfather's Grand Army of the Republic medal. Like any inquisitive youngster, I questioned my grandmother about this fantastic artifact, and she proudly proclaimed that it was her grandfather's Civil War medal.

On subsequent visits, I was continually drawn to these wonderful treasures. With a desire for more information, I questioned my father about the medal. Being a former social studies teacher, he began telling me stories about the Civil War. Then, while in junior high school, I continued my quest for more knowledge about the war and how my ancestor fit into it. My father quickly suggested that I read some Civil War books that he had, handing me Bruce Catton's classic works. I was hooked.

Shortly after beginning my teaching career at Graham High School in St. Paris, Ohio, I entered graduate school at Wright State University and chose the thesis track. Early on, I decided to research and write a regimental history. I discovered that a local regiment, the 66th Ohio Infantry, did not have a written unit history. I spent a year conducting preliminary research and was just beginning to search for primary sources when I discovered that another historian was much further along in his 66th Ohio research. After consulting with my thesis director, Dr. Edward Haas, I scrapped the project. I then jotted down information on several other local regiments and began preliminary research. As my notes mounted, I discovered that the 110th Ohio Volunteer Infantry, an organization that had seen significant action, did not have a regimental history. I also found that its colonel became a lesser known, but undoubtedly significant, figure in the Republican party.

While researching the regiment, I learned that the 110th and the rest of the Second Brigade, Third Division, Sixth Army Corps, were, in fact, the organizations that had been derisively named "Milroy's Weary Boys." In the aftermath of the Second Battle of Winchester, Maj. Gen. Robert Milroy's division had run from a numerically superior Confederate force. When the division's remnants were consolidated and assigned to the Army of the Potomac, the 110th was not universally accepted. Many Eastern Theater veterans shunned the newcomers, and Maj. Gen. Winfield Scott Hancock gave the 110th Ohio their epithet.

Many modern historians have perpetuated the inaccurate portrayal of this regiment and its brigade. I used this misnomer in the book's title because I firmly believe that the nickname should be viewed in a completely different light. Rather than accept the shame usually associated with "Milroy's Weary Boys," I believe that the 110th Ohio Volunteer Infantry should wear the epithet with honor. The 110th performed admirably during its service, and on many occasions the regiment excelled where many others would have failed. In fact, Ohio contributed approximately 175 regiments of infantry and cavalry to the Union armies, with only fifteen Ohio regiments suffering more than one hundred battle deaths. Col. J. Warren Keifer's "Weary Boys" is among this honored group.

When I began, I envisioned this book as being strictly a military history. Then, as I delved into the letters and diaries of the soldiers, I became enthralled with the human aspect and the social history. I especially enjoyed the descriptions used by the soldiers regarding the drudgery of camp life and when their emotions poured forth in postcombat writings. Whenever possible, I maintained the soldiers' exact spellings and phrasings.

As I searched and found the primary sources necessary for this study, I encountered many helpful people. I consulted many of my former colleagues at Graham High School. Many of them proofread material, and I solicited their advice on various other ideas. I must thank Mike Apswisch, Kelly Braun, Melissa Brandewie, Rich Dickert, Larry Moore, Rich Randall, Jack Wood, and the rest of the Graham High School staff for their time, patience, and encouragement. Floyd Barman, Heather Turner, and Virginia Weygandt of the Clark County Historical Society, Springfield, Ohio, were wonderful. I greatly appreciate the help, advice, and additional privileges they granted me. Nan Card and the staff at the Hayes Presidential Library, Fremont, Ohio, were of great service. Gary Arnold, archives specialist at the Ohio Historical Society helped locate many sources.

My friend and author of *A Light and Uncertain Hold,* the late David T. Thackery, gave me wonderful advice and pointed me to many sources. I sorely miss our conversations and discussions. Jim Oda, the Piqua history coordinator; the staff of the Greene County Room, Xenia, Ohio; and many others contributed greatly to this endeavor. Dr. Carl Becker and Dr. Barbara Green, both of Wright State University, offered much advice. Roger Long of Port Clinton, Ohio, made significant commentary on the final draft. I must also thank Mrs. Sue Frary of Cincinnati, Ohio, and Mr. Robert G. Hill of Sidney, Ohio, for letting me use the letters and diaries in their possession. Rick Pope did a fantastic job creating maps. John Hubbell, Joanna Hildebrand Craig, Erin Holman, Perry Sundberg, Christine Brooks, and the rest of the Kent State University Press staff were especially patient with me. They readily answered the many questions that I had and they offered excellent advice throughout the manuscript process.

Dr. Edward Haas of Wright State University, Dayton, Ohio, greatly contributed to this work. He edited the seemingly endless number of drafts and revisions. Dr. Haas taught me how to be a historian, and with words of encouragement he pushed me to excel. Though these individuals made significant contributions, I must take full responsibility for any inaccuracies and mistakes.

Finally, I must give special thanks to my wife, Carolyn. She has been especially patient with me and my obsession to complete this book. For the past four years, she has kept the household running and, quite often, pulled double duty as parent. Without the love and stability that Carolyn brings to my life, I could not have begun or completed this study.

Our Colonel has been doing his best to get us
prepared right for service and he says he thinks
he has the men to do the fighting with.
—*Pvt. John F. Rosser*

1 The Union, Now, Henceforth, Forever! Amen

Shortly after the firing on Fort Sumter, various militia organizations offered their services to the United States. President Abraham Lincoln called for 75,000 troops, and volunteers throughout the North enthusiastically responded to his request. Many men of west-central Ohio joined this show of support for Lincoln's policies. On April 17, 1861, the *Springfield Morning News* patriotically called to Clark County citizens, proclaiming that the Union faced a formidable foe, and the county must immediately raise five hundred men to defend their country. Citizens quickly formed three companies that moved to the defense of Washington, D.C. The next day, the Springfield Zouaves left Clark County and joined the 2d Ohio Volunteer Militia as Company F. Five days later, Capt. James Vananda's Springfield Washington Guards left the city. Capt. Philip Kershner's Jefferson Guards left for Columbus on the twenty-sixth. Springfield and Clark County also contributed two home guard companies and one company of cavalry. The surrounding communities reacted with similar swiftness. On April 18, the villages of Enon and Yellow Springs formed military committees to recruit and equip local units.[1]

Miami County citizens also responded quickly. The Covington Blues formed Company I of the 2d Ohio Volunteer Militia, while a company from Piqua served as Company J in the same regiment. Citizens of Xenia and Greene County also formed committees that enlisted and equipped soldiers. On April 17, local residents held their first meeting outside the courthouse in Xenia, where they started a pledge list for outfitting the companies. First on the list was John B. Allen, who pledged one thousand dollars. By April 24, two Xenia companies completed their organizations, while by May 1, a third Xenia unit formed. As the war's novelty faded and the populace questioned the conflict's length, however, enthusiasm for recruitment waned. Necessity forced Lincoln to take a more aggressive approach to filling the ranks. He pursued two different methods: drafts and bounties.[2]

The administration tried conscription first. According to the Militia Act of 1862, the Federal government established state quotas and would intervene with a state's raising of troops only when it failed to meet its goal. When this happened, Washington threatened conscription of eligible males ages eighteen to forty-five. Seeking to avoid this, on July 3, 1862, Governor David Tod issued a proclamation for additional troops. He stated that for Ohio to avoid conscription, it would have to raise forty thousand recruits. Each county was responsible for filling its share of the quota, and if a county did not meet its number, conscription would result.[3]

On July 8, 1862, in response to Governor Tod's plea, the Clark County Bar Association inquired about raising multicounty regiments. Commissioned by the organization, Judge William White and Col. Harvey Vinar contacted the state Adjutant General's Office and coordinated this recruitment effort with neighboring counties. This idea was apparently consistent with plans that the office itself developed. State authorities divided Ohio into districts and subdistricts. The Fourth Military District consisted of Montgomery, Preble, Butler, Greene, Darke, Miami, and Clark Counties. The first three composed one subdistrict, while the latter four were formed a second subdistrict. On August 13, the Adjutant General's Office authorized the formation of two regiments, later designated them the 94th and the 110th Ohio Volunteer Infantry Regiments, in the Fourth Military District's northern subdistrict.[4]

Col. Warren Keifer. Courtesy of Brad Pruden.

During a meeting of the district's board, the members elected regimental staff officers for the 110th. They appointed Lt. Col. J. Warren Keifer of the 3d Ohio Infantry, a prominent lawyer from Springfield in Clark County, as colonel of the 110th. The board then selected Capt. John Drury of Troy in Miami County as the regiment's lieutenant colonel. Albert Stark of Xenia (Greene County) and Capt. Charles Matchett of the 40th Ohio Infantry, a resident of Greenville (Darke County) held the offices of quartermaster and major, respectively. Each appointment was a unanimous decision, and the officers' residence played a factor in the process.[5]

Prominent local citizens typically recruited the companies, therefore each had a distinct regional flavor. Enterprising individuals received a commission as captain with the understood condition that they must produce a predetermined number of recruits. If they could not meet their quota, their commission then passed to another man. The men of each unit elected most of the noncommissioned officers, though the captains and the Military

Commission appointed some sergeants. The Military Commission usually found a respectable person whom local men would follow.[6]

Officer changes appeared quite frequently throughout the war. In the early stages, when enlistment was a key to company formation, the various military boards positioned individuals primarily for recruitment purposes. Local men typically wanted respected leaders from their area as officers. Use of influential individuals in these roles was essential, and in many instances, upon this assignment's completion, such officers resigned. Apparently, this was the case with William Yeazell and Jason Young. The Adjutant General's Office commissioned both men to raise companies. Yeazell recruited much of what would become Company I of the 110th Ohio, but he never mustered with the regiment. Captain Young recruited what would become Company B, mustered and trained with the regiment, but on December 18, 1862, resigned his commission.[7]

John Drury, selected as lieutenant colonel of the 110th, never mustered with the unit. He remained captain of Company B of the 94th Ohio and, on October 8, 1862, died at the Battle of Perryville, Kentucky. Charles Matchett also remained with his original regiment, the 40th Ohio Volunteer Infantry. In their stead, the Fourth District Military Commission appointed prominent Miami County individuals. On September 1, 1862, Otho Binkley, a well-known Republican in Troy, became acting major. Twelve days later, William N. Foster, the mayor of Piqua and a very influential Miami County Democrat, filled Drury's position as lieutenant colonel.[8]

In July 1862, Clark County began organizing its companies. The Military Commission sanctioned Capt. Nathan S. Smith and Capt. William Yeazell to raise companies. Smith's unit mustered in as Company C, while Yeazell's became Company I. Captain Smith gathered the requisite number of recruits, but he did make several return trips to Springfield in September for further recruiting.

To meet their goals, Clark County recruiters held a mass meeting at the county fairgrounds. The guest speaker was G. Volney Dorsey of Piqua. During the Civil War, Dorsey, a powerful regional Republican, served as Ohio's secretary of treasury. On August 22, the push for recruits was successful despite a heavy morning rain that reduced attendance. After the weather improved that afternoon, attendance increased and twelve men enlisted.[9]

This mass meeting did not end recruiting efforts in Clark County. Being unable to fill his company, Captain Yeazell never mustered with his unit, and his commission passed to Luther Brown, a prominent businessman. Brown, a major in the Springfield Independents militia organization, completed Company I's recruitment. He filled the company roster with twenty-five more men and then assumed command. Throughout the month of September, Captains Smith and Brown returned to Springfield to continue their efforts. Work proceeded from the recruiting office first located at the Henkel Law Offices. The new regiment's needs were diverse. A *Springfield Republic* advertisement, for instance, reported that during one of Brown's recruiting trips, he sought the enlistment of forty cooks of African descent. Captain Brown later used enticements that remained consistent with government regulations, offering $302 for new recruits and $402 for veteran recruits, with $75 paid upon enlistment and the balance upon completion of service.[10]

To encourage enlistment, the county governments enticed individuals into military service with bounties. Under state government authorization, counties established bounties at a rate necessary for filling their portion of the state's forty-thousand-man quota. According to the Ohio General Assembly, counties could levy taxes, sell bonds, or borrow money to provide sufficient resources. The state legislature, however, restricted the bounty system by setting the maximum interest rate on borrowed money at 6 percent per annum. Another restriction disallowed the transfer of surplus funds from bounty coffers. Dependents of bounty recipients killed in Federal service received the recruit's unpaid balance.[11]

The counties paid bounties by various methods. Some governments divided payments into three equal allotments, but overall they paid some bounty upon enlistment with the balance upon completion of service. The bounty offered for recruits in Xenia, for example, was $140. Greene County paid $65 of its bounty at enlistment and the balance upon completion of three years service. The amount differed for the neighboring Miami County towns of Piqua and Troy. Each offered a $35 bonus at enlistment. In one instance, a Greene County recruit's bounty was $100, of which county officials paid only $25 at enlistment.[12]

Company D, which organized in Greene County, had trouble receiving their money altogether. In their case, county authorities postponed payment, though the recruits continued to fulfill their obligation. Through bureaucratic oversight, this delay continued into December 1862. Greene County authorities, finally, addressed the issue after a *Xenia Torchlight* editorial informed local residents that some of the men's families faced eviction.[13]

Miami County recruitment centered on three individuals: Joseph C. Ullery, William D. Alexander, and William R. Moore. Captain Ullery filled what would become Company G with men from the western portion of the county. His recruits came mainly from the villages of Pleasant Hill, Laura, and Covington and their surrounding townships. Piqua men dominated the rolls of the future Company A. Their captain, William D. Alexander, a prominent Democrat in Piqua, taught school in Troy.[14]

William R. Moore, a lawyer from Lena, Ohio, who had previously taught school in Troy with Captain Alexander, recruited Company E from Miami County's eastern section. Moore's recruitment efforts focused on the town of Troy and the villages of Casstown, Lena, Conover, and Fletcher. Additional men for Company E came from Elizabeth, Brown, and Lost Creek Townships. Recruitment of this area, however, did not end in October 1862. After the 110th Ohio mustered into service, Lt. Joseph McKnight conducted many recruiting trips through April 1864. His later visits covered the regions where these three companies formed.[15]

These communities' influential citizens contributed greatly to recruitment efforts. No matter how noble the cause, however, this type of system lent itself to corruption. Use of personal influence usually carried consequences or contained hidden agendas. In one instance, Rev. Lucius Chapman willingly aided Sgt. Wesley Devenney's recruitment efforts in exchange for Captain Moore's effort to secure Chapman's commission as regimental chaplain. Similarly, in a letter to Sergeant Devenney, Dr. Thomas Beamer of Fletcher, Miami County, reminded the sergeant of the political power that Dr. Beamer wielded and how that power secured Devenney's office with the Military Commission. Beamer then asked Devenney to secure James Howell's selection as second sergeant in Captain Moore's Company E, which was then forming in the Fletcher and Brown Township region. Ultimately, Sergeant Devenney acquiesced and secured Howell's appointment.[16]

This type of politicking and use of influence was not atypical. Further investigation, however, revealed Dr. Beamer's true motives. In his letters, Captain Moore described James Howell's unfortunate situation and suggested that he "should return home with his rifle and shoot Dr. Beamer and Mrs. Howell for the way they are carrying on."[17]

Jason Young and Joseph Snodgrass primarily recruited in the southern portion of Darke County. The villages and townships surrounding Greenville and Arcanum produced the most soldiers for Companies B and H. Captains

William S. McElwaine and Aaron Spangler, with authorization from the Military Commission, raised two companies of Greene County men. Their recruitment efforts focused on the towns of Xenia, Fairfield, and Osborn, though a small percentage of the men came from outlying townships.[18]

During the last half of August 1862, these companies reported to Camp Piqua. Captains Alexander, Yeazell, and Young reported there first, bringing in part of their commands while still filling their companies. Originally, these three commanders recruited for the 94th, but each failed to complete their organization in time. They subsequently continued enrolling men and entered service with the 110th.[19]

On the nineteenth, the morning reports of Camp Piqua showed that the companies of W. D. Alexander, W. E. Yeazell, and J. Young totaled an aggregate of 99, 67, and 80 men and officers respectively. The commands of Alexander and Young continued their growth and increased to 102 and 108 men. Captain Yeazell's company aggregate, however, stagnated at 79, which then gave Luther Brown his opportunity to complete the organization.[20]

Six days later, Captains Joseph Snodgrass and Nathan Smith arrived at Camp Piqua. Their companies reported with complements of more than 100 men. Capt. William Moore's unit arrived with 62 men on the twenty-sixth, while Captains William S. McElwaine and Aaron Spangler arrived in the command of 102 and 88 men respectively on August 27. That same day, an additional detachment arrived for Captain Moore's company and swelled his command to 86 men.[21]

By October 1862, counties had to fill their quota or institute a draft. Draft records for the military subdistrict of Clark, Darke, Greene, and Miami Counties revealed that only Darke and Greene resorted to conscription. The Adjutant General's Office ordered Clark and Miami to draft 75 and 205 men respectively. Although they never indicated how many men volunteered in Clark County, the records show that there were no draftees enrolled by October 28. By then the Adjutant General's Office had credited Miami County with 266 volunteers and therefore excluded it from conscription.[22]

State authorities additionally ordered Darke County to draft 458 men. At the end of October, it had accredited 141 volunteers to the books and subsequently drafted 317 men. To fill its quota, Greene County needed to draft 150 men, though with 25 recruits credited toward its quota, the Adjutant General's Office reduced the draft requirement to 125 men. By October 28, records indicate that 25 men were draftees and another 72 were volunteers, leaving a balance of 28 men.

Other Ohio counties also failed to meet their quotas and conscripted individuals into service. Many men in Company K, led by Capt. John M. Smith, for example, were draftees. They resided in the Massillon area and in mid-November 1862, entered into service at Camp Mansfield.[23]

During the regiment's years of service, 1,240 individuals served. Of these, 769 enlisted during August 1862, while 43, 18, and 57 enlisted in September, October, and November respectively. August recruits accounted for 62 percent of all enlistments. Company B claimed 95 recruits for that month, and these composed 82.6 percent of their total company organization. This represents the greatest total by volume and by percent for individual companies' August recruits. The regiment's 341 recruits after November 1862 accounted for 27.5 percent of the men who served. There were 63 draftees and 85 substitutes in the regiment, with Company K claiming 24 and 30 of each. Regimental draftees constituted 5.1 percent of the total enrollment, while substitutes accounted for an additional 6.9 percent.

The men came from a full range of ages, sixteen to fifty-five years old. Three boys sixteen years of age served in the regiment: George Huffman of Company C enlisted on August 16, 1862, and died in a hospital in Cincinnati on October 15, 1864. Samuel Simpson enlisted in Company G on October 3, 1862, and on September 6, 1863, received a discharge with a surgeon's disability. On August 16, 1862, Frederick Pinkerton of Company E also enlisted. Captured at Winchester on June 15, 1863, he eventually mustered out with the regiment on June 25, 1865.

Several men over forty-five years old enlisted in the 110th Ohio. At fifty-five years of age, Pvt. John McNamee was the regiment's oldest soldier. On October 5, 1862, he enlisted in Company D as a substitute, and on April 15, 1864, transferred to the Veteran Reserve Corps. Privates James Turner and James Underwood, ages fifty and forty-eight respectively, mustered in with Company F, and on December 8, 1863, Pvt. Timothy Green, forty-eight years of age, enlisted in Company I. On August 18, 1862, at forty-seven years of age, Pvt. Samuel Canaday enlisted in Company C. Mustering out with the regiment on June 25, 1865, Timothy Green was the only one of these men who completed his full length of service.

The regiment's mean age was 24.6 years old, with Company A offering the youngest mean of 22.1 years and Company C offering the oldest mean at

27.2 years. The median age was 23 years, with little deviation among the companies. The regiment's mode age was 18 years old. Company D was the only group that varied, with a mode of 19 years old.

A numerical analysis shows that the number of enlistments per age divided into distinct groups. Only 22 recruits were under eighteen years old, while 185 recruits were eighteen years old at enlistment. The ages of nineteen to twenty-three rendered from 78 to 109 men per age, while ages twenty-four to twenty-seven inducted from 54 to 65 men per group. Men aged twenty-eight to thirty-two entered from 32 to 34 men per age, with thirty-one-year olds offering only 17 men to the regiment. From 11 to 17 were aged from thirty-three to forty years, while the over-forty age groups offered fewer than 11 men per age category.

On October 2, 1862, the regiment's original nine companies mustered into Federal service at Camp Piqua. The mustering officer was Capt. Edward A. Drake. Afterward, the 110th remained at Camp Piqua for another two weeks while it continued to train and drill. Colonel Keifer, a veteran of the Civil War's Western Theater, understood the necessity of proper preparation. He wanted the 110th to be proficient at drill before the regiment first experienced combat. Efficiency in company and battalion maneuvers, in his opinion, promoted regimental combat effectiveness and ensured the men's lives and safety. Keifer's passion for drill indeed never abated. After the 110th Ohio Infantry left Camp Piqua for the Eastern Theater, and as weather permitted, he regularly drilled the regiment.[24]

While at Camp Piqua, the 110th received French muzzle-loading rifled muskets, primarily for drilling purposes. Colonel Keifer continually petitioned the Adjutant General's Office and Governor David Tod to acquire Springfield rifled muskets. On December 12, 1863, while it was stationed at New Creek Station, Virginia, the regiment finally received their Springfield rifles. Colonel Keifer upgraded the regiment's weapons on May 23, 1863, by acquiring Henry rifles, weapons that could shoot sixteen times before reloading, for the regiment's sharpshooters. These procurements caused considerable jealousy among Ohio regiments stationed in the Shenandoah Valley.[25]

On many occasions, Union infantrymen exchanged seasonal items. The soldiers requested their boots, gloves, coats, and other winter necessities during the fall and just prior to entering winter quarters. The colonel gave his wife, Eliza, specific instructions regarding his winter necessities.

The officers and men of the 110th conducted a similar exchange each spring just prior to the start of the campaign season. They sent their winter accouterments to their homes or to storage in Washington, D.C. Members of the regiment sent home extra belongings via express box, by friend, or in the case of army-issued supplies, through the quartermaster department. Colonel Keifer also sent material home via recruiting officers and camp workers. He additionally shipped to Ohio materials by way of the sutler, Harry C. Smith, who did not have authorization to travel with the army on campaign, on one occasion entrusting Smith with his horse. In the fall of 1863, Colonel Keifer requested that his wife send a box containing his buffalo robe and overcoat with Captain Brown, who was then recruiting in Springfield. At the end of October, however, Keifer received the aforementioned items from Smith, who had just returned after the campaign season.[26]

Union infantrymen supplemented their normal complement of material by purchasing goods from their regimental sutler. These enterprising individuals received government permission and established supplemental stores within the confines of individual regiments. The goods that they sold were not government issue. Only one sutler received commission per regiment and, therefore, had a local monopoly on supplemental supplies. Harry Smith of New Carlisle was the man for the 110th.

Soldiers often viewed the sutler with contempt. Though vital in supplying the army, the merchant charged exorbitant prices for his goods, gouging his clients. Pvt. Robert Baird listed, to cite one example, the prices that he encountered at the sutler's store: "10 cents for 4 small apples, 7 cents per pound for cornmeal, 60 cents per pound cakes, figs 3 for 5 cents, oranges 5 cents a piece and about the size of a walnut."[27]

Baird further revealed his disgust for the sutler in a letter that described Smith's fright, and subsequent flight, prior to the spring campaign of 1864. The private and several other men guarded the camp, while the balance of the regiment skirmished with Rebel troops. When the Army of Northern Virginia moved and threatened the possibility of a spring offensive, sutler Smith panicked and hastily prepared to leave the vicinity. In his haste, Smith packed his wares with the help of the guard detail and fled from the region. Baird and the detail "helped him to pack up. I got all the apples I could eat besides the other little things that tasted pretty good in the shape of figs, cakes, candy, oranges, and cigars. I was tempted to steal a piece of beef but I dident know what to do with it after I got it so I left it!" He and the other soldiers thus achieved a measure of retribution for Smith's abuse of the system, "no harm stealing from the sutler for it is the onely way we can get even with him the way he cheats us is a sight!"[28]

Additionally, Cpl. John Rhoades wrote about other abuses of the sutler system. Smith, for instance, issued checks for the men but charged a high interest rate for them and granted loans that carried a heavy interest burden. He additionally exchanged notes and materials for a price. Rhoades believed that each practice was offensive, but a twenty-five-cent surcharge for exchanging any bills especially angered him.[29]

Union soldiers also received a significant amount of material from home. Family and friends used various methods to ship goods to loved ones in the Army of the Potomac. The use of express boxes was apparently the most common method. These carried a full range of goods to the 110th. On one occasion, Rhoades requested that his wife "send three pounds of butter, dried fruit, tea, and thread."[30]

According to many soldiers, abuses by inspectors took a heavy toll on material shipped to the army. On one occasion, Lt. William Hathaway lost all things of value from an express box. Robert Baird reported that another sent to the Harmony boys of Company I was missing items. To avoid additional inspection by thieving detectives at the post office, family and friends took many precautions when shipping goods to the army. Colonel Keifer, for example, recommended the use of strong wooden boxes that were tightly sealed. The men also strongly suggested the inclusion of packing lists.[31]

Sending parcels with men returning from furlough was the second most common method used to ship goods. Officers and men returning to the regiment from leave and officers returning from a recruiting trip often carried packages. For example, on June 2, 1864, a notice posted in the *Piqua Enquirer* clearly illustrates this practice. "Lieutenant John Shearer and John Cotterman will start for the 110th, on Monday next, and those wishing to send small packages, such as letters & c., can do so by leaving them at Williamson's or Davis's grocery stores." In a letter dated February 2, 1863, Cpl. John Rhoades thanked his wife, Sarah, for sending a letter and package with William Heath; Rhoades added that the food tasted great.[32]

On numerous occasions, soldiers used these same methods to send items home. They adhered to the same precautions when using express boxes to send goods home. On rare occasions, persons entrusted with goods for men in the regiment failed to fulfill their obligation. Near the close of the

110th Ohio Field Officers. *From left:* Lt. Col. William Foster, Col. J. Warren Keifer, Maj. Otho Binkley. Courtesy of Larry Strayer.

war, Corporal Rhoades sent books home with William Starry, but he later heard that Starry left the books at the rail station.[33]

In answer to the Federal government's call for troops, the State of Ohio and the Fourth Military District recruited a new regiment, the 110th Volunteer Infantry. The eight hundred soldiers who initially formed the unit came from diverse backgrounds. Well-respected men of these various communities such as Luther Brown, William McElwaine, William Moore, and Joseph Snodgrass recruited the companies. Likewise, the Military Commission selected respectable and influential local men to lead the regiment, including J. Warren Keifer, William Foster, and Otho Binkley as colonel, lieutenant colonel, and major, respectively, of the 110th Ohio. Each one was well known in his hometown and in neighboring cities as well.

When we left for Piqua, we were just

playing soldiers; now we are soldiers.

—Pvt. Charles H. Berry

2 Now We Are Soldiers

In the second week of June 1863, the regiment fought its first general engagement at the Second Battle of Winchester. Later that year, the 110th Ohio participated in Maj. Gen. George Meade's fall offensive, such as it was. And they endured Grant's spring offensive of May 4–June 22, 1864. The soldiers, however, had much idle time July–November 1863 and again from December 1863 through April 1864, during which they filled their time in camp with a variety of duties and leisure activities. Jubal Early's audacious raid in the summer of 1864 spread panic throughout Maryland and Pennsylvania. In response to this, the Sixth Corps, which included the 110th as part of the Third Division, separated from the Army of the Potomac. The regiment first moved to Maryland and then continued to the Shenandoah Valley. For over three months, the Sixth Corps chased the army of Confederate lieutenant general Jubal Early. During this period, the corps fought three skirmishes and three general engagements. Then, in December 1864, it transferred to Petersburg, south of Richmond, and participated in siege operations there. Until May 15, 1865, the 110th Ohio helped occupy southern Virginia. Finally, after nearly three years, the regiment moved to Washington, D.C., to muster out of Federal service.[1]

By orders of Col. Warren Keifer, the 110th Ohio practiced company and battalion drill on a daily basis. Keifer delineated the details of a typical day:

5 A.M.	rise
6 A.M.	eat breakfast
7 A.M.	Surgeon's call - sick and in quarters
8:30 A.M.	Guard mounting
9 to 10 A.M.	Squad drill & Officer drill
10 A.M. to 12 P.M.	Company drill
12:30 P.M.	dinner
2–5 P.M.	Battalion drill
5 P.M.	Dress Parade
6 P.M.	Supper
7 to 8 P.M.	School of Instruction for Officers & Noncommissioned Officers.[2]

Each Sunday morning, Cpl. John Rhoades observed, began with an inspection. After buckling on their cartridge boxes, the men fell into two lines and the officers called roll. Afterward, with four paces separating the lines, each man executed order arms by placing the butt of his musket on the ground next to his right toe and putting the muzzle near his right shoulder. To complete the order of inspection arms, each soldier turned to the right, drew his bayonet, and affixed it to the barrel. With a sudden upward movement of the musket that caused the rammer to rebound, the officers checked each weapon for cleanliness. Before dismissing the men, they also inspected the soldiers' knapsacks. Each man held open his knapsack, and the officers checked to make sure all items were clean and in order.[3]

When the regiments were not on a campaign or consumed with drill, other duties occupied the soldier's time. For example, picket duty was an essential function of the infantrymen. Established one and one-half miles from the divisions of the corps, this early warning system prevented a surprise enemy attack. The corps officer of the day established this nine-mile length of picket posts. Normally, he was a brigade commander, with this responsibility rotating throughout the corps. After each army movement, the officer of the day used a specific procedure when posting the pickets. In the fall of 1863, after one such relocation, Colonel Keifer was officer of the day and established the picket line. He placed thirty three-man posts sixty yards apart. The soldiers of each alternately walked their assigned sixty-yard front. Two hundred yards behind these, Keifer positioned three reserve forces of 30 men each. Thus, he covered a one-mile front with about 180 men. After Colonel Keifer properly established the perimeter, "even a single man could not enter the line by day or night without his being discovered."[4]

The infantrymen served three days on picket duty and maintained their posts despite the season or weather. In April 1864, Pvt. Robert Baird picketed as "it rained and snowed nearly all the time we was out." He and his companions made a shack from pine bushes, but it proved ineffective, and the rain soaked the privates' blankets. To combat the cold and wet weather, they made a fire. Since the only wood available was unseasoned, the privates could barely keep the flames alive.[5]

Pickets proved vulnerable to capture once the enemy began a campaign. When the Army of Northern Virginia moved through the Shenandoah Valley in June 1863, the Confederates captured some members of the 110th Ohio who were on picket duty near Winchester. On the fifteenth, the Confederates captured Lieutenants Thomas Weakley and Charles Gross and sixty men from Companies G and I. Other hazards also endangered the pickets. For example, on December 23, 1862, Stephen Ransom fell into a well while on duty near Moorefield, Virginia. His comrades rescued him using ropes and a ladder.[6]

When the armies were not on campaign or the men were not otherwise occupied, soldiers spent time on guard duty. Wherever the army stationed the regiment, the troops alternated guard-duty assignments in the camps and forts with other garrison units. While occupying Winchester, Virginia, for example, the regiment rotated duty with other troops when manning the fortifications there.[7]

During their first occupation of Winchester, various companies of the 110th guarded the many supply trains traveling between Winchester and Halltown. On one occasion, two companies went with the wagons; Company E was in the vanguard, while Company G guarded the rear. On May 26, 1863, Company G once again accompanied a supply train as it foraged in the vicinity of Winchester.[8]

Noncommissioned officers rotated the schedule for picket- and guard-duty assignments. Guard duty for Division Quartermaster Headquarters rotated every eighty minutes. On one occasion, Cpl. John Rhoades needed to repair or replace his broken pocket watch so he would know when to change out the men.[9]

Fatigue-duty assignments consumed much time for the soldiers and varied considerably. While stationed at Winchester, the men labored many hours improving the forts and breastworks that surrounded the town; Company E worked regularly at this. On May 2, 1863, Corporal Rhoades complained about working on the fortifications, while two weeks later, Captain Moore noted that the company again received that detail. These assignments continued throughout the war.[10]

Fatigue duties also consisted of building improvements for winter quarters. During the winter of 1864–65, for example, Corporal Rhoades constructed a variety of headquarters buildings and stables. Similarly, during their first occupation of Winchester, Pvt. Henry Kauffman of Company I repaired the surrounding forts. The army placed large-caliber guns in one fort, and "next week we will have to move outside and have our fort repaired also and are going to put in five field pieces in it." As Kauffman noted, this construction project soon displaced him and his comrades.[11]

Soldiers spent many hours building their winter quarters. After the fall campaign of 1864, Rhoades constructed a temporary shelter, writing that the other "boys are beginning to fix up tents by cutting and splitting timber into slabs making a square pen then fixing their shelters on for a covering." Long periods in winter camps required that the soldiers build more permanent housing. The cold necessitated the establishment of "chebangs," as some called their shelters. On several occasions after the men in the regiment completed their quarters, orders would require that the 110th move to a new locale. They therefore constructed new buildings or renovated the structures already in existence at their new site. On April 1, 1864, after the reorganization of the Army of the Potomac, the regiment moved with its new parent organization, the Sixth Corps. Because of this, three companies were without quarters, and Companies A, B, and F consequently built new shacks.[12]

During the Mine Run campaign of November–December 1863, Union troops crossed the Rappahannock River. At the conclusion of this maneuvering, the 110th occupied the winter shelters that had once housed Confederate soldiers. Private Baird described the new accommodations as measuring twelve feet by ten feet and sheltering four men each. Colonel Keifer moved into a hut originally built for a Confederate general.[13]

Accordingly, company officers and regimental staff had many other duties as well. Officer-of-the-day responsibilities fell to various levels of command, not just to Colonel Keifer. Immediately after a relocation, this assignment required the reestablishment of picket posts. If the army remained idle for any length of time, the officer of the day rode and monitored the picket line the entire day. Company-grade officers commonly received assignments as division officer of the day; the responsibilities were similar to those of the corps officer of the day.

Officers filed many reports on a daily basis. They also forwarded various reports from regiment to brigade headquarters at specified intervals. The headquarters staff of the 110th Ohio routinely submitted the following information:

List of Returns and Reports to Be Forwarded to Brigade Head Quarters
  1. Monthly Returns on or before the last day of each month;
  2. Tri-Monthly Reports on the 6th, 16th, and 26th of each month;
  3. Nominal Statement of Casualties on the 6th, 16th, and 26th of each month;
  4. Description Lists for Deserters and men returned from Desertions Monthly;
  5. Nominal List of Commissioned Officers absent without leave on 14th and last day of each month;
  6. A summary of the proceedings of Regt'l Court Martials every Friday;
  7. Chaplains Monthly Reports on or before the 2nd of each month for the month preceeding;
  8. Ordnance Report by 8 o'clock A.M. every Friday;
  9. A Report of Enlisted Men employed as servants on the 29th of each month at 10 o'clock A.M.;
  10. Weekly report of Unequipped Men, when joined, where from & c, and loss and gain due on every Friday 9 o'clock A.M.;
  11. Report of Men discharged for disability within the Corps on the 6th, 16th, and 26th of each month.[14]

Additionally, officers filed official reports at the conclusion of each campaign. Colonel Keifer reported his command's role in each campaign. Whether he led the 110th Ohio or the Second Brigade, Third Division, Keifer filed reports for the Second Battle of Winchester, Bristoe, Mine Run, Wilderness, Opequon Creek (Third Battle of Winchester), Fisher's Hill, Cedar Creek, Petersburg, and Sayler's Creek. During the war's final year, while Colonel Keifer commanded at both the brigade and division levels, Maj. Otho Binkley commanded the 110th, and he too filed official reports after each campaign.[15]

Military units large or small moved on their stomachs, and the 110th Ohio was no exception. The U.S. government supplied rations for the soldiers. The most typical fare consisted of beef, beans, bread, potatoes, and coffee, an offering that remained consistent throughout the war. Usually, the company's cooks fried the meat for the dinner. Describing his turn at cooking, Corporal Rhoades "stoped & cooked some beef & bread for dinner. I put some sow belly in the pan & set it over the fire while I prepared my beef. . . . after frying beef I put in my bread which had got dry in the pan then poured watter over it and fried it in the gravy. So I had a nice dinner."[16]

On many occasions, the soldiers supplemented their rations with confiscated goods. In the summer and fall of 1864, as the Sixth Corps moved into the Shenandoah Valley, the enlisted men seized fresh produce and livestock from the local citizens. John Rosser and John Rhoades frequently wrote about getting fresh corn, potatoes, and onions. Rhoades sympathized with the women and children of the region, and he never invaded the local houses, unlike many of his comrades. Nevertheless, he acknowledged the need for such unwelcome entries. When he did enter local homesteads, Rhoades took only corn, apples, and salt, while younger soldiers chased geese, chickens, and other livestock. Occasionally, the men of the regiment "confiscated hogs, butchered and cooked them, then sold the hind quarter. Men without money received the front quarter."[17]

Packages from home also supplemented the soldiers' diet. Express boxes and men returning from furlough often arrived with a variety of foods. Comments about dried and canned fruit, butter, apple butter, and tea appear most often in letters. Rhoades requested "Hourhound Candy" for his cough and "if extra send dried or canned fruit." He told his wife, Sarah, not to send any chicken because the meat would likely spoil along the way.[18]

The sutlers and local citizens offered perishable goods and some delicacies for a price. Sutler Harry Smith commonly sold fruits and vegetables at his store. On July 24, 1864, Rosser noted the appearance of small watermelons priced at one dollar each. On November 6, Rhoades bought bread and butter from a local citizen for fifty cents. Private Kauffman complained that apples could be purchased for "five cents each, though that is rather steep for a boy of my cloth to buy."[19]

Major holidays that did not occur during the campaign season allowed the officers and men to receive additional food offerings. The Quartermaster's Department supplied individual dinners for the soldiers in celebration of each holiday. Meanwhile, the officers observed such days as

Christmas and New Year's Eve in grand fashion. For instance, in January 1864, they held a Third Corps Ball. Several weeks later, Maj. Gen. David Birney also held a dinner party with many influential Philadelphians in attendance. Several regiments also sponsored dances during this winter.[20]

After completing drills and fatigue duties, the men received some leisure time for various activities. Many men often used their free time to write relatives. The most prolific writer of the regiment was its commander, Colonel Keifer, who corresponded with his wife regularly. For more than one year, Keifer wrote daily; during the last year of his service, however, he wrote only three times a week. Keifer's correspondence to his wife, Eliza, contains more than eight hundred letters. The colonel's letters at first were usually four pages in length, but as the war progressed, he reduced this to about two pages. His letters are eloquent, revealing an individual who was exceedingly intelligent and well educated.

Some men of the 110th informed the readers of their local newspapers about the condition of the men, the experiences of the regiment, their campaigns, and casualties. In a lengthy letter to the *Troy Times,* Major Binkley described the campaigns of 1864. Other men from Companies A, E, and G also wrote to the *Troy Times.* Lt. Henry Y. Rush, for example, informed readers of events occurring with Company E. Soldiers using the pseudonyms Davis, Incog, and Joppa, described events from the perspective of enlisted men in Company G; the fifth sergeant of Company A also wrote several letters to this newspaper.[21]

Upon one occasion, a debate developed in the press between Companies A and G. In a letter printed in the *Troy Times* on April 23, 1863, Incog accused Company A of having too many city boys. Accordingly, they had trouble keeping pace during a scouting mission near Winchester, Virginia. On May 14, the fifth sergeant of Company A replied to Incog's reputedly slanderous remarks.[22]

The *Xenia Torchlight* also received letters from several individuals representing different companies. Whereas the letters to the *Troy Times* highlighted the distinctions between the Miami County companies, the letters to the *Xenia Torchlight* focused on the similarity of the Greene County volunteers' experiences. Pvt. Lewis Bell and Lt. Jacob Mill Conwell of Company F and Cpl. Frederick LaRue of Company D sent many letters to the *Xenia Torchlight* that addressed events the 110th had experienced.[23]

Many soldiers also sent letters to the *Springfield Evening News* and the

Springfield Republic. Henry H. Stevens of Company C and Luther Brown of Company I, for example, contributed much information about the regiment to these newspapers. So too did Elias A. Barr and John R. Lippincott, both privates in Company I.[24]

After the engagement in the Wilderness, a frenzied debate ensued between Capt. Luther Brown and W. A. Lamme. On Thursday, May 17, 1864, the *Springfield Evening News* listed Pvt. Edwin H. Lamme as wounded. In the issue dated Monday, June 20, Captain Brown contradicted the newspaper's earlier claim, writing that Lamme was not wounded. Private Lamme, contended Brown, was in the rear, unhurt, and enjoying himself like most stragglers, while his comrades continued to fight nobly. On July 8, the *Springfield Republic* published an anonymous response that challenged Brown's accusations and his method of censure. The author claimed to know for a fact that Lamme was sick in the hospital. The unnamed author stated that "base and unprincipled is the officer that would stoop to such means to tarnish the fair name of a mere boy." Two weeks later, the *Springfield Republic* published Captain Brown's claim that he had signed affidavits to prove Private Lamme's dereliction of duty.[25]

The controversy took a new direction when W. A. Lamme, Edwin's father, entered the fray with Captain Brown. In a letter dated June 23, 1864, W. A. Lamme defended his son's actions; he then verbally attacked Captain Brown and the actions of the Sixth Corps and the Army of the Potomac. The elder Lamme argued that his son wrote in a letter that he was sick, continuing, "It is not reasonable to suppose the surgeons would keep a well man in the Hospital 2 or 3 weeks when they wer [*sic*] crowded for room." W. A. Lamme continued the assault by stating that if young Lamme lied, he had learned that ability while serving in Captain Brown's company. According to the father, since the war began, the *Cincinnati Gazette* had not published such a letter as Brown had published in the *Springfield Republic.* He faulted Brown for "stopping in the midst of a battle to parade the failings of a boy in his company before the public." He additionally accused the officers of searching for a scapegoat to cover their own shortcomings.

Lamme then recounted the "cowardice" that the entire Sixth Corps displayed at Wilderness, Maj. Gen. George Meade's cowardly action when he drummed an eastern correspondent from the army, and Maj. Gen. George McClellan's cowardice at Malvern Hill in 1862, when he commanded the troops from the protection of a Union gunboat in the James River.[26]

Captain Brown responded in a letter addressing each of W. A. Lamme's issues. Brown asserted that he could prove that Edwin Lamme was well when he absented himself from his company. Green Ramey, William Wise, Leroy Lowman, and T. G. Green of the 110th and Willard Childs, the surgeon in charge of the hospital, signed affidavits that confirmed Brown's accusations. The captain sent copies of these affidavits that supported his position regarding Eddy's absence. "His absence was published in the Republic on the 22nd of June. (I think) Certainly he had plenty of time to have returned to the company before he was exposed as a 'straggler.'" Brown also observed that many of the hospital personnel were not as honest as the elder Lamme would suppose. According to the officer, men sometimes fooled the doctors or worked for the hospital to avoid combat. Brown nonetheless informed Lamme's father that he would fully reinstate his son if he returned to his duty. If Edwin continued on his chosen course, however, young Lamme would have to suffer whatever consequences the military bestowed upon him. Addressing the severity issue, Brown then argued for punishment through the use of public humiliation with the statement: "I am informed upon good authority that not less than forty men in this army have been publicly shot for the crime of 'straggling.' In comparison is my mode of punishment severe?"

Pvt. Edwin Lamme did not return to Company I until November 1864. During the period of his absence, he worked in the Army of the Potomac's hospitals. Lamme served mainly as a guard in the various hospitals, particularly those near City Point, Virginia. In January 1865, a general court-martial found Private Lamme guilty of desertion. The court's sentence was lenient when compared with many other decisions—the soldier forfeited seven months pay.[27]

Most correspondence between the men of the 110th Ohio and people at home was not so inflammatory. In many instances, the soldiers inquired about local events and friends and family. Corporal Rhoades continually advised his son Willy to always be good, to go to school, and to attend Sabbath school. Rhoades also urged him to use thought and correct spelling in his writing, to control his passions, and to think before he spoke.[28]

Those officers in the 110th with significant political clout corresponded with judges and congressmen. For example, Capt. William Moore of Company E, a Douglas Democrat, regularly wrote to Congressman Frank McKinney of Piqua, Ohio. During the winter of 1864, Moore scheduled a trip to visit McKinney in Washington, D.C., but he canceled it due to an illness. When McKinney learned of Captain Moore's condition, he sent a package of goods to the officer. Before the two men could actually meet, however, Captain Moore died from his disease. One source claimed the cause of death was typhoid fever, while another cited dysentery.[29]

In letters to his wife, Colonel Keifer often mentioned Judge William White of Springfield, Ohio. Keifer regularly communicated with the judge. On many occasions, he wanted Eliza to exchange pleasantries with White and his family. Other letters reveal a deeper relationship between Keifer and the judge. The colonel apparently used White's sponsorship in several failed attempts at promotion. Previously, he had obtained letters of reference from notable individuals such as Major Generals Joseph Reynolds and Robert Milroy and Brig. Gen. James Garfield. These letters highlighted Keifer's exemplary performance and enhanced the probability of his promotion to brigadier general. Then, armed with these references, Judge White went to Washington, D.C., using his influence in Keifer's behalf.[30]

On one occasion, Judge White turned the tables and solicited advice from Colonel Keifer. White considered running for a higher public office, possibly for the office of U.S. representative for his district. Believing that it was in Judge White's best interest, however, Keifer recommended that he pursue the office of state supreme court justice rather than declaring his candidacy for Congress. The colonel warned his friend that a congressional campaign would be hotly contested, while any judicial competition would be limited.[31]

The men of the 110th Ohio spent much of their leisure time reading. When the army was idle, several men would read books for pleasure and improvement. When the army was on a campaign, however, soldiers gleaned information from the newspapers, which also distracted them from campaign hardships. The men usually selected books on education and philosophy as well as the Bible. Corporal Rhoades spent many hours reading the Bible and other works. Keifer passed many evenings reading military manuals on tactics and strategy but also dedicated time to reading the Bible. Private Kauffman of Company I rejoiced upon the arrival of his Bible via express box and deeply regretted its loss during the evacuation of Winchester.[32]

Soldiers read their hometown newspapers whenever possible. In many letters to the editors, soldiers requested that copies of the newspaper be forwarded to their company. In letters sent to relatives, the men mentioned the receipt of newspapers and how much the men appreciated those publications. On January 12, 1865, Sgt. Richard Pearson of Company G thanked the editor of the *Troy Times* for sending his paper to the regiment for the past two years. Sporadically, the soldiers read large circulation newspapers such as the *Cincinnati Gazette,* the *National Tribune,* and the *Philadelphia Enquirer.*[33]

Religion played an important role in the lives of some men. Individuals such as Corporal Rhoades spent as much leisure time as possible pursuing their faith. In 1863, while serving on garrison duty at Winchester, Rhoades attended church in town whenever possible. On February 18, he attended service for the first time since leaving Ohio four months earlier. Rhoades noted that Colonel Keifer also attended Winchester's only church.[34]

During their time with the Army of the Potomac, regular church services were not always available for the soldiers. Therefore, devout individuals devised a meeting place for themselves. If the army might move soon, these devoted men met for prayer meetings in tents or clearings. When the army settled in one location for an extended period, they often constructed a regimental and a brigade church. On January 14, 1864, Corporal Rhoades discussed construction of a church with twelve to fourteen Methodists in his company. Only five days later they completed the construction of a building. Subsequently, these men held regular church services and evening prayer meetings in their new chapel.[35]

The men entertained themselves by various methods, including games of chance. Cards became especially popular among enlisted personnel; euchre and draw poker ranked among their favorites. On payday, many men entertained themselves by gambling. Dice games, horseracing, cockfighting, and poker enjoyed wide popularity on these occasions. Corporal Rhoades noted that most of those awaiting exchange at Camp Parole had nothing to do except play cards. According to him, these same men were extremely vulgar and habitually used profanity. During his own stay at Camp Parole, Rhoades occupied his time by bathing and eating.[36]

Many individuals drank alcohol to relieve tension and to reduce boredom. Keifer believed that drinking among officers was excessive and therefore abstained from alcohol during most of his time in service. He imbibed only during the holiday season or on special occasions. When officers visited each other, they were customarily offered whiskey and water, but Keifer considered this conduct a "barbarous custom." On several occasions, he remarked in his letters on alcohol-related incidents. Only three weeks after mustering into Federal service, for instance, he "reduced a prominent Miami County citizen from sergeant for drunkenness." Keifer later declared, "all drunkenness shall be punished." Another incident occurred when part of the brigade moved from Burlington, Virginia, to Winchester. Due to intemperance, many officers of the 116th Ohio Infantry were unfit for duty. Only fourteen officers of the 116th made the march, while the 110th Ohio furnished thirty-three officers for the trek.[37]

The emancipation issue deeply divided the regiment. Colonel Keifer, for one, backed President Abraham Lincoln. He joined the Republican party in 1856 and supported many abolitionist policies. After reading the Emancipation Proclamation, Keifer "endorse[d] the President's 1st of January Proclamation." Later, during the movement from Burlington to Winchester, he celebrated the enactment of the Emancipation Proclamation with Major General Milroy, an active abolitionist.[38]

Some members of the regiment, however, opposed freeing slaves. Captain Moore fought for the preservation of the Union and for the protection of the U.S. Constitution. He vehemently opposed emancipation. Moore would rather "resign my commission before I have a nigger cook in my company."[39]

Others in the regiment also held conflicting political views. Many members were Democrats, for example, Lt. Col. William Foster, who served as mayor of Piqua before his enlistment. Capt. William D. Alexander, commander of Company A, was an influential member of the Miami County Democratic party before the war. Capt. William R. Moore of Company E claimed to be a Douglas Democrat, but many members of his wife's family were reputedly Copperheads, pro-Southern Democrats. As mentioned earlier, Captain Moore had a close relationship with Democratic congressman J. Frank McKinney of Piqua. Moore, however, disliked Congressman Clement Vallandigham's peace proposals and vowed that he would never support Vallandigham or anyone of his ilk. Moore believed that the U.S. Constitution and the Union must be preserved. Vallandigham's ideas, therefore, were antithetical to the captain's beliefs. After the Urbana newspaper printed Frank McKinney's speech that mentioned him by name, Moore reaffirmed his position regarding the conduct of the war. He did not approve of people at home "wearing butternut" and believed that Democrats should "arm themselves with the principles of the constitution and the laws," advocating a "vigorous prosecution of the war under them." He argued for similar behavior among Republicans. Colonel Keifer, however, was a Republican who had campaigned for John C. Frémont during the 1856 presidential contest. Major Binkley was also a member of the Republican party. After the war, he served as mayor of Troy, Ohio.[40]

During the 1864 elections, the regiment voted heavily in favor of Union candidates. According to Private Kauffman, 54 of 58 Clark County voters cast their ballot for the Union ticket in support of Abraham Lincoln. Corporal Rhoades believed George McClellan and the Chicago platform would lose; he further stated that "Copperheadism" was not for soldiers. Of 241 voters in the regiment, Rhoades predicted that Lincoln would garner 200 votes.[41]

Sporadically, soldiers received furloughs to visit their homes. Normally, officers received leave to complete regimental business such as recruiting. Lieutenant McKnight and Captain Brown, for instance, returned to Miami and Clark Counties on numerous occasions to enlist more men. Officers or noncommissioned officers who received furloughs frequently carried money home to the families of the men in their companies. When the soldiers of the 110th received pay on March 28, 1863, Colonel Keifer detailed men from each county to take money home. With April 10 specified as the date for his return, Captain Moore carried home some of this cash for his soldiers of Company E. Men also traveled to Ohio on passes because of personal illness or severe illness among or the death of family members. During the first two years of the war, however, some men abused the absences allowed for sickness, in the process sometimes creating an acute manpower shortage. These furloughs consequently became more difficult to obtain.[42]

The army limited visitation from civilians. While a part of Milroy's division, the regiment garrisoned Winchester, with many spouses visiting the officers. During the winter of 1863 and again in 1864, Eliza Keifer traveled to Virginia to visit her husband. Lieutenant Colonel Foster's wife also visited him on numerous occasions during the winter and spring of 1863. On May 22, 1863, Colonel Keifer noted the spouses in camp at Winchester: Foster, Harvey, McCandliss, McKnight, and Boyer.[43]

On one occasion, however, these visitations created a significant problem. As the campaign season approached, military authorities ordered civilian visitors to leave the vicinity. Despite these orders, many civilians remained with their spouses in Winchester. On June 13, 1863, the Army of Northern Virginia's Second Corps besieged Winchester while the civilians were still present. Milroy's division of the Eighth Corps fought its way out of the city, but they had to leave behind many civilians as well as Chap. James Harvey and Dr. Robert McCandliss to care for the sick and wounded. These people soon fell into the hands of the Rebels. Among the captured civilians were Mrs. Foster, Mrs. Boyer, and Mrs. Shaw. The Confederates transported these noncombatants to Richmond, where authorities imprisoned them for a short period in Castle Thunder. On July 4, the Confederates released them, and several days later these officers' wives met the 110th Ohio in Washington, D.C. That October, the Confederates exchanged Chaplain Harvey, and on November 24, they released Dr. McCandliss.[44]

A civilian, in one instance, was less fortunate. Daniel Gearhart was a wealthy and influential citizen of Miami County. Coming to Winchester in the spring of 1863, he visited his son, Silas, who was a private in Company E. Confederate forces captured the elder Gearhart and sent him to Richmond. This Miami County resident remained a prisoner through much of the war. Fifteen months later, Confederate Agent of Exchange Robert Ould recommended that the sixty-year-old Gearhart's detainment continue. According to Ould, the Miami County citizen's imprisonment ensured the proper treatment of influential Confederate citizens captured by Federal authorities.[45]

Being captured by the Confederates was a danger for all Union soldiers. During intermittent periods throughout the conflict, the opposing governments exchanged prisoners of war. Feeding one's own soldiers on a large scale was traditionally a serious logistical problem. Consequently, feeding prisoners of war was an additional supply burden that governments attempted to avoid. The Federals and Confederates, being no different than other adversaries, exchanged tens of thousands of prisoners to reduce this drain on their supplies. Government authorities usually exchanged prisoners in numbers approaching two hundred men at a time.

On June 28, 1862, to address the need for temporary housing for the exchanged prisoners, the Federal government established three camps, one of which was a converted camp of instruction at Annapolis, Maryland. Known as Camp Parole, this site provided a mechanism for the orderly exchange of prisoners. Men who had been captured spent time in Camp Parole waiting for the filing of the proper papers to complete the exchange process. They did not receive furloughs nor could they join their regiments until the completion of a formal exchange.[46]

The barracks at Camp Parole were one hundred feet long, twenty-two feet wide, had a nine-foot ceiling, and accommodated 120 men. Each building also had eight windows and four doors. A kitchen was built for every three barracks in the camp. The Quartermaster Department also added new construction projects to the camp as fully completed annexes. When these opened at Camp Parole, they each accommodated an additional 360 men. At its zenith, the camp's maximum capacity was 8,200 men.[47]

While at Camp Parole, the soldiers had a light duty-schedule. Each day, the soldiers answered reveille at 5:00 A.M. and taps sounded at 9:00 P.M. Mealtime lasted one hour for each of the three meals. Twice a day the soldiers spent one and one-half hours policing the grounds. Every day, surgeon's call lasted three and one-half hours. Sunday morning inspection offered the only variance from the daily routine.[48]

After being captured by the Confederates at Winchester, several members of the 110th Ohio described their tenure at Camp Parole. Corporal Rhoades, for example, believed the men had too much idle time that encouraged personal vices. Numerous men played cards for many hours, but Rhoades did not know how to play nor care to learn. Private Kauffman also disliked idle time. After he and several others attempted to walk home, three provost marshals captured him and returned him to camp. Pvt. Harrison Potts of Company E, however, escaped from Camp Parole when several farmers aided his temporary return to Miami County. Corporal Rhoades also contemplated desertion and wrote his wife that he "will try to walk home it will take about twenty days." He further commented that many deserters from Camp Parole got caught and that such failed attempts were costly.[49]

On occasion, influential individuals visited the regiment. The death of Captain Moore brought Representative Frank McKinney to camp. During the extensive periods the men spent in the trenches surrounding Petersburg, the 110th Ohio performed review for others. On March 7, 1865, Generals George Meade and Horatio Wright, Mrs. Ulysses Grant, Secretary of War Edwin M. Stanton's niece, and Judge and Mrs. Woodruff of New York City watched as Colonel Keifer paraded the Second Brigade, Third Division, Sixth Army Corps, through review. While they were at Petersburg, the 110th also participated in many brigade and division reviews for Major Generals Andrew Humphreys, Gouverneur Warren, Horatio Wright, and George Meade. Prior to the spring campaign of 1864, the Sixth Corps paraded in review for Lt. Gen. U. S. Grant.[50]

My officers and men knew that everything depended upon this effort. There was a solemn calmness about each. The order "forward" was given and nobly obeyed.

—Col. Warren Keifer

3 Everything Depended upon This Effort

The 110th trained at Camp Piqua in northern Miami County. On the banks of the Great Miami River, the campsite was at the Johnston Farm, formerly the homestead of eighteenth-century Indian agent Col. John Johnston. The companies arrived in late August 1862, and they remained there for two months. On October 19, they moved to the Eastern Theater. Three weeks before the companies mustered into Federal service, however, the men endured their first casualties. On Monday, September 15, Pvt. John Williams of Company H died of typhoid fever. That same evening, Pvt. J. F. Garrett of Company C apparently committed suicide owing to serious domestic problems.[1]

Training and drills were the major components of camp life at Camp Piqua. Squad, company, and battalion drill made up most of the schedule, but the companies also performed guard and fatigue duties, which early on included the construction of shanties. The military established Camp

Piqua as a temporary training site, a facility that lacked the proper equipment and buildings. The 94th Ohio Infantry, also training there, occupied crude shelters. Shortly after arriving, the men of the 110th constructed their own shelters.[2]

Through a rotating schedule, the recruits served as cooks. According to Josiah Hill, the fare was not extraordinary, and quite often the food was unpalatable. On one occasion he complained of the "two year old bacon furnished us it cant be eaten maggots without number." On September 21, 1862, Hill mentioned that they had only hard bread to eat because they had no cook that day. The next day, he again complained "about the meat that is being furnished us I was the first to grab a piece and cary it back and throw it in to the commisary."[3]

Pvt. Lorenzo Barnhart of Company B and the soldiers in the 110th ate outdoors. They put their dishes on crude tables and while standing ate their food. According to Barnhart, the men ate in this manner regardless of the weather.[4]

During the early stages of their military experience, the new soldiers lacked discipline. Men regularly absented themselves without leave. On August 31, 1862, just eight days after he had arrived in camp, Private Hill of Company E went home. In late September, he again took leave because he did not get a furlough. On Saturday, September 27, he first waded the Miami and Erie Canal and then the Great Miami River to get home. Returning the next day, Hill "left home for camp at two o'clock rode in a buggy as near as [he] dared and then took it a foot trusting to luck and [his] legs." Two weeks earlier, after guard duty, Private Hill stated: "Last night the boys had a good time 200 broke gard in the night they came stragling in with many chickens."[5]

On October 1, his company comrades elected Josiah Hill as fourth corporal. With his new position, he regularly acted as corporal of the guard. On one occasion, Hill ironically "had a lively time catching the boys that had crossed the line."[6]

The regiment left Camp Piqua on October 18, 1862. After traveling by railroad from the camp, they changed to water transportation. In Zanesville, five companies loaded on board the steamer *Jonas Powell,* while the remaining four companies embarked on the steamer *T. J. Pattin.* Because of shallow water several miles below the town, the men got out and walked downstream before taking other boats to Marietta. Private Barnhart and some men stopped to eat wild grapes while they walked along the bank of the river. In Marietta the men again loaded into railroad cars and later unloaded on the north side of the Ohio River across from Parkersburg, Virginia. Finally, three days after the regiment departed Camp Piqua, the men climbed into boats to ferry the river.[7]

During their thirteen-day stay at Parkersburg, the Ohioans spent many hours in drill. While there, the Quartermaster Department issued the 110th heavy canvas Sibley tents, which according to Private Rosser repelled water well and kept the wind from passing through. Since the unit had not yet arrived at its duty station, the quartermaster would not issue stoves. The men consequently crowded six to each tent in order to keep warm.[8]

When they were off duty, some soldiers wrote letters and went to town; others explored the countryside. Henry Kauffman, John Chatterton, Lt. Thomas Weakley, and several others went to the Little Kanawha River to wash clothes. There on the riverbank they discovered some boats. Weakley, Kauffman, and Chatterton climbed into a boat and took a ride. Later, the two privates dropped Lieutenant Weakley on the shore and continued their excursion. Kauffman and Chatterton rowed one mile upstream when a bullet suddenly flew over their heads and splashed twelve feet from their boat. "We looked up the hill and saw two bushwackers there and so we lowed we had better get to shore and before we got out they had fired at us three times but they did not hit us."[9]

On November 3, 1862, the unit loaded on cars of the Baltimore and Ohio Railroad and moved to Clarksburg, Virginia. On their eighty-three mile journey, Corporal Rhoades estimated that the train passed through at least twenty-two tunnels. According to Corporal Hill, the train passed "through a wild and romantic country only distinguished for its patriotism and poverty."[10]

During their stay at Clarksburg, the 110th camped in the bed of a dry run for ten days. The men of Lorenzo Barnhart's tent dug a fire pit inside their tent and maintained a fire for warmth. One night, the fire spread from the pit to their straw flooring and sent the men running. "We jumped up and tore the tent down and grabbed our blankets and knapsacks from the blaze and saved them; we staked our tent down at another place and slept the best we could that night." After remaining at Clarksburg for several days, the men of Hill's mess went to town and purchased a stove for heat.[11]

On Saturday morning, November 15, the regiment left camp. The Ohioans again traveled by rail and passed through many tunnels, several of which were over a mile long. The journey was slow and arduous, and the cold weather made the men miserable during the trip. At 3:00 A.M. the next day, they finally arrived at New Creek Station, Virginia.[12]

For nearly a month, the 110th remained at Camp Jessie near New Creek Station. During this extended stay, the regiment drilled at regular intervals. Occasionally, drill lasted five hours. On November 18, Maj. Gen. Robert Milroy arrived; four days later, he reviewed the troops. After the men readied themselves, they moved to the parade ground, where they waited while officers arranged the brigade in lines. The "glittering arms" of thousands of soldiers combined with General Milroy's presence impressed Corporal Rhoades. After Milroy reviewed all branches of the division, each brigade marched around the parade ground. Rhoades was especially impressed by the artillery procession. "It was a grand sight to see six horses hitched to a wagon and a large piece of hollow iron fastened on the hind part marching round in regular lin one after another in precise order." According to Corporal Hill, the troops stood fully accoutered for four hours. He claimed to be very tired after this affair.[13]

While at Clarksburg and New Creek Station, Colonel Keifer commented on his fellow officers in letters to his wife. For example, he wanted to remove Adj. Joseph Van Eaton because he had a "poor voice and cannot read or write worth a cent." Keifer also thought Lt. Col. William Foster and Maj. Otho Binkley possessed little strength, but he believed they were "agreeable gentlemen and good workers." Colonel Keifer praised Capt. Luther Brown, observing that he was a good officer who succeeded at drilling and disciplining his men. Keifer rated Capt. Nathan Smith as an excellent man, however, Smith lacked the ability to keep his men moral.[14]

Colonel Keifer also expressed his opinion regarding his superior officers. Major General Milroy's arrival on November 18 drew a terse comment from Keifer: "I know Milroy quite well but have not the highest estimate of his military character—I believe him subject to rashness." Keifer also approved of Maj. Gen. George McClellan's removal from command of the Army of the Potomac. McClellan had failed to pursue Lee's army after the Antietam campaign. Following November's midterm elections, the hesitant general became politically dispensable. Consequently, on November 4, President Lincoln relieved McClellan of command. Keifer, however, believed that a major cause for the dismissal was McClellan's avowed disapproval of Don Carlos Buell's earlier removal from command of the Army of the Ohio.

Colonel Keifer rejoiced at Major General Buell's arrest. While serving as major and then lieutenant colonel of the 3d Ohio Infantry, Keifer participated in Buell's 1862 campaign against Chattanooga following the siege of Corinth, Mississippi. As part of Maj. Gen. Ormsby Mitchell's division, Keifer had personally witnessed Buell's slow movement east. Reluctant to live off the land, Buell's four divisions depended upon the tedious supply line of the Memphis and Charleston Railroad. Confederate forces under Maj. Gen. Braxton Bragg consequently reinforced the Tennessee town before the Army of the Ohio arrived. Like many of the early Union commanders, Buell fought a limited war and refused to trample upon the constitutional rights of Confederate citizens. In Keifer's opinion, sufficient evidence existed and warranted further investigation into the general's motives and actions. Keifer believed that the War Department should prosecute Don Carlos Buell for treason, not incompetence.[15]

Though treason was a serious offense and punishable by death, U.S. military authorities executed only 391 officers and men during the Civil War. Disease killed 224,586 men and proved to be a much greater threat to the volunteers. Recruits from states west of the Appalachian Mountains proved to be especially susceptible. Men from rural areas had not been exposed to diseases such as measles, mumps, and chicken pox. As they encountered large population centers such as the Army of the Potomac, they contracted infectious diseases and other childhood maladies to which eastern troops were apparently immune. Men of the 110th Ohio proved to be no different from other westerners. Company H's John Williams was the first mortality from disease. On December 24, 1862, Pvt. Levi Trumbo of Company C also died of typhoid fever at Moorefield, Virginia. Military authorities tried to cope with the problem. Earlier, while the 110th was at New Creek Station, the men received smallpox vaccines. On November 28, Captain Moore of Company E observed that these had caused many sore arms in camp that day.[16]

During the occupation of Winchester, the troops noted outbreaks of disease in the region. On February 8, 1863, in a letter to his sister, Private Kauffman wrote that "here are not 45 men fit for duty in our Company. The mumps is whats the matter." Colonel Keifer hoped that his wife, Eliza, had heeded his advice about inoculation for smallpox because shortly after her visit to Winchester, Captain Alexander of Company A contracted the disease. During the second week of April, a typhoid epidemic swept through the town, and Colonel Keifer quickly moved his troops farther away to avoid the illness. He later reported that 115 men of the 110th contracted typhoid during this outbreak.[17]

These rampant diseases undoubtedly prompted Colonel Keifer to criticize the doctors stationed at Winchester and the medical profession as a whole. On February 14, he complained that the surgeons had not been caring properly for the sick. He intended to expose them to the public and the authorities in Washington, D.C., if they did not change their methods. Keifer thought that most doctors were "mean, little, narrow-minded, and selfish."[18]

While they were at New Creek Station, the 110th exchanged their weapons. Private Barnhart described their old weapons as "old Knocemstiffs" that his grandfather used in the War of 1812. On December 12, 1862, Colonel Keifer procured Springfield rifles for the regiment and distributed them among his troops that same day.[19]

Afterward the unit moved from New Creek Station. Although the enlisted men were unsure as to where they were going, Colonel Keifer knew their destination. Corporal Rhoades, however, correctly surmised that they were moving to occupy Winchester. On the first day, the regiment marched fourteen miles in seven hours, arriving at 5:00 P.M. in Burlington, Virginia. In his letter dated December 14, Colonel Keifer informed his wife that Mrs. Brown and Mrs. Foster, the wives of two officers, started home on the same day that the regiment left New Creek. Mrs. Foster, however, wished to accompany the army and requested to ride in the ambulance. According to Keifer, "Dr. Pixley [regimental surgeon Sumner Pixley] talked her out of it using words and terms that astonished her."[20]

On December 15 and again the following day, the soldiers of the 110th continued their march, during which they carried knapsacks that weighed forty pounds. On the first day, the men marched sixteen miles, and on the next, they marched another fourteen miles. On December 18, the 110th moved to Moorefield, a distance of eleven miles. While they were there, they stayed in the courthouse and in a deserted church. Colonel Keifer, however, commandeered a room at a Confederate-sympathizer's hotel. He delighted in the knowledge that the room previously served as General Frémont's headquarters.[21]

Ten days later, the 110th left Moorefield for Winchester. Over the next three days, the men marched sixty miles. While en route, bushwhackers attacked the brigade supply train, inflicting twelve casualties and capturing forty horses. On January 1, 1863, the regiment finally arrived at Winchester.[22]

Corporal Hill estimated the population to be fifteen hundred people. He also commented on the beauty of the town as seen from the forts that surround it. Hill remarked particularly about the splendid view of the Shenandoah Valley. In 1863, three forts, Fort Milroy, West Fort, and Star Fort, guarded the city. Fort Milroy's location was in town, while West Fort and Star Fort protected the northern and western sides of Winchester.[23]

A variety of details and duties now filled the soldiers' days. After they finished their regular drill sessions, the men spent many hours repairing the forts. Pvt. Charles Berry and Company I spent three days a week on picket duty and worked one day on the fortifications. During the first half of 1863, this pattern of picket and guard duty plus work remained constant. Illness, poor weather, and expeditions caused the only schedule changes. On May 24, Corporal Rhoades described the defenses around Winchester to his son, Willy. "Two regular forts plus three smaller forts protected the city, and rifle pits surrounded each fort. The forts contained fourteen cannons with four of those being twenty-pound guns capable of firing shell two miles."[24]

Daily chores occupied the three remaining days there. Tents, the parade ground, and the campsites required regular upkeep and maintenance. Soldiers also mended their own clothes. When Sarah Rhoades asked about her husband's ability to wash clothes, the corporal replied that he and Alpheus Line would take two kettles, a tub, and a washboard to the spring. There they scrubbed their clothes in a cold bath and then followed that with an additional wash in a hot bath, rinsing their clothes in warm water. After hanging them until dry, the men folded and placed the clothes in their knapsacks, where the articles remained until Sunday morning inspection.[25]

Many other duties occupied the time of officers. Though he preferred to stay with his men, Colonel Keifer presided over the military commission assigned to Winchester. The colonel served in this capacity throughout the occupation of Winchester. The case of George Kitchen was the first brought before Keifer's court, which found the local resident not guilty of espionage. During the first two weeks of April 1863, Keifer presided over Jonathan McFarland's murder trial. The colonel later commented that President Lincoln must uphold the court's decision.

The military commission became an institution of Milroy's division and met regularly until the Confederates drove the division from Winchester in mid-June. Several trials for violating the oath of allegiance and for horse thieving took place. Colonel Keifer noted during Joseph Puffenbarger's murder trial that the accused had resided in Sharpsburg and knew Keifer's father, Joseph.[26]

Companies of the 110th often went on foraging expeditions or accompanied supply trains to Harpers Ferry, which normally consumed several days. On April 28, several companies left with a supply train to Harpers Ferry. On Friday, May 1, they returned to Winchester.[27]

The regiment also participated in many scouting missions. On January 12–13, 1863, Colonel Keifer, Major Binkley, and five companies went on their first reconnaissance to Front Royal. The expedition, expecting to fight two regiments of cavalry, charged the town. They captured four Confederate soldiers and confiscated the Confederate mail as well as a large supply of tobacco. According to Keifer, a cavalry squadron that accompanied his command caught the "notorious" Captain Hilliard while he slept at a friend's house.[28]

Six days later, a portion of the 110th went on another scouting mission. This force, consisting of four companies of the 110th and five companies of the 122d Ohio Infantry, marched to Thompson Station, Virginia. On January 19, after arriving at 2:00 A.M., the men searched the town and found one shotgun and lots of liniment. The soldiers slept a few hours and then began their return trip. According to Rhoades, they marched for almost sixteen hours without much rest, and he almost gave out on the way back to Winchester.[29]

On April 12–13, Colonel Keifer led the 110th and 122d Ohio Infantry Regiments, the 13th Pennsylvania Cavalry, and one section of Battery D, 1st West Virginia Artillery, on an expedition. His force first raided a Confederate tannery in the vicinity of Capon Springs, West Virginia, then scouted a short distance up the Shenandoah Valley. The Federals encountered no Confederate troops before encamping near Columbia Furnace. That night the men were miserable as they attempted to sleep through a steady rain without tents. They returned to Winchester on the thirteenth. Colonel Keifer complained about the 13th Pennsylvania Cavalry's poor performance. Henry Kauffman also noted the unreliability of the Pennsylvanians, claiming that once while on picket duty, they apparently ran from the enemy, a retreat that caused the loss of more than one hundred men.

Keifer later lambasted these men from the Keystone State: "the 13th Pennsylvania's officers sustain their reputation of drunkenness and cowardice; as a body they are most unreliable men in word and act." In a letter to the *Springfield Republic,* Elias Barr mockingly reported that on their recent excursions the Federals had "killed one snake, captured two dogs, one contraband, and one grasshopper. Taking into consideration that this is not the season for grasshoppers, this capture perhaps will turn the balance in our favor."[30]

During early May, the 110th again scouted in the Shenandoah Valley. On Tuesday afternoon, May 5, four infantry regiments, one cavalry regiment, and nine pieces of artillery moved south toward Strasburg and Woodstock. Over the next four days, the men traveled 104 miles, confiscated a fifty-pound barrel of flour, captured a dozen prisoners, and released some slaves. The command lost four men from the 122d Ohio Infantry who went to a barn in which the Confederates captured them. Two weeks later, the 110th Ohio Infantry, a squadron from the 13th Pennsylvania Cavalry, and one section of artillery conducted still another reconnaissance. This expedition captured seven Confederates: one captain, one lieutenant, and five enlisted men. On May 29, a similar scouting party brought in eleven bushwhackers and twenty-six horses.[31]

The following day, under a flag of truce, Colonel Keifer met with Confederate troops at Middletown. He left his escort, the 18th Connecticut Infantry and two companies from the 13th Pennsylvania Cavalry, at Newtown. On a hill one mile south of the town, Keifer, Captain McElwaine, two other officers, and six enlisted men waited until noon, when ten Confederate officers and forty enlisted men arrived. The parties moved to the hotel in Middletown, where they talked humorously about the war and other events. The meeting went on for three hours and ended with an exchange of newspapers and mail. Keifer sent letters to officers of the 3d Ohio Infantry who were in Libby Prison. The reason for the truce was to safely allow the movement of refugees between the lines. Keifer professed that all participants of the meeting enjoyed themselves and that there was a "free flow of fine spirits."

On June 8, Keifer reported how his men had captured fourteen Confederate cavalrymen earlier. The Rebel army permitted dismounted cavalrymen to steal horses to replace their worn-out mounts. As a preventative measure, Keifer stationed small outposts at crossroads that allowed people into the area, but the guards stopped the men who tried to exit the region, either capturing or shooting anyone who attempted to escape the trap. According to the colonel, the men of the 18th Connecticut Infantry really enjoyed this work and were especially good at it.

While stationed in Winchester, Colonel Keifer performed two functions besides his assignments as colonel of the 110th and presiding officer for the military commission at Winchester. He positioned the outposts and organized the espionage efforts for Milroy's division of the Eighth Army Corps. Occasionally, he forewarned his wife, Eliza, of the hazards of occupying Winchester. If the Army of Northern Virginia invaded the North via the Shenandoah Valley, the Confederates would have to clear Federal troops from Winchester. Early in their occupation assignment, Major General Milroy had indicated that he would not abandon the town for slight provocations. Colonel Keifer at that time questioned Milroy's leadership ability. In addition to this November statement, Keifer now professed that Milroy knew nothing outside his own headquarters.

In late May 1863, Keifer alerted his wife about "important movements" that would occur very soon. If Union commanders faltered, he commented, the Confederates would take the initiative. On the twenty-ninth, the colonel wrote that the Rebels had made a strong movement on the Rappahannock River. A day later, he informed her that sixteen thousand Confederate troops occupied Fisher's Hill near Strasburg, Virginia. Keifer believed that General Lee would soon cross the Rappahannock and that a "terrible action will ensue." During the first two weeks of June, the colonel continually advised his wife about the increase of Confederate forces in the Shenandoah Valley. It was his opinion that Harpers Ferry, Martinsburg, or points in Pennsylvania would be the target of the impending Confederate strike. Keifer predicted that the Rebel offensive would still occur even after their defeat at the cavalry engagement of Brandy Station (June 9).[32]

During the second week of June, Colonel Keifer's prediction became reality. Keifer, however, underestimated the audacious movement that Gen. Robert E. Lee planned. Earlier, the Union officer predicted an opposing force of 20,000 men, but when General Lee struck, he brought the entire Army of Northern Virginia, estimated at 75,000 men. The movement's vanguard was the Second Corps, now under the command of Lt. Gen. Richard S. "Old Bald Head" Ewell. Directly in the Rebels' path was General Milroy's imperiled command of 6,900 effectives.[33]

On June 13, Union troops first encountered Ewell's forces on the Front Royal Road. The 13th Pennsylvania Cavalry and the 87th Pennsylvania Infantry surprised elements of the 1st Maryland (Confederate) Cavalry, killing fifty men and capturing another thirty-seven. Later that morning, General Milroy sent the 110th, the 123d Ohio Infantry, the 12th West Virginia Infantry, the 12th Pennsylvania Cavalry, and Battery D of the 1st West Virginia Artillery to patrol the Strasburg Road. At two o'clock that afternoon, Brig. Gen. Washington Elliott, commanding the patrol, ordered Colonel Keifer to make a reconnaissance toward Kernstown. Keifer, in command of the 110th, the 12th Pennsylvania Cavalry, and one section of the artillery, pushed Confederate pickets nearly to Kernstown. The Federal force fulfilled its job by unmasking a body of Confederate infantry. Eventually, a brigade of Confederate infantry threatened to flank Keifer's command, which retreated from its exposed position and joined the forces that remained with General Elliott on Bower's Hill, south of Winchester.

Enemy troops massed along the Front Royal Road, threatening the command of Col. William Ely of the 18th Connecticut Infantry. General Elliott, therefore, pulled his troops back and positioned them in supporting distance of Ely's forces. During the skirmishing that continued until dark, a prisoner from Brig. Gen. Harry T. Hays's Louisiana Brigade first informed the Union officers that Milroy's command faced Ewell's entire Second Corps. At two o'clock Sunday morning, Elliott's command moved through Winchester into the forts north of town.[34]

At dawn, the 110th, Capt. F. H. Arkenoe's company of the 116th Ohio, and Battery L, 5th U.S. Artillery, manned the earthworks west of town. This position, known as the West Fort, guarded the approaches to Winchester from the Pughtown and Romney Roads. Throughout the day, the Confederates remained quiet. At two o'clock Sunday afternoon, Captain Morgan and two companies of the 12th Pennsylvania Cavalry reconnoitered west on the Pughtown Road. Morgan's scouts found no trace of the enemy. According to Pvt. Lorenzo Barnhart, "everything was quiet the boys were laying on the parapets in the sun." The Union troops in the West Fort believed that the Confederates were keeping their distance.[35]

As the Union troops in the West Fort relaxed, General Ewell ordered Maj. Gen. Jubal Early's division to the west of the town. Early moved undetected around Apple Pie Ridge and placed twenty cannons on Little North Mountain. When they opened fire at 4:00 P.M., the Rebel artillery

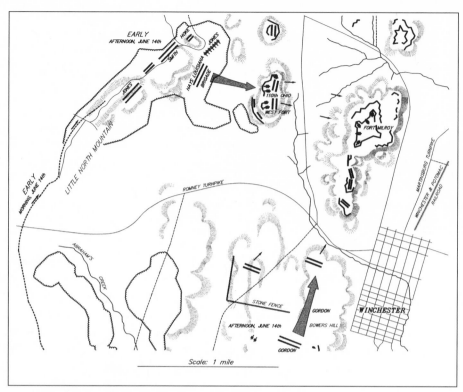

Second Battle of Winchester, afternoon of June 14, 1863.

dominated the small Union earthworks and surprised Private Barnhart and the other Union soldiers. "All at once . . . here came a shower of shot and shell the boys tumbled off the parapets behind them like turtles drop off a log into the water." Lt. Wallace Randolph's Battery L returned fire, but after a two-hour duel with Early's twenty guns, the small Federal battery was overwhelmed. About six o'clock, the bombardment of West Fort abated; it rendered four guns of Battery L unserviceable, leaving only two cannon to oppose the anticipated Confederate assault. The Union troops watched for movement in the brush to the west, and officers ordered the men to load their weapons and affix their bayonets.[36]

While the bombardment kept the Union troops undercover, General Hays's Louisiana Brigade moved into position. As the cannonading ceased, Hays's five regiments of infantry assaulted West Fort. According to Private Barnhart, the Louisiana Brigade emerged from a nearby ravine in dress parade order. The Yankees, however, were ready. As Hays's brigade approached, the Federals loosed a devastating volley that created gaping holes in the Southern lines. The Confederate veterans, however, quickly closed these large gaps, and the assaulting column never slowed. The Louisiana Brigade stopped in front of the West Fort and fired a volley. Then, in column formation, Hays's infantry charged "with bayonets and yell[ing] like indians."[37]

According to Colonel Keifer, "many Confederate officers and men were seen to fall, and the head of the column wavered, but there were no trenches or abatis to obstruct the enemy's advance." During the volley, a Confederate bullet struck Sgt. Mathias McAnally, slightly wounding him. After the Louisiana infantry swarmed inside the fort, McAnally fell under a clubbed musket. Once inside, a Confederate major prematurely demanded that Cpl. John Rhoades surrender, but the Ohio corporal bayoneted him. As Rhoades tried to withdraw his bayonet, a musket crashed down upon his head. Catching a glimpse of the incoming blow, Rhoades partially deflected the musket with his arms. The gun's lock, however, split his scalp. As the dazed and bloody Federal rose, another Confederate soldier leveled his musket at Rhoades. Luckily, a Confederate officer intervened and saved the corporal.

Only after the Ohio troops were outnumbered in the fort and their exposed flanks were threatened did the colonel order retreat. The Federals now fled in great disorder toward Fort Milroy. According to Private Barnhart, it was "every man for himself." He narrowly escaped through a ravine. The final stretch of ground between the retreating soldiers and Fort Milroy was a wide-open meadow. "While crossing this [I] was in plain view of them they sent the shot after me but [I] would not halt and went ahead towards the Fort with there bullits plowing the ground around my feet." Believing he would be hit at any moment, Barnhart reached the safety of Fort Milroy. Justifying his run, Barnhart wrote he did "not want to serve time in a confederate prison that is why I undertook to run the gauntlet."[38]

Sunday, June 14, closed with the 110th Ohio in Fort Milroy. Although the Confederates bombarded the position until nine o'clock that evening, the fighting that involved the regiment had ended. During the conflict at West Fort, the unit suffered forty-five casualties, including the capture of Lt. Paris Horney of Company C and Sergeant McAnally and Corporal Rhoades of Company E. In 1864, Lieutenant Horney died while confined in a Confederate prison in Columbia, South Carolina.[39]

Soon after the shelling ceased, General Milroy called a council of war with his three brigade commanders: General Elliott, Colonel Ely, and Col. A. T. McReynolds, who commanded the First, Second, and Third Brigades respectively. Rather than surrender their commands or fight until annihilated, the group decided that they should attempt a breakout. To succeed, the division needed to move quickly and quietly. The troops, carrying full packs, secured their possessions to prevent them from making too much noise. They destroyed all of the wagons, spiked their cannons, and threw their remaining stores into the forts' cisterns.[40]

On the night of June 14, a detachment of sixty men from the 110th under the command of Lieutenants Thomas Weakley and Charles Gross served on picket duty. They remained at their posts until captured the following morning. Asst. Surgeon Robert McCandliss and Chap. James Harvey stayed at the hospital with the sick, which included Lieutenants William Cron and George Miller. Early in the morning of Monday, June 15, Milroy's division started down the Martinsburg Road, marking another Union evacuation of Winchester. According to Colonel Keifer, the 110th marched out with nineteen officers and four hundred men.[41]

The 110th and 126th Ohio Infantry Regiments led the division's movement. At four o'clock in the morning, after traveling four miles on the Martinsburg Road, the Union troops heard squeaking hubs. This sound alerted the vanguard to the presence of Confederate artillery. Rebel brigadier general Edward Johnson had positioned his division on the Martinsburg Road to prevent a Union escape in that direction. The noise that the moving artillery created, however, forewarned the Federal troops of the Confederate presence.[42]

After turning east on the Charles Town Road and traveling a quarter mile, the Union advance units confronted one section of the 1st Maryland (Confederate) Artillery guarding the bridge over the Winchester and Potomac Railroad tracks. The Stonewall Brigade quickly came to the support of the two Confederate guns. Gen. "Allegheny Ed" Johnson consequently won the race to entrap Milroy's division. In a Herculean effort, the regiments of Milroy's Second Brigade briefly knocked the door ajar and allowed some Union troops to escape. According to Colonel Keifer, "the attempt to cut out through superior and well posted forces, and without artillery ourselves was the most desperate ever attempted." As the fire from the Confederates increased, Keifer received permission to charge the Rebel force before him. According to the colonel: "My officers and men knew that everything depended upon this effort. There was a solemn calmness about each. The order 'forward' was given and nobly obeyed."[43]

Surprising the Confederates, the 110th Ohio, supported by the 122d Ohio Infantry, charged the Rebel infantry and artillery posted in the woods along the road and almost drove into their camp. According to Private Barnhart, the two Buckeye regiments "went in with a double quick. When we got close enough we gave them a volley of minnie balls for there breakfast." For a brief time, the unexpected assault dumbfounded the Southerners. After they recovered, however, the Rebels replied with such heavy artillery and musket fire that many nearby tree limbs were knocked down.[44]

General Elliott then ordered the 123d Ohio, 87th Pennsylvania, and 18th Connecticut Infantry Regiments to assault the woods to the right of the 110th. The distance between the opposing lines varied from fifteen to one hundred feet. For nearly two hours an uneven battle raged until the exhausted Union troops ran low on ammunition. The 110th repeatedly assailed the Confederate position. On one occasion, the Ohio troops drove the Rebels past their artillery support, and the Union troops killed many of the Confederate artillerymen and their horses, rendering the battery immobile. The 110th Ohio, 122d Ohio, and a part of the 87th Pennsylvania then extricated themselves from the Confederate trap. The other Union regiments in the woods, however, were not so fortunate. The 123d Ohio, 18th Connecticut, and the balance of the 87th Pennsylvania, unable to disengage, surrendered to the Confederates en masse.

After maneuvering away from the contest near Stephenson's Depot, Colonel Keifer led the 110th and 122d Ohio Infantry Regiments to Harpers Ferry; Generals Milroy and Elliott accompanied them. Within a twelve-hour span, the Union soldiers traveled thirty-five miles and fought a two-hour battle with the enemy. The 110th escaped with 18 officers and 305 enlisted men. The 122d Ohio escaped with numbers equaling the 110th. Most other units reported to Harpers Ferry with fewer than 100 men. The 110th suffered 315 casualties during the engagements of June 13–15. On the latter day, Gen. Edward Johnson netted 2,400 prisoners from Milroy's division. The Federals suffered a total of 3,826 casualties during the fiasco at Winchester.[45]

For two weeks, the 110th remained at Harpers Ferry. Because Keifer's men left many items at Winchester, the colonel requisitioned clothes and tents for his troops. He obtained some material but asserted that the regiment needed a complete refit. For many rainy nights, Corporal Hill and the others slept without tents.

While at Maryland Heights, the Ohioans strengthened the fortifications and then prepared for an evacuation to Washington, D.C. While leading the Army of the Potomac in its pursuit of Lee's army, Maj. Gen. Joseph Hooker inspected the positions around Harpers Ferry. On June 27, Captain Moore observed that Hooker looked like everybody else, but he wore more buttons.[46]

Lieutenant General Ewell's Second Corps proved to be just the vanguard of Lee's invading army. After destroying Milroy's command at Winchester, Ewell moved his corps into Pennsylvania. The rest of Lee's Army of Northern Virginia followed. The Confederate army took Chambersburg and bombarded Harrisburg before Lee concentrated his army at Gettysburg.

The Army of the Potomac pursued the Rebels north. On June 28, President Abraham Lincoln replaced General Hooker with Maj. Gen. George Meade. The new commander pursued the Army of Northern Virginia. Three days later, the two armies collided. Gettysburg's three-day engagement was the bloodiest of the Civil War.

On July 1, while the battle raged in Pennsylvania, the Union garrison evacuated Maryland Heights. The 110th moved in the first three boats, and their new assignment was to protect the approaches to the Potomac. Two days later, Captain Spangler and Company F confronted two companies of Confederate cavalry that threatened Edward's Ferry. The next day, the boats safely reached Washington, D.C.[47]

On July 6, in the aftermath of Gettysburg, the 110th Ohio left Washington to join the pursuit of Lee's retreating army. The units that retreated from Harpers Ferry formed a new command, the Third Division, Third Corps, Army of the Potomac. The remnants of Milroy's division became the Second Brigade, under the command of Colonel Keifer. Brigadier General Elliott received command of the division, while Maj. Gen. William French took over command of the Third Corps from the wounded Maj. Gen. Daniel Sickles.

Maj. Gen. Henry Halleck, meanwhile, ordered the arrest of Major General Milroy. Military authorities court-martialed Milroy for not evacuating Winchester. The general, however, showed evidence that he was not ordered to abandon the town. For one week, Colonel Keifer visited Washington, D.C., and testified on Milroy's behalf. Later that summer, a court of inquiry convened to decide General Milroy's fate but made no formal report on the matter. Ten months later, Judge Advocate General Joseph Holt exonerated Milroy. Authorities did not formally punish any officers associated with the Winchester debacle. But Maj. Gen. Robert Milroy remained inactive while awaiting his fate. After being exonerated, he reported for duty in Nashville, where he recruited and organized militia regiments.[48]

The soldiers of the 110th Ohio captured at Winchester were moved to Richmond. These prisoners marched to Staunton and then boarded a train bound for the Confederate capital. Upon arrival, all of them spent the night in Libby Prison. In the morning, the enlisted men were transferred to Belle Isle. One soldier was glad to leave the confines of Libby Prison, formerly a tobacco warehouse, even though the treatment at Belle Isle was "barbarous, inhuman and worse than cannibalism." Rations consisted of rotten red beans boiled in dirty river water. For drinking purposes, the prisoners filtered river water through sand. In his letter of July 23, Corporal Rhoades informed his wife that the residents of Richmond faced starvation. He listed some of the prices in the Confederate capital: "Wheat per bushel $7.00, Flower barrel $33 to 35, . . . coffee pound $4.00, Sugar pound 1.25, Beans Bushel $18.00 to $20.00, . . . Potatoes $14.00, Salt 45 cents, Whiskey $25.00, Wood cord $23.00, Butter pound $1.25." On Thursday, July 23, the Confederates paroled the enlisted men. A day later, though saddened by the thought of leaving their officers in Libby Prison, the soldiers of the 110th sailed for Camp Parole in Maryland, where they awaited exchange.[49]

During the spring and summer of 1863, Federal authorities faced the possibility of a serious manpower shortage. The terms of enlistment for over one hundred volunteer infantry regiments would soon expire. Attempting to avoid the potential crisis, Republicans passed conscription legislation. This draft mechanism, however, proved to have flaws. The draftees could hire substitutes to fill their positions or they could pay a commutation fee of three hundred dollars. Low-income workers consequently were susceptible to the draft; through the use of their wealth, upper-class men could avoid conscription.

The Democratic machinery of New York City easily persuaded the low-income workers of the city to oppose emancipation. Already threatened by inflating prices that were outpacing wage increases, these workers believed that after the war, freedmen would migrate to Northern industrial centers and cause greater employment competition. They also viewed the substitute and commutation clauses of conscription as another injustice aimed at the lower classes.

On July 11, in New York City's Ninth Congressional District, officials from the Provost Marshal's Bureau drew names for the first draft lottery. Three days later, the city erupted in riots. Workers attacked everything they associated as the cause of the perceived injustice, namely conscription and emancipation. Mobs destroyed draft offices and attacked the officers and clerks assigned there. They also assaulted and, in some instances, killed policemen who opposed them. City and state authorities were unable to get assistance from the militia because those regiments were in Pennsylvania to oppose Lee's invasion. For three days in mid-July, many workers in New York City rebelled. Federal authorities delayed enforcing conscription there until twenty thousand soldiers from the Army of the Potomac arrived. On August 19, 1863, the draft in New York City resumed.[50]

This unrest soon affected the 110th Ohio, although while the riots raged the regiment generally experienced a quiet time. The month of July and the first two weeks of August proved uneventful for those who were now part of the Third Corps. On August 15, however, the army ordered Colonel Keifer to move to Alexandria, Virginia, with the 110th and 122d Ohio Infantry Regiments. After waiting four days for the transport *Atlantic* to arrive, the Buckeye troops instead boarded the steamship *Mississippi* for transport to Governor's Island, New York. From August 23 to September 6, the 110th remained in New York on garrison duty, enforcing the draft laws and escorting conscripts to their transports.[51]

When this duty ended, the 110th embarked on a ship bound for Alexandria, Virginia, where they unloaded two days later. The regiment camped at Alexandria for an additional two days before marching to rejoin the Third Corps. According to Josiah Hill, "not a man wants to go back to the Potomac army they say send me to south America Texas or the North pole any wher but save us from this degradation."[52]

For the next four days, the troops marched to join the Army of the Potomac near Fayetteville, Virginia. On September 13, while en route to the Third Corps, these Ohio troops traversed the Bull Run battleground. Corporal Hill bemoaned the treatment of the Union corpses: "Oh what a sight bones and bodies being scattered over the ground I saw to graves almost on the road with hands and feet protruding one of the legs was torn of and lay some distance away." Corporal Hill considered the sight a disgrace, "the Bodies of our soldiers killed in battle lying uncovered on the ground their bones coming apart." Upon reaching the army's position, the 110th Ohio officially became part of the Second Brigade, Third Division, Third Army Corps. Colonel Keifer resumed command of the brigade, and later he reorganized its staff.[53]

Over the next three weeks, the 110th moved only once. During this period, Hill and several other members of the regiment became sick and consequently lagged behind. They caught up with the regiment several days later. By the time he finally found the new camp, Hill had missed the distribution of rations. He and the others received no rations and did not eat for two days.[54]

While the Army of the Potomac had a brief lull in its 1863 campaign season, the Army of the Cumberland suffered a humiliating defeat at the Battle of Chickamauga. Josiah Hill expressed his concern that the setback might prolong the war twelve months. Colonel Keifer also lamented the loss. He argued that the men and officers displayed much bravery, but Union generals lost the battle on the second day because of their poor leadership. Keifer "always believed General [Alexander] McCook was a failure: look at Perryville, Stones River and Chicamauga." He continued his verbal attack by commenting that General Halleck "is at least incompetent in his position and is responsible for our many disasters and slow progress."[55]

Brigadier General Elliott transferred to the Army of the Cumberland on October 3. Though unpopular with the troops, Keifer remarked that Elliott had always treated him with kindness. The colonel assessed Elliott as having good business qualifications and being a strict disciplinarian. But he contended that General Elliott never distinguished himself for bravery at Winchester. Keifer assumed that Elliott would become Maj. Gen. William Rosecrans's chief of staff, filling the void that opened with Brig. Gen. James Garfield's election to Congress. Captain Moore of Company E rejoiced at General Elliott's departure. "Nothing could give the soldiers of our Brigade . . . more real pleasure than the fact of his going they made the woods resound with cheers when they heard of the fact." Captain Moore maintained that the general "had neither the confidence or respect of officers or men under his command." Elliott's replacement was Brig. Gen. Joseph Carr. Even though Colonel Keifer did not know him personally, he understood that Carr was a New York Republican with important political connections.[56]

On October 10, hostilities resumed after the Army of Northern Virginia crossed the Rappahannock and threatened to flank the Army of the Potomac. When the Confederates crossed, Major General Meade countered Lee's advance by ordering a retrograde movement for the Army of the Potomac. In preparation for battle, orders required the distribution of eight days' rations to the soldiers. On that first day, the army moved approximately one mile. The 110th subsequently remained on the move for the next fifteen days. According to Hill, the men marched during the day and spent many evenings on guard or picket duty: "Well the day is done and . . . after the hardest marching I ever done We are ordered out on picket duty and passed a rainy night."[57]

During the Bristoe campaign, Ohio troops cast ballots for the gubernatorial race between John Brough and Clement Vallandigham. On October 14, the men of the 110th voted. According to two members of the regiment, they believed that Brough would garner most of the Union soldiers' ballots. Corporal Hill worried that fighting might interrupt their chance for voting, and if that occurred, "I am afraid Val[landigham] will be elected as more than 4/5 of the soldier's will vote against him." According to Keifer, while skirmishing with the enemy, "ballot-boxes were opened, and a regular election was held for the Ohio troops, both the boxes and ballots being carried to the voters along the battle-line so they might vote without breaking it." After the tabulation, the colonel observed that "no Clark County man voted for Vallandigham."[58]

On several occasions, the 110th functioned as the rear guard for the army's movement. On October 13 and again two days later, the 110th skirmished with the enemy. Colonel Keifer's Second Brigade delayed A. P. Hill's Confederate divisions so that the Union Third Corps gained a sizable lead on the pursuing Confederate forces. In the afternoon of October 15, as Keifer's command rapidly moved away from Hill's force, the colonel and an orderly stopped on the high ground that overlooked Broad Run and its fords. While there, they shared a lunch of sardines and hardtack. As the two Yankees ate alone, the unsuspecting forces under Union general G. K. Warren and Confederate general A. P. Hill both prepared to cross Broad Run, and the vanguard of the two corps collided. Colonel Keifer had the rare opportunity to witness the whole battle: from chance encounter to withdrawal from the confrontation. "From my position I could see between the lines of the opposing forces; and I could note the maneuvers of each separate organization; and I could almost anticipate to a certainty the result of the attacks and counterattacks." This chance engagement turned quickly into a bloody contest as both sides were unsure of their opponent's size and intentions. The Confederates sustained 1,378 casualties, while General Warren lost only 546 men.[59]

General Lee's advance ended with Hill's defeat at Bristoe Station. The Confederates recrossed the Rappahannock River and settled into winter quarters near Brandy Station. The Army of the Potomac followed them and then established quarters on the north side of the Rappahannock at Catlett's Station.

General Meade, however, never intended to remain at Catlett's Station for the winter. On November 7, the Third Corps massed near Kelly's Ford, and the next morning, two brigades of the First Division forced a crossing there. The rest of the Third Corps followed and deployed for battle.[60]

Orders from the corps and division commanders detailed a portion of Keifer's command to capture Miller's Hill. This position, two miles north of Brandy Station, served as a forward observation post for the Confederates, and General Meade wanted the enemy infantry and artillery posted there removed. Meade took this action because he believed that Lee had deployed the Army of Northern Virginia behind the eminence.[61]

Keifer described a humorous episode prior to the assault on Miller's Hill. As the men of the 110th lay exposed to artillery fire, the shells that fell nearby covered them with dirt, and shrapnel passed among them. One man had his knapsack knocked off while another man had his tin bucket shot away from his belt. While the men hugged the ground, one of the new recruits "very innocently asked whether 'those things would hurt a feller if they hit him.'" Pvt. Ben Fye of Company C wryly told Captain Brown that he "thought it was about time to compromise this thing or some of them would get hurt."[62]

Colonel Keifer implored General Carr to use the entire command to secure the hill. Carr, however, ordered Keifer to capture the position using only two regiments. Accordingly, the 138th Pennsylvania and the 110th Ohio made the assault. The 110th deployed to the right, while the 138th Pennsylvania went on the left. The 6th Maryland and 122d Ohio Infantry Regiments supported the assault. While he watched the attacking troops move forward, Colonel Keifer noticed that the 110th moved too methodically. According to Keifer, Lieutenant Colonel Foster "would only obey an order literally, and I feared an accident, so I thought best to be upon the ground myself. I say . . . without arrogance, that I knew that my presence with the men, was worth a great deal." As the Confederates fiercely held their ground against the Pennsylvanians, Keifer pushed the skirmishers of the 110th to the crest of the hill, precipitating a Confederate withdrawal.[63]

Keifer praised Colonels William Ball, Matthew McClennan, and John Horn as "men of fine judgement and excellent executive ability. They obey my orders willingly and promptly." He praised Lieutenant Colonel Foster and Major Binkley, for they "exhibited their usual bravery." Keifer, however, criticized Foster and Binkley for their lack of dash.

The 110th Ohio's successful assault on Miller's Hill concluded their action in this campaign. The brigade suffered light casualties. One notable exception was the loss of Capt. Lazarus Andress of the 138th Pennsylvania, who was mortally wounded during the attack. After this engagement, Gen. Robert E. Lee's army crossed over the Rapidan River and assumed defensive positions farther south. The 110th subsequently moved a few miles north of the new Rebel site and occupied the winter quarters that the Confederates had recently constructed.[64]

Over the next two weeks, the soldiers of the 110th Ohio encamped near Brandy Station, drilling regularly. They also returned to their routine of fatigue, guard, and picket duties.

On November 26, the Army of the Potomac left its winter quarters and started on a new campaign. The Third Corps crossed the Rapidan River at Jacob's Ford, while the army's other corps crossed at Germanna Ford, Culpepper Mine Ford, and Ely's Ford. The Third Corps artillery, however, could not negotiate the steep banks at Jacob's Ford and later crossed at Germanna Ford, rejoining their corps the next day. This unforeseen problem, however, delayed Maj. Gen. William French's movements. When his artillery finally reunited with the column, French's corps was only three miles south of the river.[65]

Late the next morning, the Third Corps trekked south from Jacob's Ford toward Robertson's Tavern, with Brig. Gen. Henry Prince's Second Division in the van. As his column approached the Raccoon Ford Road, Prince's command collided with the lead elements of Richard Ewell's Second Corps. The brigades of the Third Division, Third Corps, deployed on the left of Prince's troops.[66]

The 110th assaulted Confederate positions on a small ridge that dominated the Union line. Colonel Keifer, upon his own initiative, assaulted and held the ridge until the First Brigade of the Third Division arrived in support. The 110th and 122d Ohio Infantry Regiments captured the summit of the ridge, while the 6th Maryland and the 138th Pennsylvania held the left flank. During the encounter, the Second Brigade repelled three Confederate counterattacks. Finally, as darkness fell, the advance troops of Maj. Gen. David Birney's First Division relieved the 110th and the rest of their brigade. This process required intricate maneuvering. To conduct a passage of lines without creating a serious breech in a defensive position could prove risky. At General Birney's request, Keifer's brigade laid down to let the First Division walk past.[67]

The two opposing armies quietly faced each other for the next two days. On November 29, Gen. G. K. Warren believed that an attack on the Confederate right could succeed. He proposed the idea to General Meade, who ordered that both Confederate flanks be assaulted early the next morning. The Third Division of the Third Corps moved into position to strengthen Warren's assault on the Confederate right. At four o'clock in the morning, the division marched to its jumping-off point. At dawn, though, the sunlight revealed the strength of the enemy's position. After a preparatory bombardment began promptly at eight o'clock, Colonel Keifer noticed that "not unfrequently through the column there could be seen on a soldier's breast a paper giving his name, company, regiment, and home address, so, if killed, his body could be identified." General Warren, upon further consideration, doubted the assault's chance for success and convinced Meade that an attack would be disastrous. For the next two days, the two armies remained in close proximity. Then, at dusk on December 1, the Army of the Potomac crossed the Rapidan. The men of the 110th Ohio returned to their camp near Brandy Station and established winter quarters.[68]

General Meade's Mine Run campaign was a failure. The Army of Northern Virginia remained in its defensive position south of the Rapidan, and the Army of the Potomac returned to its original position to the north. The 110th suffered thirty-one casualties: six killed and twenty-five wounded. Colonel Keifer lamented the death of Lt. James A. Fox, who perished during a Confederate counterattack. On November 27, the men buried Fox "at midnight, in full uniform, wrapped in his blanket, behind a near-by garden fence."[69]

During the winter months, Colonel Keifer filled the ranks of the regiment, as recruiting officers trekked to their respective counties for more men. On December 23, 1863, Lt. William Hathaway returned to Clark County for this duty. On January 4, 1864, the Henry Hawkens Band of Springfield arrived. Its arrival delighted Colonel Keifer since the musicians would now become the regimental band. Early recruiting efforts paid dividends when twenty-two new soldiers arrived on February 20, 1864.[70]

While in winter quarters, fatigue and picket duties occupied much of the soldiers' time. Paperwork and officer-of-the-day routines filled the officers' time. During the winter of 1863–64, many commanders within the army shifted positions. On December 22, 1863, Lieutenant Colonel Foster resigned and returned to Piqua. Major Binkley advanced to command the regiment and Captain McElwaine moved into Binkley's slot as major. During the fall of 1863, Binkley had become unpopular. Colonel Keifer hoped that trouble would not come from his promotion. According to Capt. William Moore, Binkley "succeeded in rendering himself odious and hated by everybody in the regiment." During these winter months, Colonel Keifer served on several courts-martial as the army attempted to rid itself of incompetent and inefficient officers. Following the engagement at Mine Run, for instance, Keifer noted that the army dismissed for cowardice Maj. Joseph Peach and Capt. Orlando Farquhar of the 122d Ohio Infantry.[71]

Many other changes occurred in the Army of the Potomac during the winter. On December 12, 1863, Colonel Keifer evoked confidence in the army's commander. He believed that "General Meade [was] the right man for the Army of the Potomac, but there are too many discordant parts for it to operate successfully." In early January 1864, General Meade applied to the War Department to consolidate the Army of the Potomac. Twice, consolidation rumors had spread through the brigade. On March 4, 1864, the army finally reorganized. The First and Third Corps dissolved and their components distributed to the Second, Fifth, and Sixth Corps. This move consequently displaced many division, brigade, and corps commanders. Major Generals William French and John Newton returned to Washington, D.C., to await other commands. The Third Division of the Third Corps consolidated with the Sixth Corps, becoming its Third Division. The dispersal of several other commands caused the demotion of other officers. Brig. Gen. James B. Ricketts became the new divisional commander, replacing General Carr. Colonel Keifer, who had served as brigade commander, now returned to command of the 110th Ohio. During the next two months, Brig. Gen. Henry Prince, Col. Benjamin Smith, and Brig. Gen. Truman Seymour each commanded the brigade for short periods.[72]

The transferred units also received new flags. The presentation of its new colors finalized the transfer of the 110th to the Sixth Corps. In a formal ceremony on April 8, 1864, Chap. Lucius Chapman presented these new flags to Colonel Keifer. Much controversy, however, surrounded the presentation because Keifer received the old flags as well. Some members of the regiment believed that the old colors should be returned to the ladies of Piqua, who had donated them.[73]

During the first seventeen months of their service, the men of the 110th traveled from west-central Ohio to northern Virginia, participated in three general engagements, and fulfilled the reserve role in another engagement. They experienced garrison duty and the life of soldiers in a campaigning army. After the humiliation at Winchester, many members of the regiment spent time in Confederate prisons. After these engagements, the men, with great reservation, became part of the Third Corps of the Army of the Potomac. During the reorganization in the spring of 1864, the unit then transferred to the Sixth Corps, which created even greater consternation among the Ohioans. This reorganization, however, caused command changes that many of them ultimately viewed in a positive fashion.

Well, I am still alive, but the scenes

of today pass description.

—Pvt. Josiah Hill

4 Well, I Am Still Alive

During the first two years of the Civil War, a pattern developed within the Army of the Potomac. Each spring, the Federals crossed the Rappahannock and Rapidan Rivers and fought the Army of Northern Virginia. Each engagement ended in Union defeat. The Federal commander subsequently retreated across the rivers, sometimes as far as the outskirts of Washington, D.C. After much haranguing, President Lincoln would replace the general. Each newly appointed commander of the Army of the Potomac spent several weeks reorganizing the staff, and then he planned to meet and defeat the Army of Northern Virginia. Confederate forces foiled each advance.

The spring of 1864, however, promised to be different. As the Union army awoke from its winter slumber, officials changed and reorganized the Army of the Potomac's composition. The first step reduced the command structure from five corps to three. Second, to fill the depleted ranks in the Army of the Potomac, Federal authorities pursued a vigorous recruiting program. In May 1864, they also reduced the size of the Union garrison at Washington, D.C. Many of these heavy artillery regiments that protected the capital reinforced the Army of the Potomac. In many cases, these regiments joined established brigades throughout the army and fought as infantry. The last and perhaps most important change occurred at the top of the command structure. On March 10, 1864, Lt. Gen. Ulysses S. Grant took command of all Union forces. Grant, however, established his headquarters with the Army of the Potomac, and the stage was set for a bloody contest.

As the weather permitted, the Federal troops participated in reviews and drills. With increased regularity, these became an important part of their schedule. Josiah Hill and other members of the 110th Ohio Volunteer Infantry noted that drill and review exercises became weekly events. Army dignitaries on many occasions watched as the regiment marched in division and corps reviews. On February 25, 1864, Pvt. Robert Baird and Col. Warren Keifer noted that Maj. Gen. William French and Brig. Gen. Joseph Carr attended one such review. On April 18, Lieutenant General Grant and Maj. Gen. George Meade reviewed the Sixth Corps.[1]

In April, target practice also became part of the schedule. On the seventh and again two weeks later, the regiment had target practice. In his letter of that day, Private Baird of Company I told his sister, Carrie, that he needed to clean his gun due to the firing that day. Later that same day, he continued the letter and informed her that he fired his weapon only once that day, but tomorrow, he expected to shoot more. Placing time constraints on target practice, General Meade required the completion of all firing between 9:00 A.M. and noon.[2]

During the last two weeks of April, the Army of the Potomac prepared for its spring campaign. On the fourteenth, the regiment's sutler, Harry Smith, left camp. Keifer also sent Duke, his favorite horse, home with Smith. Later, to replace Duke, the colonel purchased a bay mare for $125. As further evidence of an anticipated movement, the Quartermaster Department carried away all excess baggage and supplies.[3]

A distressing topic arose as these preparations continued. Governor John Brough apparently promoted some men in the 110th. This, however, enraged the personnel in the regiment. Though he approved of the recent promotions of Joseph Van Eaton and Joseph McKnight, Cpl. John Rhoades thought that the governor "does not necessarily promote qualified individuals." Cpl. Josiah Hill believed that the recent promotions "makes us feel like poor dogs rather than men for the officers that have been placed over us but I will leave the matter none can help it We are all dissgraced together." Colonel Keifer too was a harsh critic of Governor Brough. He

Adjutant Joseph Van Eaton. Courtesy of USAMHI.

stated that "[Brough] has done more to injure the service by his mode of appointing officers than he can ever do good as governor." According to Keifer, Brough's system demoralized many regiments. He argued that the governor's "promotions in my regiment have with few exceptions been of the worst kind. He has gone outside of his own declared rule to appoint and commission the worthless, cowardly and incompetent." According to the colonel, Governor Brough apparently gave Ohio troops orders that conflicted with those issued by the War Department. Keifer added that many Ohio officers did not recognize the governor's authority in this matter. The criticism also produced a ripple effect. After Col. William Ball of the 122d Ohio Infantry publicly denounced the promotion policy, Governor Brough attempted to have him dismissed.[4]

Some members of the 110th evaluated the leadership of the Army of the Potomac. Colonel Keifer voiced his reservations about General Grant. In March 1864 he asserted, "I will not detract from his greatness, but I want to be well satisfied with the man before I pronounce him superhuman." On April 18, after Generals Grant and Meade reviewed the Sixth Corps, Keifer met the lieutenant general. Afterward, he again expressed his doubts about Grant: "I am not of exalted opinion of him, but I hope to be disappointed in my estimate of him." Conversely, Pvt. John Rosser declared, "I think General Grant is the man to plan a campaign and indeed to execute it too." Continuing, he praised the Army of the Potomac as a force that is "irresistible." Similarly, Corporal Rhoades wrote that all the men have confidence in General Grant.[5]

Even though the men believed in Grant's ability, they understood what his leadership meant. For the upcoming spring and summer of 1864, Rhoades and Rosser knew that the 110th would face an extremely difficult campaign. Corporal Hill doubted that he was ready for such a hard experience. On May 1, Colonel Keifer believed the next battle would be the "bloodiest of modern time." Two days later, on the eve of the campaign, Keifer sent home his last will and testament, noting that he had not changed it for fear that it would destroy its integrity.[6]

At four o'clock on the morning on May 4, 1864, the Army of the Potomac opened its spring campaign. Grant planned to turn the Army of Northern Virginia's right flank and force Robert E. Lee to fight somewhere south of the dense thicket known as the Wilderness. Maj. Gen. Winfield Hancock's Second Corps crossed the Rapidan River at Ely's Ford and proceeded to the vicinity of Chancellorsville. Gouverneur K. Warren's Fifth Corps crossed at Germanna Ford and moved toward Wilderness Tavern. Maj. Gen. John Sedgwick's Sixth Corps followed Warren across at Germanna and bivouacked on the heights south of the ford. Lee, however, planned to strike the Federal army as it passed through the Wilderness. By doing so, he would offset the Army of the Potomac's manpower advantage.

On the campaign's second day, the Fifth Corps marched on the Orange and Fredericksburg Plank Road. The Second Corps moved toward Todd's Tavern, while the Sixth Corps followed the Fifth. Just before noon, the Fifth Corps collided with Confederate general Richard Ewell's Second Corps. The Federals deployed along the road, and the Sixth Corps came into line on its right. General Sedgwick, however, detached two elements of his command. Brig. Gen. George W. Getty's division moved to the intersection of the Brock and Orange Plank Roads and awaited the arrival of Hancock's corps. The Second Brigade of the Third Division, including the 110th Ohio, held the heights south of Germanna Ford and awaited the arrival of Maj. Gen. Ambrose Burnside's Ninth Corps.[7]

At ten o'clock that morning, Burnside finally reached Germanna Ford. Released from its duty, the Second Brigade moved forward and joined the rest of the Sixth Corps. The regiments filed into line on the right of the Gen. Horatio Wright's First Division. At the same time, Brig. Gen. Truman Seymour, the brigade's new commander, reported for duty. Colonel Keifer returned to command of the 110th, supplanting Lt. Col. Otho Binkley. Seymour conducted a brief reconnaissance and concluded that the Second Brigade overlapped the Confederate line. The 6th Maryland and the 110th Ohio deployed in the front line from left to right. Capt. Luther Brown, with Companies A and I, and Capt. Clifton Prentiss with one company of the 6th Maryland, then advanced as skirmishers. The 122d Ohio, 138th Pennsylvania, and 126th Ohio Infantry Regiments formed the second line. On the afternoon and evening of May 5, the 110th held the extreme right of the Army of the Potomac.[8]

At five o'clock that evening, Colonel Keifer was ordered to assault the Confederate flank with the brigade's front line. This attack would consequently rout the Confederates, and Lee's left flank would crumble. As the Union front line traversed the wooded, undulating ground, the 110th Ohio and the 6th Maryland came over a small rise and encountered entrenched Rebel forces. Doubting the success of a frontal assault, Keifer sent for confirmation of the order. Two hours after receiving the initial order, a second one arrived demanding an immediate attack on the works, which Keifer ordered. Capt. Luther Brown's Company I, deployed as skirmishers, immediately engaged sharpshooters from Brig. Gen. John Pegram's Virginia brigade. With the increased sound of firing, the 6th Maryland and 110th Ohio fixed bayonets and moved to within 150 yards of the Rebel fortifications. Pegram's Virginians then rose from behind their breastworks and delivered a devastating volley that halted the attack. The two Union regiments remained in their advanced positions and awaited the First Division's promised support. Contrary to Seymour's reconnaissance, the Federal line did not overlap and flank the Rebels. Rather, the Confederate line overlapped the flanks of the 6th Maryland and the 110th Ohio, and both suffered

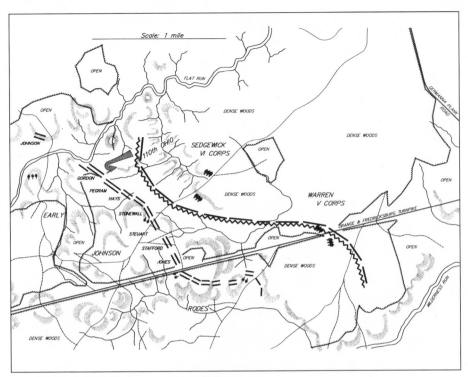

Battle of the Wilderness, evening of May 5, 1864.

heavy casualties from oblique fire. As evening fell, the 6th Maryland and the 110th Ohio remained in close proximity to the Confederates, and the opposing sides continued their destructive fire for three hours. According to Lieutenant Colonel Binkley: "it became so dark that our aim had to be guided by the flash of the enemy's guns. . . . [They] had the advantage of fighting behind breastworks, our men stubbornly held their position until the order was given to fall back." With their ammunition exhausted, the 110th "formed in rear of the second line, and laid on arms all night."[9]

Maj. William McElwaine died during the assault, and the flames that subsequently engulfed the region also consumed his corpse. Capt. John Smith of Company K and Lt. Joseph McKnight of Company E were mortally wounded. On May 6, Pvt. Robert J. Baird of Company I died from wounds received during the previous evening's attack. At half past eight that evening, a minié ball smashed both bones in Colonel Keifer's left forearm. Thirty minutes later he relinquished command of the 110th to

Capt. John Smith. Courtesy of Margaret S. Hedden.

Lieutenant Colonel Binkley and proceeded to a hospital in the rear. For the next three months, Keifer convalesced in Springfield, Ohio. During the evening assault of May 5, the 110th lost one officer and thirteen enlisted men killed, and six officers and ninety-three men wounded, for a total of 113 casualties. Similarly, the 6th Maryland suffered heavy losses. The two regiments together took 262 casualties that evening, or 27 percent of their effective strength.[10]

On the morning of May 6, the Second Brigade once again assaulted the enemy works. After the Confederates repulsed this second attack, the 110th retreated a short distance and constructed breastworks. At 2:00 P.M., Brig. Gen. Alexander Shaler's brigade of the First Division extended the Union right, relieving the Ohioans as the extreme right of the army. Skirmishing continued until sunset, when Confederate general John B. Gordon's brigade attacked and turned the Union right flank. Shaler's brigade melted before the onslaught. To stop this new threat, Lieutenant Colonel Binkley changed the facing of the regiment's right flank, but his attempt at holding the position failed. Retreating Union troops, closely pursued by Gordon's soldiers, created too much confusion. Most of the Second Brigade retreated with Shaler's brigade. During this tumult, General Shaler and the recently arrived General Seymour tried to rally the troops, though with little success. The two Union generals became separated from the main body of Northern soldiers, and the Confederates captured both. The remnants of the shattered brigades fell back about a mile before establishing a new defensive position. These troops, augmented by other Sixth Corps units, then repulsed a second Confederate assault in this sector. On May 6, the Ohioans' losses were relatively light: three enlisted men killed, seventeen wounded, and fourteen missing for an aggregate of 34 casualties. During two days of fighting in the Wilderness, the 110th Ohio suffered 134 casualties, including its colonel and major.[11]

The next day, the 110th, as part of other Sixth Corps movements, captured the ground that it had lost the previous day. Like most of the soldiers in the two armies, the Ohioans rested the remainder of the day. Rather than continue the battle in the Wilderness, General Grant ordered the Army of the Potomac to move south. Later that night, Union troops marched toward the crossroads village of Spotsylvania Court House. The Fifth Corps was in the vanguard on the Brock Road, while the Second and Sixth Corps moved on the Orange Plank Road and the Orange Turnpike. Following the army's trains, the Ninth Corps was in the rear. Lieutenant Colonel Binkley reported that "about 10 o'clock on the evening of the 7th we left our position and marched all night and until about 4 P.M. the next day, passing through Chancellorsville, to the vicinity of Spotsylvania Court-House." For four hours, the regiment occupied one position before changing to another location. According to Binkley, this change "consumed the balance of the night."[12]

Robert E. Lee, however, anticipated Grant's move, and rushed the Confederate First Corps, now commanded by Maj. Gen. Richard Anderson, to

Spotsylvania to prevent its capture by the Federals. The Army of the Potomac, therefore, would have to fight to seize this important crossroads. When Lee's forces reached Spotsylvania, they entrenched. From May 8 to May 12, Union forces repeatedly assailed the fortified Confederate position.

On the ninth, a Confederate sharpshooter killed Maj. Gen. John Sedgwick while he investigated the disposition of the enemy's forces. Maj. Gen. Horatio G. Wright replaced him as commander of the Sixth Corps. On the twelfth, part of the Sixth Corps assaulted the salient protruding from the center of the Confederate lines. The 110th skirmished with Rebel troops while other Sixth Corps units made the assault. During the fighting around Spotsylvania Court House, the regiment's losses were comparatively light and included four enlisted men killed and two officers and twenty-eight men wounded for an aggregate loss of thirty-four men. The 126th Ohio Infantry of the Second Brigade, Third Division, by comparison, suffered more severe casualties while attacking the salient, amounting to 25 percent of its effective strength.[13]

On June 27, 1864, Pvt. Elias A. Barr of Company I described the first two engagements of the spring campaign. For more than nine consecutive days, recalled Barr, there was fighting between the two sides, with the 110th under fire for seven of the nine days. The troops marched, entrenched, and fought during the day and night. According to Barr, "little time was given for repose and recreation, and the men became so exhausted and sleepy that some actually fell asleep while marching along slowly after night." The exhaustion became so great that soldiers slept while occupying an advanced line. Some weary men even dozed through skirmishes and cannonading. "Yes, they slept, as only a weary soldier can sleep, in the midst of tumult and danger; and perhaps dream of home and its endearments."[14]

After Spotsylvania, during the next week the two armies briefly tended to their wounded and rushed in reinforcements to fill their thinned ranks. Though skirmishing daily, both sides avoided another general engagement at Spotsylvania. On May 19, Ewell's corps attacked the Union left and discovered that Grant had begun another flanking movement around the Confederate right. During the night of May 20, the Army of the Potomac moved south, led by Hancock's Second Corps; Grant's objective was to cross the North Anna River near Hanover Junction. According to Lieutenant Colonel Binkley, the 110th "remained until about 10 o'clock at night, when we quietly moved out; marched all night and halted after daylight at

Guiney's Station." On Sunday, May 22, the regiment marched a short distance before halting at midday. The troops resumed the march at three o'clock and stopped for the night at Lebanon Church. The next day, the 110th served as rear guard. At midnight, the Ohioans finally crossed Pole Cat River and bivouacked. General Lee's successful defense at Spotsylvania Court House preserved for him the most direct route, though. Lee's army left the morning after Grant's movement began. Approximately one day before the Federals got there, the Confederate army arrived at the bridge.[15]

The Third Division of the Sixth Corps was not engaged at North Anna River. On May 26, it began another night march to turn Lee's flank, with the 110th Ohio and the 10th Vermont Infantry serving as pickets. The division moved out at dusk. At eleven o'clock, the guarding regiments finally crossed the North Anna River. According to Binkley, the men "marched all night, arriving at Chesterfield Station about noon next day, where three days' rations were issued. We then continued our march and rejoined the brigade just after dark." They then encamped on the Taylor Plantation in King Valley.[16]

During the movement from the North Anna River, Cpl. Fred LaRue of Company D complained, "on account of the great number of dead horses along the road. The rebs had skinned them, which did not add to their sweetness." Private Rosser, who enlisted at forty-one years of age, found that this march was extremely difficult. He complained that previous rains adversely affected the road conditions and made the trek more difficult. He commented that "it had rained during the day and night, and the roads were worked up awfully, some places knee deep." The men marched all night. At nine o'clock the next morning, they stopped for coffee, and a short time later, the regiment resumed the march. During this, the column moved twenty miles. "It was a very hot day," complained Rosser. "Oh I was awful near played out, so were many others younger than I."[17]

From the opposite sides of Totopotomy Creek, the two armies briefly confronted each other. There they rested and avoided a general engagement. On May 30, the 110th moved four miles to the left and again the next day. The Army of the Potomac continued its flanking movement. This time the objective was the crossroads at Cold Harbor. Grant had dispatched Maj. Gen. Philip Sheridan with two divisions of cavalry to capture and hold the location. Sheridan's troopers drove off Fitzhugh Lee's two Confederate cavalry brigades. Later on May 31, elements of Maj. Gen.

Richard Anderson's Confederate corps vigorously attacked the Union troopers, causing Sheridan to call for immediate infantry support.[18]

The Sixth Corps and the Eighteenth Corps, from the Army of the James, converged on Cold Harbor the following day and relieved Sheridan's troopers. Leaving at 2:00 A.M., the 110th marched through the night, arriving at Cold Harbor at 10:00 A.M. Binkley, 250 men of the 110th Ohio, and 150 men from the 87th Pennsylvania then deployed as skirmishers while the rest of the division constructed breastworks. After the balance of the corps reached the field, Binkley's skirmishers advanced and developed the enemy's position. The Eighteenth Corps followed the skirmish line toward the Rebel entrenchments. That portion of the 110th that was not on picket duty assaulted the Confederate positions with the rest of the Second Brigade, which attacked in four waves, and deployed as skirmishers. The 6th Maryland and 138th Pennsylvania were in the front line, while the second and third lines consisted of the recently arrived 9th New York Heavy Artillery. The 122d and 126th Ohio Infantry Regiments deployed as the brigade's fourth line. When one wave stalled, the next one moved past and continued the attack. The Federals subsequently captured the Confederate's first line of fortifications; Union troops converted them into defensible positions the next day.[19]

In the morning of June 3, the Sixth Corps renewed its assault on the Confederate works. Positioned from left to right, the 110th Ohio and 122d Ohio formed the front line of the Second Brigade, Third Division. The 9th New York Heavy Artillery formed the second and third lines. The 6th Maryland, the 138th Pennsylvania, and the 126th Ohio formed the fourth line. The Second Brigade assault advanced 175 yards, however it severed the connection between the 110th Ohio and the Second Division and exposed the regiment's right flank. Portions of the 110th returned Confederate fire, while the balance of the regiment constructed crude fortifications. Lieutenant Colonel Binkley said that the fire "proved so destructive that it became necessary to protect ourselves in some way. The men commenced making excavations, by digging with their bayonets and scooping up the earth with their tin cups and plates." Eventually, the men got shovels and vigorously constructed their breastworks under fire. After this disastrous assault, Corporal Hill wrote in his diary, "Well, I am still alive, but the scenes of today pass description."[20]

For the next week, the two armies remained in close proximity. The

110th rotated with other regiments on the picket line, ultimately serving there on three different days. The regiment, in each instance, occupied the frontline trenches for twenty-four hours. Private Rosser informed his wife, Lucy, that the Union lines consisted of three entrenchments and that each day the regiments rotated forward a line. Beginning at the third line, each unit moved up until it finally reached the front. After one day there, it then rotated to the rear and rested for twenty-four hours. According to Rosser, they "have not laid in a tent for near three weeks, lay right down on the ground with Gu[m] blanket around us and if there is not too much firing we sleep like tops." The Ohio private noted that, under these sleeping arrangements, "a man does not take cold as easily as a person would suppose, to lie down on the wet ground, a person would suppose it would kill any one, soon, but not half so soon as one would suppose."[21]

During their picket duty on June 11, the 110th marched to the left part of the line and relieved the 39th Wisconsin. The Confederate entrenchments nearby had a protective ditch that was four feet wide and three feet deep. On many occasions, when the Confederate and Union soldiers were in such close proximity for an extended period, they exchanged information and goods. Corporal Rhoades explained that "the rebs would hold up a paper and wave it then our man would do the same then the reb and our man would start and meet halfway and exchange then go back." He recalled, "It looks so strange to see men meet like brothers bid each other good by, go back to their works and commence shooting at each other." The opposing pickets eventually agreed upon an informal cease-fire. LaRue said that "there was but little firing in our front. The Johnnies called over for us not to fire and they would not."[22]

During this campaign, distribution of rations was a problem for the Quartermaster Department. Occasionally, members of the 110th noted the scarcity of food or the hazards entailed when preparing a meal. On May 18, Corporal Hill's supper that evening was the first meal he had eaten in twenty-four hours. Nine days later, he again complained about the lack of rations. Rhoades complained on May 31 that the men ate six hardtack per day and supplemented this thin fare with confiscated hogs, chickens, and geese. On one occasion, while the 110th was entrenched at Cold Harbor, Rhoades rummaged through the haversacks of dead Confederates to find food. The men risked being shot if they attempted to cook or to retrieve water. Private Rosser begged his wife to send him fifty cents because he spent the last of his money on food. He explained, "I was so starved out that I bought some cheese and other little things to eat." Because of these hardships, Hill, Rhoades, and Rosser commented that the people at home would not recognize the haggard members of the regiment.[23]

After ten days at Cold Harbor, Grant continued his sidling movement. On June 12, 1864, the Sixth Corps was the last to move south and cross the James River. Four days later, units of the Sixth Corps, including the 110th, boarded the transport *Star* and crossed to Bermuda Hundred. For two days, the regiment remained in positions preparatory to an assault on the Confederate entrenchments. According to Corporal Rhoades, the opposing fortifications covered forty acres. He estimated that the wall was eight feet wide and that a ditch twenty feet wide and eight feet deep protected the fort. Abatis guarded the front, and artillery posted in the vicinity covered the approaches to the fort. While waiting for the assault orders, Rhoades "had to lay in time of action by the side of a dead man who had ben killed a day or two before." The corpse "smeled so bad that I could hardly stand it, [but] we have become so used to it that we hardly notice at all."[24]

The Union troops at Bermuda Hundred, however, never assaulted the enemy position. After spending two days there, the 110th crossed the James River on a pontoon bridge to join operations against Petersburg. For the next two weeks, the regiment operated on the left wing of the army. The men spent several days on picket duty and skirmished with the enemy. On July 2, the Ohioans raided the Weldon Railroad. Four days later, they embarked on the transport *City of Albany* and arrived in Baltimore six days later. There, the Third Division, Sixth Corps, loaded into cars of the Baltimore and Ohio Railroad and rushed to Monocacy Junction, Maryland, where they reinforced Maj. Gen. Lew Wallace's small command.

During the spring of 1864, the Army of the Potomac's Overland campaign was devastating to many commands. Like other regiments in the Second Brigade, Third Division, Sixth Corps, the 110th Ohio Volunteer Infantry suffered extensive casualties. The campaign was physically, mentally, and emotionally difficult for the troops. In a period of just six weeks, the soldiers marched in the Virginia heat from Culpepper Court House to Petersburg, a distance of more than one hundred miles. During this period, the soldiers ate reduced rations and often occupied exposed positions on the picket line for great lengths of time. Opportunities for cooked meals were few. The soldiers of the 110th, in many instances, served twenty-four hours on picket duty and later that same day undertook a twenty-mile march. One night, for example, the regiment conducted a forced march and by midmorning had reached the distant battlefield of Cold Harbor, where they deployed as skirmishers and then assaulted the Confederate entrenchments.

The soldiers endured incredible physical abuse that eventually contributed to the extensive casualty list. During Grant's spring offensive, the Army of the Potomac suffered 54,926 casualties. Among these were the 235 suffered by the 110th. In a letter to his wife, Private Rosser agonized that the regiment had "marched with 550 men, we have not now got 200. Our Major McElwaine is killed Colonel Keifer severely wounded. . . . I must close by sending my love and the hope that we may yet meet when this cruel war is over to part no more. Yours till death."[25]

Lieutenant Colonel Ebright was Killed. My noble friend Colonel Horn was mortally wounded. The mention of the two names above brings to my eyes tears drawn from the deepest sorrow.

—Col. Warren Keifer

5 Tears Drawn from the Deepest Sorrow

On May 21, 1864, Maj. Gen. David Hunter assumed command of the Department of West Virginia, and sixteen days later, when Hunter's troops entered Staunton, he achieved the Union's deepest penetration into the Shenandoah Valley. After capturing and burning Lexington, the Federals threatened Lynchburg and Charlottesville. Gen. Robert E. Lee needed to suppress the threat that Hunter's forces created.

Lee quickly dispatched Maj. Gen. John Breckinridge to Lynchburg with two brigades of infantry, and on June 18, at great risk to the Confederate army and capital, he also dispatched Lt. Gen. Jubal Early and the Second Corps, Army of Northern Virginia. After defeating Hunter and driving him from the Valley, Early would later cross the Potomac River and threaten Washington, D.C. Lee hoped his ambitious plan would draw the Army of the Potomac, or at least elements of it, away from Richmond and Petersburg. On June 22, after Early chased Hunter for three days, he turned his

Southerners north. Ten days later, when Early's corps emerged from the Shenandoah Valley, the citizens of Washington, D.C., and Baltimore raised an alarm.[1]

Maj. Gen. Lew Wallace, whose department Early's invasion seriously threatened, moved to meet the Confederates as far west of the Union capital as possible. Wallace positioned his twenty-three hundred men at Monocacy Junction, three miles east of Frederick, Maryland. With many inexperienced National Guard regiments in his command, he understood that the Confederate veterans would oust him from his position. Wallace's goals, though, were to force Early to deploy for battle and to determine his objective.[2]

Lt. Gen. Ulysses Grant reacted to Early's invasion by dispatching five thousand Yankee troops to Baltimore. On July 6, the 110th Ohio boarded the transport *City of Albany.* That night, as the transport moved from the James River to Chesapeake Bay, Pvt. Joseph Warfield, a Clark County farm laborer who served in Company I, fell overboard and drowned. On July 8, Brig. Gen. James B. Ricketts's division unloaded at Baltimore, and the general hurried his available troops to the Monocacy River. From 1:00 A.M. to 3:00 A.M. July 9, his ten regiments unloaded at Monocacy Junction. Later that morning, three more of Ricketts's regiments, which were delayed during transport, left Baltimore bound for Monocacy Junction. The 6th Maryland, 67th Pennsylvania, and most of the 122d Ohio were scheduled to arrive at Monocacy about one o'clock that afternoon.[3]

The banks of the Monocacy River were steep. With few places to ford, the three bridges that crossed the river three miles east of Frederick—two wooden spans for the Baltimore Pike and the Washington Pike and one of iron for the Baltimore and Ohio Railroad—were strategically important. Selecting these few bridges and fords for his defensive line, Wallace placed his green troops to the right. These inexperienced soldiers guarded the Baltimore Pike Bridge and Crum's Ford. On his left, Wallace then positioned Ricketts's ten regiments. He gambled that Early's butternut soldiers would cross the Monocacy River at the Washington Pike and railroad bridges to assail the Union left, and so deployed Ricketts's Sixth Corps veterans to hold the vital crossings where he guessed there would be the heaviest fighting.[4]

On July 9, General Ricketts deployed the First Brigade, under the command of Col. William S. Truex of the 14th New Jersey, on his left, and the Second Brigade, Col. Matthew McClennan of the 138th Pennsylvania commanding, to the right. The Union troops hastily constructed earthworks

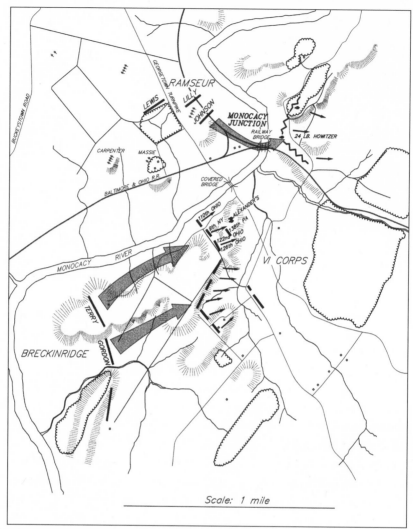

Battle of Monocacy, July 9, 1864.

that overlooked the river crossings. Lt. Col. Otho Binkley and the 110th held the Second Brigade's left flank, where the two Sixth Corps brigades connected. The 9th New York Heavy Artillery, under the command of Lt. Col. William H. Seward Jr., filed into line behind Binkley's Buckeyes.

At eight o'clock that morning, Confederate infantry emerged from the outskirts of Frederick. General Early then deployed his only available cavalry, Brig. Gen. John McCausland's unreliable brigade. McCausland's "buttermilk rangers" scouted beyond the Union left looking for an alternate crossing. A local farmer showed the Confederate cavalry commander a little-known farm ford at the mouth of Bellenger Creek, the McKinney-Worthington Ford. The cavalry dismounted and sent their horses back across the river. Believing that they only faced Union militia, the Rebel horsemen confidently prepared to fight dismounted.[5]

Ricketts realized that McCausland's crossing threatened the entire Union position. Truex's First Brigade refused the left flank and extended their line from the Thomas House to the Baker Valley Road. From left to right, Truex deployed four companies of the 8th Illinois Cavalry along with the 10th Vermont, 87th Pennsylvania, 14th New Jersey, and the 106th and 151st New York Infantry Regiments. Companies B and C of the 122d Ohio dashed forward and strengthened the 10th Vermont's skirmish line on the Worthington property.[6]

Believing that they would quickly defeat Wallace's command, McCausland's dismounted troopers advanced in line of battle. The sheer strength of the cavalry assault sent the skirmishers tumbling back to the main Union line. When McCausland's troopers cleared a fence that separated the Thomas and Worthington properties, Truex's brigade greeted the surprised Confederates with a devastating volley. The Sixth Corps veterans' fire smashed McCausland's attack and littered the Thomas property with Confederate dead and wounded. McCausland and the remnants of his shattered brigade, however, were not to be bested by Union militia. The Rebel cavalryman reinforced and extended his line of battle, attempting to find the vulnerable Union left flank.[7]

Ricketts hurriedly maneuvered to counter McCausland's new threat. The Union infantry extended their line and retreated a short distance to a small roadside ditch paralleling the Washington Pike. Ricketts doublequicked the 138th Pennsylvania and a battalion of the 9th New York from their riverbank entrenchments into the ditch on the 10th Vermont's left. Ricketts's Second Brigade now redeployed with the 126th Ohio and the remaining 9th New York battalion adjoining Truex's right. Binkley's 110th Ohio now refused their left flank and connected with the right of the 9th New York Heavy Artillery. When the second Rebel assault appeared, the Sixth Corps veterans again unleashed a volley that again devastated the dismounted Confederate troopers.[8]

When Ricketts's veterans stopped McCausland's second assault, the

Federals surged forward and drove back the Confederate brigade. With their right flank advancing along the river, the 110th was struck by a "murderous fire of Musketry and Artillery, the latter coming obliquely from the front and rear, and directly from the right." Binkley's Buckeyes pursued McCausland's troopers to the Worthington property. "Finding it impossible to hold [their] position . . . , [the 110th] fell back a few rods and formed along a cut in the Washington Turnpike." When the Union counterstroke stalled and pulled back, a Confederate bullet struck Cpl. John Rhoades's "napsack hitting the side of panhandle then passing through a towel doubled then through a shirt doubled . . . then through five folds of gum blanket the ball lodging in blanket[;] thus [he] was mercifully preserved."[9]

Though McCausland's first assault was disastrous, General Early now knew where he could flank the strong Union position. The Confederate cavalry's severe repulse also warned Early that there was more across the river than just Union militia. "Old Jube" deployed his as yet uncommitted infantry. Maj. Gen. John Breckinridge quickly marched his two divisions to the McKinney-Worthington Ford. While Brig. Gen. John Echols's division remained in reserve on the west bank, Breckinridge led forward Maj. Gen. John B. Gordon's hard-hitting division. Not wanting to waste time, Gordon pleaded with his brigades to cross without removing their shoes. Responding to his call, Gordon's Virginians, Georgians, and Louisianans plunged across the river.[10]

Gordon's three brigades double-quicked to the Worthington property and formed in line of battle. From left to right, Gordon deployed Brig. Gen. William Terry's Virginia brigade, Brig. Gen. Zebulon York's Louisiana brigade, and Brig. Gen. Clement Evans's Georgia brigade. The Confederates deployed in three lines of battle and advanced en echelon toward the Union line.

Evans's Georgians climbed the fences and marched through the wheat fields north and east of the Worthington house. As they approached the Thomas farm's outbuildings, Truex's line exploded with a maelstrom of fire that rocked the Confederate line. Still, the Georgians pressed forward. During the ensuing fight along the Baker Valley Road and the Thomas farm, both sides inflicted heavy casualties, with some Georgia regiments suffering 50 percent casualties. General Evans fell when a Yankee minié ball smashed his pocket housewife and entered his side, driving many needles in with it. For many years afterward, Evans would pull pins and needles from his side. The Georgians' constant pressure and an acute shortage of ammunition took its toll on Truex's men. The Union left flank, however, held.

York's Louisianans then struck the juncture between the two Union brigades. A small ravine concealed York's approach, and the Louisianans unexpectedly burst upon the 151st New York and 126th Ohio. The fighting quickly devolved into hand-to-hand combat, but the small Louisiana brigade was unable to break the line. York's men retreated a short distance and exchanged fire with the two Union regiments. The loss of three color-bearers in both Union regiments attests to the contest's ferocity.[11]

Terry's Virginians, however, were the key to the Confederate assault. To strengthen his left flank, General Ricketts had stripped regiments from his right. Only two units now held the weakened Union right, one battalion of the 9th New York "Heavies" and the 110th Ohio. As Ricketts's division refused its left flank, these two Union regiments were pulled from their entrenchments facing the river. After smashing McCausland's assault, Lieutenant Colonels William H. Seward Jr. (son of Lincoln's secretary of state) and Otho Binkley deployed their small force in an abandoned road cut. From here, the Union regiments faced the Confederate veterans of Terry's brigade, including the remnants of the famous Stonewall Brigade.

After advancing through a cornfield and driving back the Union skirmishers, the Virginians tore down a rail fence and pressed forward. General Gordon accompanied Terry's brigade and restrained the Virginians from needlessly chasing the fleeing skirmishers. Gordon wanted his troops to conserve their energy until they contacted the main Federal line.[12]

Company F of the 151st New York held the skirmish line in the cornfield. At the appearance of Terry's Virginians, the New Yorkers fired a shot each and then ran back to McClennan and Truex's position. Binkley and Seward now prepared their men for the expected Confederate assault. The two officers had chosen a good defensive site. The Confederate's new axis of attack rendered ineffective the Union rifle pits along the river. The 9th New York and 110th Ohio, however, took advantage of the abandoned road cut near the Washington Pike.

When Terry's brigade closed to within one hundred yards, the two Federal regiments rose and fired a volley that halted the Rebel advance. The two lines then continuously exchanged volleys, but the New Yorkers and

Ohioans held firm. While the other nine partial Confederate regiments exchanged fire with the Federal troops, General Terry sent the five fragmentary regiments of Col. J. H. S. Funk's consolidated Stonewall Brigade to flank Binkley's and Seward's stubborn Yankees. Funk's men followed the Worthington Spring hollow to the banks of the Monocacy River. The remnants of the old Stonewall Brigade emerged near the 110th Ohio's right. Funk's Confederates then wheeled left and fired into the 110th Ohio's unprotected flank. After enduring enfilading artillery fire for the past two hours, the fire of Funk's men from an unexpected direction broke the 110th Ohio and the 9th New York Heavy Artillery. The two Union regiments ran pell-mell for Gambrill's Mill. As the 110th raced from the field, the regimental color-bearer fell mortally wounded, and it appeared that the colors would be lost. At great personal risk, however, Cpl. W. R. Moyer of Company H dashed back to the road cut and snatched the flag to safety.[13]

The rout of Binkley's and Seward's men completely unhinged Ricketts's line. The collapse of the right flank had a domino effect on each successive regiment. Soon, Ricketts's entire division fled the field. Union officers desperately tried to stem the flow, and some men rallied near Gambrill's Mill. But after briefly exchanging volleys with the pursuing Confederates, this line too collapsed.[14]

The Federals left most of their casualties on the battlefield. In his official report, General Wallace lambasted the Baltimore and Ohio Railroad agent for removing a nearby train. According to him, Federal authorities had assigned this train to transport casualties. For lack of transportation, therefore, Wallace's veterans begrudgingly abandoned their fallen comrades. During the remainder of the day, Wallace's shattered command marched to Ellicott's Mills, where they bivouacked for the night.[15]

Other members of the 110th Ohio were not as fortunate as Rhoades or Moyer and were counted among the Union casualties. Cpl. Frederick LaRue and Pvt. John Rosser were among the Yankees captured at Monocacy. A Confederate minié ball struck Capt. Luther Brown of Company I in the shoulder and exited from his neck, severely wounding the Clark County native. During the Federal retreat, Cpl. Charles Berry and several other men of Company I carried the disabled officer from the field but abandoned him when pursuing Confederate cavalry almost captured the group. Early newspaper reports proclaimed Brown's wound mortal. When Union troops later entered Frederick, they found that the captain had indeed

Pvt. John Free. Courtesy of Larry Strayer.

survived. He eventually spent a lengthy convalescence in Springfield, Ohio, and later returned to the Third Division as its provost marshal.[16]

Sgt. James Howell of Company E fell when a Confederate ball struck and broke his leg. Since he was unable to leave the battlefield, the Rebels captured the wounded man, and doctors amputated his leg. Two days later at Frederick, Sergeant Howell died from his wound. During the fighting on the Union left, Pvt. John Free of Company A was killed. After being shot in the arm, Cpl. Josiah Hill spent the next three weeks in Baltimore and Annapolis hospitals. During the month of August, Hill went home on furlough. On September 2, he returned to the hospitals in Baltimore and

Washington. The next month, Hill reported to Harpers Ferry and on November 27 finally returned to active duty.[17]

General Wallace's force suffered 1,294 casualties, primarily soldiers from Ricketts's command. The First Brigade lost 505 men, while the Second Brigade suffered 567 casualties. The 110th Ohio accounted for 11 percent of the total Federal casualties at Monocacy. The regiment lost 1 officer and 3 enlisted men killed, 5 officers and 77 men wounded, and 2 officers and 50 enlisted men captured or missing, for an aggregate of 138 casualties.[18]

On July 10, Early's force continued its march east. The next day, these Confederate troops reached the outer fortifications of Washington. As Early approached Fort Stevens on the northwest corner of the capital, the first elements of the Sixth Corps arrived from City Point. Realizing that additional Union reinforcements must be coming, Early retreated to the relative safety of the Shenandoah Valley. The Sixth Corps and the recently arrived Nineteenth Corps pursued the Army of the Valley around the Blue Ridge Mountains and through the many gaps.[19]

Ricketts's Third Division arrived in Washington on July 14 and, after marching nearly forty miles in the next three days, finally caught up with the Federal main body at Hamilton, Virginia. On July 20, Maj. Gen. Horatio G. Wright's corps began a retrograde movement. Three days later, the Union veterans marched across the Chain Bridge into Washington, D.C.

On July 26, Wright's command moved along the northern bank of the Potomac River and three days later crossed the Potomac at Harpers Ferry, camping near Bolivar, West Virginia. The next morning, the Federals again crossed the Potomac. On July 31, they finally encamped for two days near Frederick, Maryland. Wright's command crossed the Monocacy River on August 3 and camped near the Third Division's battlefield.[20]

During this two-week span, the Union troops marched approximately 170 miles. Corporals Rhoades and Hill complained about the extremely difficult conditions. Rhoades, in fact, temporarily became lame when his great-toenails blackened and fell off. On July 28, Private Rosser returned to the 110th Ohio after he escaped from his Confederate captors. During the regiment's stay near Frederick, several members visited the Monocacy battlefield. In his August 4 letter to the *Troy Times,* "Joppa" described the battle and the experiences of several men. One veteran stated that "on top of the hill there when they shelled us, I lay so flat I was'nt thicker than a side of sole leather." After the retreat began, another veteran recounted, "through that field you could'nt have seen my coat tail for dust I kicked up."[21]

As the two armies maneuvered between Winchester and Washington, General Grant decided that creating a unified command structure was the optimum means for pursuit of Early's forces. The War Department consequently created the Middle Military Division, and Grant entrusted his cavalry chief, Maj. Gen. Philip "Little Phil" Sheridan, with the new command. Observing that there were many scattered units in the Department of West Virginia, Sheridan realized he must consolidate his forces. After achieving this goal, he could then confront Early's Army of the Valley.[22]

At the end of July, General Grant ordered Sheridan to attack Early's Confederates in the Shenandoah Valley and "follow him to the death." On August 6, Major General Sheridan arrived at Harpers Ferry and began the reorganization and consolidation of his new command. To aid in the endeavor, Grant further augmented Sheridan's forces by adding three divisions of cavalry from Petersburg. The consolidation and expansion of Union arms in the region swelled Sheridan's Army of the Shenandoah to 48,000 men. On August 10, Sheridan moved and occupied Winchester. He then pursued Early up the Shenandoah Valley. As Federal troops appeared near Early's stronghold at Fisher's Hill, Grant sent word that Lee had reinforced the Army of the Valley. Sheridan consequently became cautious, and on August 21, the Army of the Shenandoah retreated to the vicinity of Harpers Ferry. Eight days later, Union troops once again pushed forward to Charles Town, Virginia, and for the next three days they camped near there. On September 3, the Sixth Corps moved to Berryville, where it remained for sixteen days.[23]

Colonel Keifer returned from his convalescence in Springfield, Ohio, on August 26, after recovering from his Wilderness wounds. Originally, he had been transported by ambulance to Fredericksburg, Virginia, where he stayed for several weeks. He had three large wounds in his arm. At first, the colonel thought his arm would be amputated, but the doctors saved the injured limb. While in the hospital at Fredericksburg, Keifer observed that the application of ice was the only pain relief that the physicians administered. He also noted that Dorothea Dix visited him during his stay.

On August 27, while at Harpers Ferry, Keifer assumed command of the brigade. For many months, however, his wounded left arm remained splinted and in a sling. According to Corporal Rhoades, Keifer "carried his arm in a tin case." Despite his disability, the colonel's return caused much satisfaction in the brigade.[24]

On September 14, Maj. Gen. Joseph Kershaw's Confederate infantry division and Maj. W. E. Cutshaw's artillery battalion departed Winchester on the Front Royal Road. The next day, Thomas Law, who regularly traveled to Winchester to peddle fresh vegetables, carried a message from General Sheridan to Miss Rebecca Wright. Sheridan implored her to help the Union cause by sending him information regarding Early's troops and their dispositions. On September 16, Miss Wright informed Sheridan of Kershaw's departure.[25]

"Little Phil" immediately recognized the information's value. The next day, Sheridan learned from his cavalry units that two Confederate divisions were at Martinsburg while the rest of Early's forces remained at Winchester. Realizing that the Confederate army was weakened and divided, Sheridan planned to crush it.[26]

On September 18, while at Martinsburg, Early learned of Grant's presence at Charles Town and surmised that Union operations would soon begin. Quickly reacting to consolidate his dispersed forces, the Confederate commander marched the two divisions at Martinsburg toward Winchester. When they bedded down that night, Early's four divisions were barely within supporting distance.[27]

At dawn the next day, Brig. Gen. James H. Wilson's cavalry division plunged across Opequon Creek and captured a small Confederate breastwork. Wright's infantry corps closely followed the horsemen. By eight o'clock, the Sixth Corps began relieving Wilson's troopers in the captured breastworks. Brig. Gen. George W. Getty's division aligned on the left of the Berryville Pike. While Brig. Gen. David A. Russell's division was the Sixth Corps's reserve, Ricketts's division formed on the right of the pike. After a delay at the Spout Spring Ford, Maj. Gen. William H. Emory's Nineteenth Corps finally crossed Opequon Creek as well. Brig. Gen. Cuvier Grover's division formed on Ricketts's right, while Brig. Gen. William Dwight's division became Emory's corps reserve.

Upon hearing the firing in front of Maj. Gen. Stephen D. Ramseur's position, Early rushed Gordon's and Maj. Gen. Robert Rodes's divisions to his aid. General Breckinridge, at the head of Brig. Gen. Gabriel Wharton's division, held the Martinsburg Pike near Stephenson's Depot. General Ramseur gained time for reinforcements to arrive by alternately fighting and retreating. At ten o'clock, Rodes's division went into line on Ramseur's left, and Gordon beyond Rodes.[28]

As the Union troops prepared for the assault, Lt. Col. Aaron Ebright of the 126th Ohio Volunteer Infantry approached Colonel Keifer. Ebright informed Keifer that he had a premonition of his own death. To alleviate his friend's apprehensions, the colonel quickly recounted the many battles that they had survived. Still, Ebright feared that he would die this day. Keifer finally reassured his friend that if he should fall, his body would be sent home for burial in Lancaster, Ohio. He also promised to write a letter to the lieutenant colonel's wife.

About 11:30 A.M., the Union troops surged forward. Ricketts's and Getty's divisions slowly advanced along the Berryville Pike. The Federals pushed Ramseur's division back to the farm owned by Enos Dinkle Sr. Keifer deployed the two thousand men of the Second Brigade in two lines of battle. The 126th Ohio deployed on the left of the front line and was to maintain connection with the Berryville Pike. Deploying successively to the right were the 6th Maryland, 138th Pennsylvania, and 67th Pennsylvania. The 9th New York Heavy Artillery deployed on the left of the second line, while the 122d Ohio and 110th extended it to the right. The brigade moved through the rugged terrain of Ash Hollow and then charged up a ninety-foot hill to reach the Dinkle farm plateau. As Ricketts's veterans drove the Confederates from the farm, seven cannon of Lt. Col. Carter M. Braxton's artillery battalion opened fire. Keifer noticed that the Rebel guns were without infantry support and quickly dispatched the 138th Pennsylvania, 67th Pennsylvania, and 110th Ohio to silence them. The three Union regiments advanced at the double-quick, and when within range, unleashed a devastating volley. The Union veterans continued their fire until they had killed the battery horses and driven off the Confederate gunners.[29]

Meanwhile, Grover's division routed Brig. Gen. Clement Evans's brigade of Gordon's division and vigorously pressed its advantage. Because Sheridan's instructions required that Ricketts's left maintain connection with the Berryville Pike, a dangerous gap between the two Federal divisions developed. The only Union troops in the gap were the three Union regiments sent to silence Braxton's guns. Rodes spotted the widening gap and exploited it by pouring his Rebel division into the opening.

As Rodes's veterans advanced, Brig. Gen. Cullen Battle's Alabama brigade charged the 138th Pennsylvania, 67th Pennsylvania, and 110th Ohio. The three veteran regiments stood firm. Battle's brigade, however, overlapped the Union line on both flanks. With devastating fire coming from their front and sides, the Pennsylvanians and Ohioans eventually broke and retreated in disorder to Ash Hollow.

Without any Union infantry to their immediate front, Rodes's Confederates poured an enfilading fire into the right flank of Ricketts's division on the Dinkle farm plateau. Subsequently, the rest of Keifer's brigade and Col. William Emerson's brigade withdrew. Since the troops on his right flank retreated, Maj. Gen. George Getty also withdrew his Second Division from the height. Ramseur's division eagerly pursued the retiring Federals. As the Second Brigade retreated, Keifer recounted that "while [Ebright] was riding near me he fell dead from his horse, pierced in the breast by a rifle ball."

The three Yankee regiments that had been in the gap between the Sixth and Nineteenth Corps, however, slowed Rodes's butternut infantry. Maj. Gen. David Russell's First Division plugged the hole in the Union line, effectively stopping the Confederate assault. Both sides lost heavily on this portion of the battlefield. Generals Robert Rodes and A. C. Godwin died during the Confederate counterstroke, as did Russell.[30]

A bloody stalemate along the Berryville Pike ensued. On Early's left, however, two of Sheridan's cavalry divisions made progress against Wharton's infantry and Col. William H. Payne's cavalry brigade. Sheridan then deployed the yet uncommitted Eighth Corps to press Early's left flank. Maj. Gen. George Crook's two divisions emerged from a morass and smashed Gordon's left. Maj. Gen. A. T. A. Torbert, leading Sheridan's cavalry, had two divisions charge across open ground, routing the Confederates. As Wharton and Payne gave way, General Sheridan rode along the Sixth and Nineteenth Corps lines urging his troops forward. His presence was unlike that of any other Union commander. Sheridan's confidence and excitement electrified his troops, and the Union veterans responded by charging the Rebel works in their front, making their victory complete.[31]

With the collapse of his left flank, Early's army disintegrated. Many Confederate soldiers fled through the streets of Winchester. Col. Thomas Munford's cavalry brigade, accompanied by artillery, occupied Star Fort. This small force made a determined stand that allowed Ramseur's division to reorganize for a possible rear-guard action. On the Senseny Road, Maj. Gen. Lunsford Lomax held at bay Wilson's Federal cavalry division, a maneuver that prevented the Union troopers from wreaking havoc upon Early's retreating army.[32]

The aftermath of the engagement near Opequon Creek showed that both armies took extensive casualties. The Confederates suffered 276 killed,

1,827 wounded, and 1,818 missing for an aggregate of 3,921. Union forces lost 697 killed, 3,983 wounded, and 338 missing for a total of 5,018. The 110th Ohio suffered 7 men killed and 5 officers and 43 men wounded for a total 55 casualties. Corporal Rosser was wounded in the leg. Lt. Joshua Deeter, correspondent to the *Troy Times* under the pseudonym "Joppa," later died of wounds received at this Third Battle of Winchester. So too did Capt. Alexander Trimble. On September 20, in a letter to his wife, Eliza, Keifer mourned that "Lieutenant Colonel Ebright was killed. My noble friend Colonel Horn was mortally wounded. The mention of the two names above brings to my eyes tears drawn from the deepest sorrow."[33]

At daybreak on September 20, the Army of the Shenandoah pursued Early's men. Later that afternoon, the Union army found the Confederates posted behind the strong fortifications at Fisher's Hill, near Strasburg. Early deployed Wharton's division on the right, while Gordon's division formed on Wharton's left. Brig. Gen. John Pegram, now commanding Ramseur's division, extended Gordon's left and Ramseur, taking over for the fallen Robert Rodes, put his division on Pegram's left. General Lomax's cavalry division held the extreme left of the Confederate line.[34]

Sheridan, realizing that his men could not capture the Confederate lines by direct assault, maneuvered to take the position with a turning column. The Eighth Corps, therefore, moved into the heavy timber near Hupp's Hill, just north of Cedar Creek. The next day, the Sixth Corps closed on the Confederate works, resulting in a severe fight for the possession of some high ground near Tumbling Run. After Ricketts's and Getty's divisions secured the position, the First Division, now commanded by Brig. Gen. Frank Wheaton, deployed to their left. On September 22, Emory's two divisions extended the Union left.

At dawn, the Eighth Corps, moving under the cover of intervening woods and ravines, marched to the western part of the valley near Little North Mountain. After Crook's corps passed, Ricketts's division extended the Union right. The Third Division now faced Ramseur's division on the Confederate left and openly showed preparations to assault the Rebel front. Confederate lookouts on Massanutten Mountain noticed Ricketts's maneuvering and informed Early that it would actually make the main Federal assault.[35]

At four o'clock, one hour after Ricketts extended the Union right, the Eighth Corps reached its position. One-half hour later, the undetected Federals stormed out of the woods and easily routed Lomax's cavalry. As

Crook's men drove east, Ramseur changed his division's front to face this new threat.

While Crook's men pressured Ramseur, Sheridan's remaining infantry began a left-wheel movement to flank Early's line. Ricketts's division charged the Confederate line to their front. After penetrating the line, his Yankee veterans turned east and maintained their advance. Getty's division continued the frontal assault and followed with a wheel left.

When Ramseur's troops left their works to face Crook's men, the 110th charged the Confederate fortifications. The timing of the Union frontal assault caught Ramseur's troops in the midst of their change. Numerous panic-stricken Confederates immediately fled or surrendered. Lt. Robert Wiley and Privates Elias Barr and William Wise of the 110th Ohio, with Pvt. O. A. Ashbrook of the 126th Ohio Infantry, for instance, captured Capt. William A. Ashby (brother of Confederate general Turner Ashby) and twenty enlisted men.

After the Federal troops turned the Confederate left flank, the resistance of Early's demoralized army quickly collapsed. The Army of the Valley fled south along the Valley Pike. This time, however, Col. Thomas Devin's cavalry brigade was in position to harry the fleeing Confederates. The Federal horsemen pursued the Rebels to Mount Jackson, where the Southerners made a stand. Devin could not dislodge this group. Sheridan subsequently sent the balance of Brig. Gen. William Averell's division to defeat these Confederates and continue the pursuit of Early's army. Instead, Averell withdrew and encamped for the evening. The Army of the Valley took advantage of the respite and marched first to Woodstock, then to New Market. On September 26, Early's army passed through Brown's Gap.[36]

The engagement at Fisher's Hill was a decisive victory for the Union troops. Not only had they routed Early's army from the supposedly impregnable position of Fisher's Hill, they had done so with ease and little loss. The Army of the Shenandoah suffered 528 casualties: 1 officer and 51 men killed, 33 officers and 424 men wounded, and 19 men missing. Early's losses were 30 killed, 210 wounded, and 995 missing, for an aggregate loss of 1,235. The Confederate Army of the Valley also lost eleven pieces of artillery.[37]

Sheridan's troops pursued the Rebels up the Valley. On September 26, Federal cavalry skirmished heavily with Early's forces near Brown's Gap, but the Union troopers avoided a general engagement. In compliance with orders from Sheridan, General Torbert destroyed the Virginia Central Railroad. He then moved his command to Staunton and destroyed an immense quantity of army stores there. Brig. Gen. Wesley Merritt moved his division to Port Republic.

Sheridan, meanwhile, consolidated his position near Mount Crawford. He posted the Sixth and Nineteenth Corps there, while Crook's Eighth Corps marched to Harrisonburg. The three infantry corps waited for the return of the Federal troopers before backtracking to the vicinity of Winchester. For about one week, the Army of the Shenandoah remained in the upper valley.

Rather than operate from an advance base there, Sheridan wanted to move his command back to the lower valley. He argued that it was not logical to operate from a long and tenuous line of communication and supply and wanted Federal troops to guard the northern exit of the valley. He further believed that as his troops retired from the area, they should leave the Valley untenable for use by the enemy. Later, after retiring from the Shenandoah, the War Department would dismantle Sheridan's army by returning many of the units to the Union lines at Petersburg.[38]

On October 6, Sheridan began his retrograde movement. As the infantry moved north, the Federal cavalry laid waste to the region. Union soldiers and troopers drove many head of livestock before the army while Union wagons carried away many perishable goods. The cavalry destroyed any other goods that they could not haul away and also demolished any means of manufacturing goods for the Confederacy. Sheridan's men destroyed "large quantities of Flour, hay and grain, that have been collected and stored for the Confederate Army." Keifer noted that the troopers also burned "all mills, barns, grain and hay stacks, driving off all horses, cattle, sheep and hogs, and bringing away all Negroes. The object seems to be the entire destruction of everything that could be of use to the rebels."[39]

This scorched-earth policy, however, disgusted some members of the 110th. Corporal Rhoades and Colonel Keifer, for instance, believed that it was necessary to bring the war to a successful conclusion. Rhoades commented that in "many places [local citizens] will get no corn because the yankeys eat all [of it.] . . . sometimes I feel sorry for the women & children but I see no other way to put down the rebellion for the rebs get their supplies from the valley . . . and we want to cut as far as we can their supplies."[40]

On October 13, Secretary of War Edwin Stanton summoned Sheridan to Washington, D.C., for further consultation. Three days later, at eight o'clock in the morning, Sheridan reported to Secretary Stanton and Maj.

Gen. Henry Halleck. He wanted to promptly return to his command after the meeting, and Stanton consequently ordered that a train be ready at noon to whisk "Little Phil" back to Martinsburg.[41]

General Early's army followed the Federal troops down the Valley. While the Federal army encamped at Cedar Creek, the Army of the Valley reestablished its position in the fortifications at Fisher's Hill. Federal troops were unaware of the Rebel presence until Confederate artillery shelled the Eighth Corps camp from Hupp's Hill. After a brief but fierce engagement, the Confederate artillery withdrew to Fisher's Hill.[42]

On October 14, the Army of the Shenandoah encamped on the northern bank of Cedar Creek. Protected by the impassable Massanutten Mountain, the Union army's left flank rested on Cedar Creek. The Eighth Corps occupied this position with Col. Joseph Thoburn's division holding an advanced post on a small rise near Bowman's Mill Ford. Col. Rutherford B. Hayes's division occupied a position east of the Valley Pike. Col. J. Howard Kitching's small provisional division camped to Hayes's left. The Nineteenth Corps occupied the line near the Valley Pike. General Emory's two divisions defended a position covering the Valley Pike bridge that crossed over Cedar Creek and also protected the Hottles Mill Ford.

The Sixth Corps extended the Union right. The Third Division adjoined the Nineteenth Corps at Meadow Brook. Keifer's Second Brigade held the left of the Sixth Corps. Wheaton's division and Getty's division prolonged the Federal right. Since Maj. Gen. Horatio Wright commanded the Army of the Shenandoah during Sheridan's absence, Ricketts now commanded the Sixth Corps, while Keifer commanded the Third Division. Col. William Ball now commanded the brigade.[43]

On October 17, unwilling to sit idle, the irascible and aggressive Early directed his subordinates to submit plans for attacking the Federal army. Pegram proposed an assault on the Federal army's right. Generals Gordon and Evans, supported by Capt. Jedediah Hotchkiss, proposed a movement against the Union left. Gordon and Hotchkiss believed it feasible to send an infantry column on a night march down a narrow path between the base of Massanutten Mountain and the North Fork of the Shenandoah River. Early assigned Gordon to command the flanking column, which would consist of Pegram's, Gordon's, and Ramseur's infantry divisions with Gen. William Payne's cavalry brigade.[44]

Shortly before 4:30 A.M., Kershaw's brigades, accompanied by Jubal Early, forded Cedar Creek and quickly subdued the pickets at Bowman's Mill Ford. About ten minutes later, Payne's cavalry splashed across the river at Bowman's Ford and captured the few sentries there.[45]

Hearing the rising crescendo of Kershaw's attack on Thoburn's position, Gordon hurried his divisions toward Hayes's and Kitchings's positions. As Hayes's regiments scurried into their fortifications, Gordon's assault force struck a sledgehammer blow against the Union troops. The Confederates, in many instances, captured or killed the soldiers as they emerged from their shelter tents. Hayes's line quickly disintegrated before the Confederate onslaught. Union losses were heavy. Crook's shattered command fled northwest toward Belle Grove and the entrenchments of Emory's Nineteenth Corps.

Alarmed at the increased firing to their east, Emory's men answered the "long roll." General Wright, after a brief visit to Hayes's position, arrived at the Nineteenth Corps headquarters. After quickly informing Emory of the army's predicament, Wright ordered the Nineteenth Corps to refuse its left flank. Emory then shifted Col. David Shunk's brigade to bolster his left.[46]

Wright informed Emory that he must hold his line until the Sixth Corps arrived. Realizing that advancing Rebel infantry seriously threatened his line of retreat, Emory sent Brig. Gen. James McMillan's brigade to neutralize the Confederate threat along the Valley Pike.

Just as Emory's men adjusted to meet the new threat, however, the Confederate assault columns joined east of the Valley Pike and struck Emory's line near the Valley Pike bridge. As four Confederate brigades attacked the Federal line where it paralleled the Valley Pike, Wharton's division charged across the bridge. Several Confederate artillery batteries then opened fire, enfilading a portion of Emory's line. The pressure quickly made Emory's position perilous.[47]

While the Eighth and Nineteenth Corps grappled with Early's army, the Sixth Corps swiftly broke camp, sent its wagons to the rear, and marched to the two imperiled Federal corps' support. Separated by Meadow Brook, Keifer's division was the nearest Union reinforcement. The Sixth Corps changed their facing from southwest to east, with the Third Division holding the right, the First Division the center, and the Second Division the left. The Third Division waded Meadow Brook south of Belle Grove, while the First Division crossed the stream north of the mansion. Getty's division crossed Meadow Brook near Middletown.

The Third Division brigades moved en echelon. Ball's brigade was the division vanguard, while the First Brigade marched to the left and rear of the Second. Ball's brigade had crossed Meadow Brook and moved up the ridge when Emory's line broke. The Second Brigade then deployed into two lines of battle, from left to right, the 126th, 122d, and 110th Ohio. In their haste to escape capture, Emory's and Crook's men poured through the 122d's and 110th's ranks, throwing the two regiments into confusion. Colonel Ball struggled to maintain the brigade's integrity. His first line retreated a short distance, while the 9th New York Heavy Artillery pushed forward to check the Rebel advance. The First Brigade of Wheaton's division suffered a similar fate as it crossed Meadow Brook.[48]

After seeing the Union line at Belle Grove disintegrate, General Wright had two choices for dealing with the Confederate onslaught. First, he could throw the Sixth Corps into the wild melee surrounding the mansion and force a final decision there. If the subsequent fighting went in favor of the Confederates, however, they would force the Union army to fight with its back to Cedar Creek, leaving the Army of the Shenandoah no avenue of escape. Pursuing his second choice, Wright pulled the First and Third Divisions back across Meadow Brook and redeployed them on the crest of Red Hill. Keifer's division held the right, with Ball's brigade composing his right and Col. William Emerson's brigade his left. The 126th Ohio, 122d Ohio, and 110th Ohio remained in the front line. Capt. James McKnight's Battery M, 5th U.S. Artillery, and Capt. George Adams's Battery G, 1st Rhode Island Light Artillery, held the junction between Keifer and Wheaton. The latter deployed Col. William Penrose's small brigade to Adams's left, while Col. Joseph Hamblin's brigade extended the First Division line farther left. Lt. Jacob Lamb's Battery C, 1st Rhode Island Light Artillery, unlimbered between Penrose and Hamblin. Capt. Greenleaf Stevens's Battery E, 5th Maine Light Artillery, and Lt. Orasmus Van Etten's 1st Battery, New York Light Artillery, soon unlimbered on higher ground to the left and rear of the First Division. Wright then moved Getty's Second Division just south of Middletown and placed it to the left of the Union batteries, with the Second Division's left flank on the Valley Pike. Getty's objective was to keep the road open. If need be, the Army of the Shenandoah could then retreat along this route toward Winchester.[49]

Gordon's and Kershaw's infantry divisions meanwhile pursued the broken remnants of the Nineteenth Corps. Kershaw, however, stopped in the ravine of Meadow Brook and reformed his disorganized command. Continuing their pursuit, Gordon's division immediately assaulted Red Hill. Emerson's brigade greeted the Southern infantry with a deadly volley. The surprised Confederates quickly retreated into the safety of the Meadow Brook ravine to reorganize.

Gordon noticed that as Kershaw's reformed division moved forward, they advanced across his front. He subsequently moved his brigades behind Kershaw, thus becoming the extreme left of the Confederate army. About 7:30 A.M., the left of Gordon's division rested on Cedar Creek near Hottles Mill Ford. Three of Kershaw's brigades were on Gordon's right, while Brig. Gen. William Cox's and Brig. Gen. Philip Cook's brigades of Ramseur's division connected with Kershaw's right. Gen. John Pegram's three brigades joined Cook's right, and Gen. Stephen D. Ramseur's two remaining brigades extended Pegram's right, straddling the Valley Pike. Wharton's division and Carter's artillery brigade then moved north along the Valley Pike to the vicinity of Middletown. Several of Carter's batteries, however, followed Gordon and Kershaw to Belle Grove, where they unlimbered and fired at the Sixth Corps line on Red Hill.[50]

The shattered regiments of the Eighth and Nineteenth Corps retreated to Dr. Shipley's residence beyond Red Hill. There, Hayes and Emory worked feverishly to restore order. Meanwhile, Wheaton's and Keifer's two divisions now faced the four victorious Confederate divisions that had routed the Union left. After the brief respite to consolidate their lines, the Rebel infantry, flushed with their earlier success, moved forward to destroy the Union's last organized infantry units on the field—the Sixth Corps. Gordon's division assailed Keifer's right brigade under Ball, while Kershaw's frontal assault hit Emerson's brigade. Meanwhile, elements of Pegram's and Ramseur's divisions attacked Wheaton's division and the Federal batteries posted behind the First Division.[51]

For about one hour, the fighting swirled about Red Hill. Yet the two Union divisions firmly held their position. Gordon's and Kershaw's divisions repeatedly assaulted Keifer's division, and each time the Union infantry and artillery greeted them with volleys of musketry and rounds of canister. During the second Confederate assault, Keifer's brigades ran critically short of ammunition. The ferocity of the fighting and the lack of ammunition forced Emerson's brigade to fall back from the crest of Red Hill. As Emerson pulled back, McKnight's and Adams's men worked feverishly to extricate their guns.

However, they abandoned three cannon after the battery horses were killed. Kershaw's men swarmed over the captured artillery. As the Confederates reformed to finish driving the Union division from the position, a Union officer arrived with two mules carrying precious ammunition.

With cartridge boxes refilled, Keifer's division was now ready to resume the contest for Red Hill. Colonel Keifer ordered Emerson's brigade to counterattack. The 10th Vermont and the 6th Maryland charged the captured guns. The fight for these became hand-to-hand, with the Vermonters and Marylanders finally driving Kershaw's disorganized troops back to the Meadow Brook ravine.

When the two Confederate divisions again emerged from Meadow Brook, Ball's and Emerson's brigades unleashed successive volleys. When the Southern line faltered, Keifer ordered Emerson's and part of Ball's brigades to counterattack. Emerson's front line and the 126th and 122d Ohio charged, and once again, drove the Rebels back into the Meadow Brook ravine.

Just past 8:30 A.M., Gordon's, Kershaw's, and Pegram's divisions slammed into the Federal line. Thus far, the fighting on Red Hill had centered on Keifer's two brigades. Now, however, the fighting moved north as five Confederate brigades hit Wheaton's line. Rebel fire hit the two First Division brigades on their front and both flanks. While Kershaw's men attacked Emerson's brigade and McKnight's and Adams's batteries, Pegram's brigades swarmed up the slope toward Penrose's and Hamblin's commands. Brig. Gen. Robert D. Johnston's brigade of Pegram's division penetrated the line near Van Etten's batteries. This breach forced Wheaton's First Division to move obliquely to the northwest. Keifer's Third Division and the remnants of the Eighth and Nineteenth Corps likewise retreated to the northwest to avoid being cut off by the Confederates. Having been driven from Red Hill, the First and Third Divisions retired about a mile north of the Shipley residence.

With the collapse of the Federal line at Red Hill, Getty's Second Division also retired a short distance to the north. He moved his three brigades to a small semicircular hill on the western outskirts of Middletown. Any assaulting units would have to advance across open ground before climbing the steep slopes of the hill to reach his infantry. This hill's defensibility allowed any artillery placed on its summit to dominate the Valley Pike.[52]

Getty's division repulsed several Confederate attacks. Col. Thomas Carter's artillery then shelled the Federal lines. As the Union infantry moved to the hill's reverse slope for protection, Battle's Alabamians moved around Getty's right flank and Col. Thomas Smith's brigade threatened the left. About 9:30 A.M., Getty retired his division north to a small ridge one mile north of Middletown.[53]

After Getty's retreat, Early halted and reorganized his army. Wharton's division and Brig. Gen. William T. Wofford's brigade moved northeast of Middletown. Carter's guns moved north of the village. From right to left, Pegram, Ramseur, Kershaw, and Gordon filed into line along the Old Forge Road. By 11:30 A.M., the Confederates completed their new dispositions.[54]

In Winchester, meanwhile, General Sheridan awoke at an early hour. Reports came to him about an increased sound of artillery from the south. Growing concerned, Sheridan and his cavalry escort, rode toward the Union camp. As the group crested a small rise several miles south of Winchester, large groups of stragglers, slightly wounded men, and baggage wagons suddenly came into view. Sheridan instantly realized that disaster had befallen his army. As Sheridan traveled on, many Union soldiers recognized him, and having the utmost confidence in his abilities, these infantrymen returned with their commander. Shortly after eleven o'clock, Sheridan, followed by many of his veterans, reached his demoralized army north of Middletown. Sheridan later recalled that after jumping his horse over the rails of a fence, he "rode to the crest of the elevation, and there taking off my hat, the men rose up from behind their barricade with cheers of recognition."[55]

After conferring with Generals Crook and Wright, the commanding general ordered Keifer's and Wheaton's divisions to extend Getty's line to the right. Emory's two divisions would then form on Wheaton's right. Custer's cavalry division would protect Emory's right flank.[56]

At one o'clock, Gordon's, Kershaw's, and Ramseur's divisions moved forward in a halfhearted attempt to drive the Union infantry from the area. The morning attack, however, had decimated the already depleted Confederate line. Additionally, many Rebel infantrymen straggled. After the Union troops destroyed the Shenandoah's resources, rations for Early's men became virtually nonexistent. The Confederate infantry was in dire need of food and clothing; Rebel troops from the western states had not received clothing and shoes for many months. Many of them now looted the abandoned Union encampments to fill their haversacks and replace accouterments. Sheridan's veterans easily repulsed the Confederate assault on their lines.[57]

The morale of the Union infantry now reached a zenith with Sheridan's arrival and the return of many stragglers. After being routed from their tents in the morning, the Federals wanted to drive the enemy from the field, recapture their camps, and recover their pride and dignity. After the failure of Early's infantry assault, Sheridan unleashed his army. Getty's division attacked south with its left on the Valley Pike. Following the removal of some interspersed Eighth Corps remnants, Keifer's division prolonged its left to make connection with Getty's right. Wheaton maintained contact with Keifer's division.

Emory's two divisions were the key to the Union counterattack. After Early's infantry drove them from the field earlier, Grover's and Dwight's divisions reformed on the Union right. During their afternoon assault, these divisions would strike the left of the Confederate line. According to Sheridan's plan, the Nineteenth Corps, after turning Early's left, would continue its turning movement and attempt to capture the Valley Pike bridge. If his plan succeeded, Sheridan would capture Early's army and eliminate this threat in the Shenandoah Valley.[58]

At four o'clock, the Union infantry surged forward. When Sheridan's soldiers emerged from the woods, Gordon's, Kershaw's, and Ramseur's men greeted them with a ferocious volley. Rocked by the Confederate fire, the advance of all three Sixth Corps divisions stalled as the men took shelter behind a stone wall and exchanged fire with Ramseur's and Kershaw's divisions.

After recovering from their initial repulse, Emory's divisions once again pushed forward. Grover's division struck York's Louisianans and Terry's Virginians, while Dwight's division assaulted Evans's brigade. After Dwight dispatched Evans's Georgians, the Rebel left crumbled, and Custer's cavalry division stormed into the Confederate rear area.[59]

Colonel Keifer, meanwhile, noticed that a transverse wall ran along the right of the Third Division line and perpendicular to the wall that the combatants used for shelter. Simultaneous with Dwight's turning movement, Keifer ordered Capt. W. H. Day, a staff officer of the First Brigade, to take a party of volunteers forward along the transverse wall. Over one hundred men crawled along it and succeeded in reaching the enemy's position. They then rose up and from an unexpected direction, delivered a volley into the Confederate ranks. Before the surprised Confederates could recover, Keifer ordered the entire division to charge and dislodged the Southerners from their defensive position.[60]

The Confederate left completely collapsed. Custer exploited the situation as nervous Rebels dashed for the bridge across Cedar Creek. Trying to avert disaster, Major General Ramseur successfully rallied his men. A Union bullet struck Ramseur, and the fall of the gallant Confederate general sealed the Army of the Valley's fate. No other Confederate units were able to make a determined stand or fight a rearguard action. Each time Early's men rallied, Union infantry and cavalry struck the Confederate line once again, sending the Rebel forces reeling. Custer's cavalry was especially effective in the pursuit.[61]

The Confederate army eventually retreated to New Market. The reversal at Cedar Creek virtually eliminated Rebel resistance in the Shenandoah Valley. Lieutenant General Early estimated his loss at "1,860 killed and wounded and something over 1,000 prisoners."[62]

Union losses at Cedar Creek were greater than those that the Confederates suffered. Sheridan estimated his loss at 644 killed, 3,430 wounded, and 1,591 missing. The total Union loss was 5,665 men. The 110th suffered little in comparison to other units. The Buckeye regiment, however, lost 5 men killed, 2 officers and 27 men wounded, and 1 officer captured for an aggregate loss of 35 men.[63]

Lt. Robert Wiley was the captured officer. During the fighting on Red Hill, the regiment ran low on ammunition. Wiley went to the supply train and forwarded several mules loaded with ammunition. When he later returned to the regiment, the division had already retreated to a position northwest of Middletown. Since he returned to the regiment's former position, now in the hands of the Confederates, Wiley became a prisoner of war.[64]

Among the Union wounded at Cedar Creek were Privates Henry Kauffman and John Rosser and Capt. Wesley Devenney. A Confederate minié ball wounded Kauffman when it passed through the fleshy part of his left leg. The Ohio private spent the next three months recuperating at the U.S. Army General Hospital in York, Pennsylvania and then several weeks convalescing at his family's home in Harmony, Ohio.[65]

Early in the engagement, Captain Devenney fell with a mortal wound. A bullet entered his breast on his right side and lodged in the small of his back. Corporal Rhoades initially believed that the captain might recover from the wound. The bullet, however, had punctured Devenney's lung. On October 23, the officer succumbed to his wound.[66]

Pvt. John Rosser fell with a serious wound at Cedar Creek when a cannonball severed his left foot. On October 22, in a letter he dictated to

Brev. Brig. Gen. J. Warren Keifer. Courtesy of Western Reserve Historical Society.

William Reed, Rosser described his ordeal. He lost his foot during the morning attack. Doctors subsequently amputated his left leg below the knee. The wound, according to Rosser, bled freely, causing the Darke County soldier to weaken. After lying in a hospital near Newtown for two days, he went by ambulance to Martinsburg, Virginia. At ten o'clock in the morning on October 21, hospital personnel loaded the Ohio private in the ambulance, where he remained until the next morning. During the twenty-four hours he lay in the ambulance wagon, the night was rainy and extremely cold, Rosser noting that the conditions caused him to suffer very much. He informed his wife, Lucy, that he would "perhaps remain here a few days and then be removed to Baltimore. I think I will get to come home in a month or two. . . . I do not want you to fret yourself about me. I am in good spirits. I am now done soldering." Two days later, on October 24, Pvt. John Frederick Rosser bled to death.[67]

After the battle, the Army of the Shenandoah remained in the Valley for another six weeks. The Sixth Corps spent the first two weeks in camp near Cedar Creek. During the second and third weeks of November, the corps encamped near Kernstown. From November 22 to December 3, it bivouacked at Camp Russell, near Winchester. The next day, the Army of the Shenandoah dissolved, and the Sixth Corps embarked on railroad cars to Washington, D.C., and from there it moved to Petersburg and rejoined the Army of the Potomac.

The summer and fall of 1864 proved to be an extremely dramatic period for the Union and its armies. While Grant besieged Lee's Army of Northern Virginia at Petersburg, elements of the Rebel army entered the Shenandoah Valley, threatening Washington, D.C. Grant responded by sending the Sixth Corps to confront the Confederates in the Valley. These troops prevented Jubal Early's forces from capturing the Federal capital. Grant also directed two other Union corps to join the newly created Middle Military Division. Under the command of Maj. Gen. Philip Sheridan, the soldiers in this new department moved to meet and defeat the Confederate Army of the Valley.

From July 9 to October 19, the two armies fought four major engagements and had numerous smaller encounters. The 110th Ohio Volunteer Infantry participated in all four engagements and witnessed the devastation of the Shenandoah Valley that left the area virtually worthless to the Confederates. During the various engagements of the summer and fall, the west-central Ohio regiment suffered many casualties: 138 at Monocacy, 55 at Opequon Creek (Third Battle of Winchester), 3 at Fisher's Hill, and 35 at Cedar Creek. During this four-month campaign, the 110th lost a total of 231 men as battlefield casualties, with the companies in the regiment suffering proportionately. On May 4, for example, when they crossed the Rapidan River, Company I numbered 65 men. By November 24, this Springfield and Clark County company mustered only 38 men.[68]

I now feel that my Children have for them a home in the land of the free and the home of the Brave. God has given us our contry he has taught the world that slavery is an evill rebellion unholy and slavery one of the blackest of crimes.

—*Cpl. John R. Rhoades*

6 The Land of the Free

The boys of the 110th Ohio Infantry believed that they would spend their winter quartered near Winchester. Though no longer on campaign, the soldiers remained active. During the six weeks following Cedar Creek, Union officers went back to their local communities for recruiting purposes. Many men also came back to the ranks after recovering from various wounds. For example, on Sunday, November 26, 1864, Josiah Hill returned to Company I after a lengthy convalescence, and on January 18, 1865, Pvt. Henry Kauffman rejoined the regiment at Petersburg. Colonel Keifer regularly updated his wife, Eliza, on the condition of his left arm. On November 13, 1864, Union doctors removed two additional bone fragments from his left forearm. He hoped that the last splinters were gone and that his arm could now heal properly.[1]

The return of many general officers concerned Colonel Keifer. On October 28, he worried about the appointment of five brigadier generals to the Army of the Shenandoah and warned that these generals returned to the frontline units only after the campaign season ended. He noted that no one wanted them. Keifer added that if the politicians placed these incompetent officers above him, begrudgingly, he would submit to their authority. In many instances, these officers had "never heard the whistle of a bullet." The recent promotions also distressed Corporal Rhoades. He similarly believed that the politicians promoted many undeserving men, bypassing more qualified individuals in Company E.[2]

On October 29, 1864, Brig. Gen. Truman Seymour returned to the Sixth Corps and to command of the division, while Keifer resumed command of the Second Brigade. Seymour's return dissatisfied Colonel Keifer. The Ohio colonel condemned the general for his poor behavior at the Battle of the Wilderness. During the conflict of May 5–7, General Seymour had failed to rally his troops. During the confusion of Brig. Gen. John Gordon's assault, Seymour became separated from the brigade, and the Confederates captured him. Keifer, begrudgingly, served under the released officer for the next six months.[3]

At noon on December 3, the 110th Ohio boarded a train for Washington, D.C. After arriving at seven o'clock the following morning, the unit embarked five hours later aboard the transport *Lizzie Baker* bound for City Point, Virginia. As the regiments that composed the Second Brigade, Third Division, Sixth Corps, moved south, the units became separated on the various transports required to move such a large body of troops. Brig. Gen. J. Warren Keifer, recently promoted for gallant and meritorious service at the Battle of Cedar Creek, moved with the first load of men. At noon on December 5, the first transport arrived at City Point, and the first regiments spent the remainder of the day there. That evening, Seymour introduced Keifer to Ulysses Grant. After the interview with the general in chief, the Buckeye brigadier revealed a changed attitude toward the lieutenant general. During the spring of 1864, Keifer was wary of the many laurels placed upon Grant. On March 29, Keifer stated that he "would not detract from his greatness but I want to be well satisfied with the man before I pronounce him superhuman." In December, however, the Clark County native reversed this early criticism and proclaimed that Grant was just the man for the job. Keifer noted that Grant was a confident man but not a braggart. The new general "was impressed with his quiet & determined manner. He seems to be fully aware of the great responsibility that rests upon him."[4]

On December 6, the brigade moved to the western portion of the Petersburg entrenchments, manning the area just west of the Weldon and

Petersburg Railroad. The regiments garrisoned Forts Keene and Wadsworth plus the connecting fortifications. Three days later, the Second Brigade went on a brief expedition to Hatcher's Run. After returning to their lines, the soldiers started construction of their winter quarters.

The winter months proved uneventful. During December, January, and February, the men of the 110th rotated picket-duty assignments. When free from this task, the soldiers performed a variety of fatigue duties. In mid-December, for example, some moved their winter shacks. According to officers of the regiment, the men had built some shanties too close to the lines, so the residents of those shelters had to tear them down and rebuild them farther to the rear. Corporal Rhoades regularly went to the woods to cut firewood. On February 2, 1865, Rhoades and a party of men cut and put handles in one thousand axes. According to the corporal, the army was on marching orders, and he expected the Union infantrymen would soon use these tools to cut a path through the Confederate defenses.[5]

In addition to these duties, the Union infantrymen at Petersburg also had plenty of leisure time. General Keifer applied for leave, and much to his surprise received a lengthy furlough. Rhoades spent much of his free time reading books and letters, writing to family, and going to prayer meetings. Corporal Hill likewise wrote to family members regularly. He also spent time reading letters from home, and on several occasions was extremely anxious to receive more.[6]

In February, the Army of the Potomac extended its lines to the left. Grant believed that eventually he would stretch Lee's forces to the breaking point. On the eighth, the Sixth Corps sidled left. The men of the 110th moved approximately one and one-half miles west. These Yankee veterans now occupied a position west of Squirrel Level Road. According to several men, the fortifications were crude and unfinished, and they quickly worked on the forts and nearby trenches. Men not on fatigue duty constructed new winter quarters. General Keifer predicted on February 9 that it would be an uncomfortable four days while they rebuilt their winter quarters. For many in the brigade, this was the third time they had constructed winter quarters that year, while for some it was their fourth. While building the new shelters, the men slept in their tents. According to Hill, his comrades in the 110th were quite uncomfortable. On February 10 and again on February 14, Hill noted that the previous nights were quite cold. Hill and his bunkmates spent the fourteenth repairing their shack so it would retain heat. The next day they passed daubing paint on their shanty.[7]

As part of the position west of Squirrel Level Road, the thirty-five hundred men of the brigade garrisoned Forts Fisher, Welch, and Gregg and the interconnecting trenches. The Ohioans of the 110th again rotated on a schedule for picket duty. In this portion of the line, however, there was fewer than one hundred yards separating the lines. Those on picket duty on both sides agreed to limit the amount of firing along this portion of the line. General Keifer noticed that the adversaries equally divided the firewood located between the lines. On February 10, while the general visited the pickets, he noticed that men from both sides cut and carried wood from the same tree. Casual conversation between the pickets was not unusual. While some conducted a steady fire along one portion of the line, other pickets a few yards away casually conversed.[8]

On February 10, a Union lieutenant engaged one Confederate picket in conversation. The Yankee informed the Rebel of the abundance of food and the good treatment inside the Union lines. Shortly after that, the picket deserted. During the winter of 1864–65, desertion became a serious problem, especially for the Army of Northern Virginia. Rebel deserters increasingly became a topic of the Ohioans' letters home. During a two-week span in February 1865, General Keifer repeatedly informed Eliza of recent defections. By February 21, though his estimates appear a bit exaggerated, Corporal Rhoades claimed that 261 Confederates had deserted. Six days later, he stated that an additional 300 Southerners had left the Confederate trenches. On February 23 and again on March 3, Corporal Hill was excited and amused at the steady stream of Confederate deserters. On March 16, Private Kauffman was on picket duty when 14 Johnnies surrendered themselves. According to Kauffman, five of the deserters brought their guns and cartridge boxes with them. On four separate occasions, Sgt. Maj. Francis McMillen noted in his diary that many deserters entered the Union entrenchments.[9]

From February 27 to March 8, Maj. Luther Brown recorded the appearance of fifty-six Confederate deserters at division headquarters. Throughout the war, though, Confederate officers rarely took "French leave." According to the *Official Records,* no general officers and only one colonel and one major deserted; it was even rare for one holding a rank as high as captain to desert. Yet Brown's list included a captain and a corporal of the

8th Florida, a second lieutenant and a sergeant of the 44th North Carolina, a sergeant of the 11th North Carolina, and fifty-one enlisted men. Three Confederate regiments greatly contributed to Major Brown's list. With numbers similarly proportionate to those in the *Official Records,* the 11th and 44th North Carolina Infantry and 10th Florida Infantry Regiments had fifteen, eight, and fourteen deserters respectively. On March 2, Confederate prisoners informed Sergeant McMillen that "their men are going home as fast if not faster than they are deserting to us."[10]

With such an exorbitant desertion rate, Confederate officers discouraged communication between the picket lines. The ever-resourceful soldiers, however, maintained contact. "The rebs had a dog that they would put a paper in his mouth and send him over to our lines [and] our fellows would give him one of ours and back he would go."[11]

Union soldiers also deserted. Pvt. James L. Hicks, 67th Pennsylvania Infantry, and another unidentified Pennsylvania infantryman forged furloughs for leave to Philadelphia.[12] The provost marshal caught the two men and returned the fugitives to Keifer's brigade. A court-martial subsequently convicted both men. As was common throughout the Civil War, though, influential politicians intervened, and the army subsequently imprisoned the unnamed man at Fort Jefferson in the Dry Tortugas. On February 27, however, the court sentenced Private Hicks to death by musketry.[13]

Believing that President Lincoln would overturn yet another capital sentence, General Keifer delayed the execution. On March 10, Maj. Gen. George Meade summoned Keifer to headquarters and berated the Clark County native for not carrying it out. As was common among West Point–trained commanders, Meade ordered Keifer to execute Private Hicks the next day. Furthermore, after Private Hicks's execution, Keifer was required to report the outcome to Meade's headquarters.

During the morning of March 11, the brigade was drawn up on three sides of a square. The fourth side remained clear with exception of a recently dug grave and the placement of a coffin beside the hole. Preceded by a fife-and-drum band that played the "dead-march," Private Hicks passed through the ranks of the brigade. "The condemned man was taken to the coffin, where he was blindfolded and required to stand in front of six men armed with rifles, five only of which were loaded with Minie balls. At the command 'Fire!' from a designated officer, the guns discharged and poor Hicks fell dead." According to General Keifer, Provost Marshal Maj. Luther

Brown executed Hicks in a "strict and calm military order." Later that same day, General Keifer received preliminary word that President Lincoln had pardoned Hicks. Two weeks later, Special Orders No. 146 arrived, belatedly pardoning the Pennsylvania private.[14]

Throughout February and March, a variety of dignitaries reviewed the 110th and the rest of Keifer's brigade. On February 21, Brigadier General Seymour reviewed the brigade. The next day, Maj. Gen. Horatio Wright, commander of the Sixth Corps, did the same with the whole division. During the evening of March 5, the brigade again turned out for parade. Two days later, Generals Meade and Wright, Mrs. Julia Grant, Judge and Mrs. Woodruff of New York City, and the daughter and niece of Secretary of War Edwin Stanton reviewed the brigade; General Keifer received only thirty-minutes notice of this one. According to Keifer, the brigade review delighted Generals Meade and Wright. The Ohioan claimed that parading before such dignitaries was an honor for the 3,300 men of the brigade.[15]

On March 9, Major Generals Meade, Gouverneur K. Warren, and Andrew Humphreys attended a musical performed by soldiers of the Sixth Corps. Afterward, the generals went to Fort Fisher to view the Confederate camps. To honor the generals, Keifer turned out the brigade for review. The next day, General Meade returned to the camp of the Second Brigade and ordered Keifer to conduct another brigade review.[16]

On Friday, March 17, the day after an extravagant St. Patrick's Day celebration that included footraces and horse races, the Army of the Potomac began its preparations for the upcoming campaign season. The men sent all tents and excess baggage from the camps. Corporal Hill complained of the discomfort the men would now endure. His only solace was the belief that this would be the final campaign of the war.[17]

During the early morning hours of March 25, Confederate general John Gordon's corps assaulted the Union lines at Fort Stedman. Gordon's assault surprised Brig. Gen. Orlando Wilcox's Ninth Corps division that garrisoned Fort Stedman. The Southerners captured and briefly held the position. While the Union troops in Forts Haskell and McGilvery rebuffed their assailants, the rest of the Army of the Potomac answered the "long roll." Nearby units, however, quickly counterattacked and recaptured Stedman.[18]

Throughout the rest of the Federal lines, the soldiers remained under arms while the general officers of the Union army reconnoitered the Confederate position. Along the front of the Sixth Corps, officers believed that they could capture the Confederate's outer fortifications. In the early afternoon, Generals Wright and Seymour visited General Keifer at brigade headquarters and ordered him to assault the Confederate outerworks with two regiments. Keifer protested when he learned that a division staff officer would lead the attack. Seymour and Wright, however, ordered the Ohioan to make the necessary arrangements. Keifer called for the 110th and 122d Ohio Infantry Regiments to assault the selected Confederate positions.

As Keifer predicted, the assault failed. Capt. Henry Stevens of Company I reported that enfilading fire forced the two units back to the Union picket line. During this assault, the two Ohio regiments quickly suffered sixty casualties. When General Seymour ordered that the attack continue, Keifer vehemently protested against "the useless slaughter of men under incompetent officers." General Wright, however, supported his division commander and ordered that the attack resume. Wright, however, acquiesced to Keifer's demands by offering the Ohio brigadier the opportunity to nominate an officer to lead the next assault. Keifer selected Lt. Col. Otho Binkley. As the two Ohio regiments prepared, Wright ordered Keifer and the balance of the Second Brigade to support the assault on the Confederate fortifications. After the regimental commanders received their assignments, the blue-clad soldiers dashed across the open terrain that separated the armies. As ordered, they withheld their fire until they reached the Confederate trenches. The Yankees breeched the Rebel works, taking three hundred prisoners. Flushed with success, the three Union generals quickly forgot their earlier disagreement.[19]

The 110th sustained heavy casualties during these two assaults. During the second attack, General Keifer avoided injury, although the concussion of nearby artillery shell bursts twice knocked him down. A Confederate minié ball, however, severely wounded Lt. Col. Aaron Spangler when it struck him in the thigh. According to Private Kauffman, Company I lost three men. Pvt. Avery Griffith died during the assault while Sgt. David King and Cpl. William Wise were among the wounded. During the initial assault, Sgt. Maj. Francis McMillen was shot. The Greene County native's life, however, was miraculously spared when the bullet pierced his diary, deflected off his pocket watch, and imbedded in his belt buckle.[20]

Over the next several days, regular skirmishing took place. Several times, the Confederates made halfhearted assaults to recapture that portion of their line held by the Second Brigade. On Monday, March 27, however, the opposing sides agreed to a truce so that they could bury the dead from the previous fighting. During this suspension of hostilities, Union and Confederate officers mingled between the lines. General Keifer noted that the Rebels were not enthusiastic about the Confederacy's chance of success.[21]

After the Sixth Corps's initial success, Lieutenant General Grant decided that the end of the siege at Petersburg was near. The impetuous Maj. Gen. Philip Sheridan proposed a bold plan to continue the movement left to overextend the Confederate lines. Sheridan first considered using only his cavalry divisions. After his initial success at Dinwiddie Court House though, he requested the Sixth Corps to support the troopers. Wright's infantry, however, was engaged along the left of the Union entrenchments, making extraction from their advanced position very difficult. Grant, therefore, sent Major General Warren's Fifth Corps to Sheridan's assistance. The subsequent success at the Battle of Five Forks on April 1 paved the way for the final assaults on the Petersburg entrenchments.[22]

In anticipation of Sheridan's success, Grant ordered the remaining Union troops to prepare to assault the Confederate fortifications. The commanding general scheduled the assault for 4:00 A.M. on April 2. During the evening, however, he ordered a preparatory bombardment of the Confederate lines. Foregoing the element of surprise for his infantry assault, Grant believed that the bombardment was necessary to prevent the Confederates from leaving the Petersburg entrenchments and overwhelming Sheridan's forces.[23]

The major push for the Union assault rested with the Wright's Sixth Corps. Since these Yankee veterans had captured the Confederates' outerworks, Grant and Wright deemed this the logical location for the main push. The Third Division was on the corps' left, while Maj. Gen. George Getty's Second Division served on its right flank. Maj. Gen. Frank Wheaton's First Division would move en echelon behind the Second Division's right flank. Maj. Gen. John Parke's Ninth Corps would continue the forward movement on Wheaton's right flank, and Maj. Gen. E. O. C. Ord would continue pressuring the Confederate line to the left of the Sixth Corps.[24]

At midnight, the units began filing into position for the anticipated assault. General Meade ordered that the divisions participating in the assault should attack on regimental fronts. He also ordered the consolidation of many of the decimated regiments with other units to make sure that the assault line was not too long and then postponed the assault until

4:40 A.M. Fire from a gun at Fort Fisher signaled the start of the assault, and the infantry units immediately surged forward. The Union troops quickly pierced the thinly manned Confederate entrenchments held by North Carolinians of Brig. Gen. James Lane's brigade of Maj. Gen. Cadmus Wilcox's division. Keifer's Second Brigade was one of the first to break the Confederate lines at Petersburg.

Men of the Pioneer Corps accompanied the head of the assault columns. These men cleared a path through the abatis and *chevaux de frise,* early antipersonnel obstacles intended to slow advancing infantry and cavalry. The Yankee veterans crossed open ground before encountering deep ditches that protected the Rebel entrenchments. Because of the nature of the ground and the extreme exposure while riding on horseback, most officers went on foot. Men in the first line did not load their rifles, though the second line troops did, for they provided covering fire for the first line whenever necessary. After crossing the open ground, many soldiers plunged their bayonet-tipped rifles into the ditches' steep embankments. The sequence of rifles projecting from the embankments then served as makeshift ladders for the assaulting Union infantrymen.[25]

During the subsequent fighting that swirled throughout the entrenchments, several members of the 110th distinguished themselves. Capt. William Shaw led a group of soldiers that captured a small Confederate fort. Shaw and his assault group took over fifty prisoners and captured four pieces of artillery. Sergeant Major McMillen, formerly first sergeant of Company C, captured a Confederate battle flag and subsequently received the Medal of Honor. Pvt. Isaac James of Company H also won the Medal of Honor after he captured a Confederate battle flag. The entrenchments that the 110th took came with a cost, though. The regiment suffered twenty-eight casualties comprising one officer and three enlisted men killed and an additional two officers and twenty-two men wounded. While Capt. William Shellenberger of Company A received a severe wound in the arm, a Confederate soldier emerged from a shelter and shot Capt. Henry H. Stevens of Company I, whose wound proved mortal.[26]

Two members of Keifer's brigade were among the many Union soldiers who exploited the breakthrough. After the Sixth Corps penetrated the Confederate entrenchments, Wright's men wheeled left and attacked other Rebel fortifications from the rear. Consecutively, Col. Andrew Nelson's brigade of Mississippians, Brig. Gen. William McComb's Maryland and

Above: Capt. William Shaw. Courtesy of USAMHI. *Below:* Capt. William Shellenberger. Courtesy of USAMHI.

Tennessee brigade, and Brig. Gen. William McRae's North Carolina brigade were driven from their entrenchments. In consequence of this, many Rebel units retreated to their innermost fortifications along the Dimmock Line. During this mass of confusion, Confederate Lt. Gen. Ambrose Powell Hill moved to the threatened region and attempted to stabilize the Confederate lines. In a chance encounter, however, General Hill and a staff member ran headlong into Cpl. Ted Mauk and Pvt. Daniel Wolford of the 138th Pennsylvania Volunteer Infantry. When the two groups exchanged shots, Hill fell dead from his horse. Corporal Mauk claimed credit for the bullet that pierced the general's heart.[27]

During the assault, Col. Clifton K. Prentiss, commanding the Second Brigade's 6th Maryland Infantry, received a mortal wound. As he led his regiment over a Confederate parapet held by a portion of McComb's Maryland and Tennessee brigade, a Rebel minié ball struck his chest, tearing away part of the colonel's breastbone and exposing his heart. Next to the young Maryland officer fell the major who commanded a Confederate battery in the parapet. Colonel Prentiss discovered that the Confederate artillerist with the severe leg wound was his brother, whom he had not seen in four years. Doctors treated the two brothers in the same hospitals until their subsequent deaths—the Confederate major died in June 1865, while Colonel Prentiss died in August.[28]

With the fortifications of Petersburg breached, General Lee informed the Confederate government that the defense of Petersburg and Richmond was no longer feasible and sent word to Confederate president Jefferson Davis requesting that he leave the Confederate capital. Davis and his cabinet quickly fled Richmond. Lee's army began its evacuation later that same night. Confederate lieutenant general James Longstreet's First and Third Corps were the vanguard of the Confederate movement. Confederate lieutenant general Richard S. Ewell, commanding the forces of the Richmond garrison, trailed Longstreet, while Maj. Gen. John B. Gordon's Second Corps formed the Confederate rear guard. Early in the morning of April 3, Grant's Federals again assaulted the Confederate entrenchments surrounding Petersburg. This time, they found that the Confederates had abandoned their fortifications. Federal troops quickly marched into and occupied Richmond. Later that day, Corporal Hill saw Abraham Lincoln as the president traveled to Richmond.[29]

After learning of the evacuation, Grant organized his forces for the pursuit of the Army of Northern Virginia. On parallel roads south of the Appomattox River, the Fifth, Second, and Sixth Corps pursued the Confederates toward Amelia Court House, with General Sheridan's cavalry divisions preceding the infantry. Traveling on a parallel route still farther south, Major General Ord's Twenty-Fourth Corps and Major General Parke's Ninth Corps moved along the Southside Railroad, the latter repairing the track as they went. After resting the night of April 5, Humphreys's Second Corps moved into line behind Sheridan's troopers. Wright's Sixth Corps was second in line, while Maj. Gen. Charles Griffin's Fifth Corps followed Wright's infantry.[30]

Sheridan's cavalry continually harried the fleeing Confederates. The Union troopers attacked the vulnerable wagon trains following Longstreet's infantry. Employing hit-and-run tactics, Union cavalry created a gap between Longstreet and Ewell. The latter, fearing for the safety of the wagons that followed him, ordered the supply train to take the Jamestown Road that ran parallel to his line of march. While on this alternate route, the supply train would be safe from Sheridan's troopers. Amid the confusion of the retreat and Sheridan's attacks, however, Ewell failed to inform General Gordon of this change. Gordon, therefore, followed the supply train onto the alternate route.[31]

As the Georgian and his troops moved onto the Jamestown Road, Wright's Sixth Corps quickly closed on Ewell's isolated command. At five o'clock that afternoon, Ewell's infantry had just crossed the pole bridge over Little Sayler's Creek near the James Moses Hillsman farm when Wright's infantry appeared. Keifer's Second Brigade of the Third Division was first to deploy in line of battle. While the Confederate infantry threw up breastworks and barricades on top of the ridge west of the stream, Col. William Truex's First Brigade, Third Division, formed in line of battle on Keifer's left. Two brigades of Brigadier General Wheaton's First Division arrived soon afterward. Col. Oliver Edward's Third Brigade and Col. Joseph Hamblin's Second Brigade extended the Union line of battle from Truex's left. Five batteries of Maj. John Cowan's Artillery Brigade, numbering twenty guns, unlimbered behind the four Sixth Corps brigades. Ewell positioned Maj. Gen. Joseph Kershaw's division on the Confederate right, while Maj. Gen. G. W. Custis Lee's division deployed on the left.[32]

As the main body of Keifer's Second Brigade was arriving, the 110th Ohio, 122d Ohio, and the 9th New York Heavy Artillery pursued a column of

Confederate wagons fleeing down a parallel route. The 110th Ohio and 9th New York Heavies, after chasing the column across the creek, encountered a section of Rebel artillery. The Confederate guns fired shot and canister into the Sixth Corps troops that were forming to assault the main Confederate defensive line. The three Second Brigade regiments formed in line of battle and assaulted the enemy guns. The section of Confederate artillery, consequently, limbered their cannon and withdrew to another position. The Ohioans and New Yorkers continued their pursuit of the Rebel artillery. As the three regiments again prepared an assault, an order arrived that delayed them: General Sheridan wanted the Union cavalry units in the area to make the assault. However, the cavalry did not attack before the Rebel section could withdraw yet again. As Binkley's expedition withdrew and rejoined the Sixth Corps, Maj. Gen. Andrew Humphreys's Second Corps deployed in line of battle.[33]

About 5:30 P.M., the Sixth Corps artillery opened fire upon Ewell's main defensive position. Thirty minutes later, General Seymour's and General Wheaton's Sixth Corps divisions charged Ewell's entrenchments. The Yankee veterans held their weapons and cartridge boxes above their heads as they crossed the four-foot depths of Little Sayler's Creek. The Union infantry withheld their fire until they were within one hundred yards of the Rebel entrenchments. But before Wheaton's men fired, Confederate infantry rose from behind their barricades and unleashed a devastating volley into the middle of the attacking lines. While the Union flanks made good progress, the center stalled. It was at this juncture that Commodore John Randolph Tucker had his Confederate Naval Brigade charge the faltering Union infantry. His two thousand men from the James River fleet and the Confederate Marine detachment emerged from a small ravine and struck the Federals. Concentrated fire from Cowan's Artillery Brigade and the arrival of Maj. Gen. George Getty's Second Division staved off disaster for the Union center. Tucker's brigade consequently retreated into a timbered area behind the Confederate entrenchments.

With Union infantry pressing both flanks, Ewell's Southerners gallantly held their ground. The appearance of Sheridan's cavalry in rear of the Rebel lines, however, caused resistance to collapse quickly. Confederate casualties along Sayler's Creek numbered six thousand, with many of those being prisoners of war. Among those captured were Generals Ewell, Kershaw, and Custis Lee.[34]

According to General Keifer, Commodore Tucker's Naval Brigade was ignorant of the Confederate surrender. Repeated attempts to contact the Rebels located in the woods failed. Now doubting the reports of a Confederate unit still in the timberline, Keifer investigated. Riding into the woods alone, he stumbled across the Confederate sailors. Keifer, realizing the precariousness of his situation, took advantage of the approaching darkness, the lack of light associated with dusk in the woods masking his identity. Keifer quickly ordered the Confederate units forward. It was not until they reached the edge of the woods that they finally recognized Keifer to be a Union general officer and prepared to shoot him. As Keifer turned to surrender, the Confederates became confused. In an incident reminiscent of what happened to Maj. Gen. James B. McPherson in fighting around Atlanta, the Clark County native immediately spurred his horse into action. Unlike McPherson, however, Keifer survived, crediting Commodore Tucker and Capt. John D. Semmes with saving his life. According to the general, the two Confederate officers knocked aside the rifles aimed at him, thereby causing the bullets to miss their target. Keifer later returned to the woods with a detachment of Union infantry and demanded the surrender of the Confederate Naval Brigade. After explaining the situation to Commodore Tucker, the Confederate officer subsequently acquiesced. Later that summer, being indebted to the two Rebel naval officers, General Keifer intervened to have Tucker and Semmes released from the prison on Johnson's Island near Sandusky, Ohio.[35]

After dark, Keifer's brigade moved from Sayler's Creek. The Union troops, after marching all day and fighting that same evening, finally bivouacked two and a half miles from the battlefield. The next morning, the Sixth Corps continued its pursuit of the remnants of Lee's shattered army. At 10:00 P.M. on April 7, the Second Brigade crossed the Appomattox River at Farmville, where they camped for the night. Over the next two days, Wright's Sixth Corps continued the chase. At 2:00 P.M. on April 9, 1865, Keifer's Buckeyes halted about six miles away from Appomattox Court House. It was here that the men learned of Gen. Robert E. Lee's surrender.[36]

After hearing the news, General Keifer described the Union troops as "drunk with excitement. . . . I have tried to restrain my own feelings of joy, in vain. Officers and men may yet be seen about the camps meeting, embracing and crying for joy." General Keifer also noted that the he and his staff tore down the cherry tree that they used for shade and used it as mementos. Corporals Rhoades and Hill described the reaction of their comrades as joyous. While the Sixth Corps maintained its bivouac near Appomattox Court House, the men relaxed and began greeting each other on social rather than military terms.[37]

On Saturday, April 15, bad news reached the Army of the Potomac. During the evening hours, General Keifer received word of President Abraham Lincoln's assassination. After receiving a copy of the telegram bearing the news, Keifer ordered Colonel Binkley to report to Second Brigade headquarters with one company of the 110th. Binkley quickly arrived with a fully accoutered company. General Keifer feared that the Union troops would seek reprisals on unarmed Confederates once they learned the news. He, therefore, wished to use the armed company for crowd control during his announcement of President Lincoln's death. While addressing the troops, General Keifer urged the soldiers to use "moderation, conciliation, and magnanimity." In his April 15 letter to his wife, he described his feelings about Lincoln's assassination. The traitorous act of the Southern conspirators enraged Keifer. He pledged to fight for "the complete annihilation of the Southern Slaveholding race. . . . Humanity revolts at the thought of waging war against the existence of our fellow men, but our country's future prosperity, and *retributive justice,* seem to demand it." Keifer, however, took some solace in knowing that President Lincoln lived to see the capitulation of the Army of Northern Virginia. He presciently wrote, "President Lincoln's course with regard to slavery will render his name immortal."[38]

While the regiment remained near Appomattox Court House, the 110th presented flags to Maj. Gen. George G. Meade. During the final campaign, the soldiers of the Second Brigade captured six Confederate battle flags, more than any other brigade in the Sixth Corps. Since the men of the 110th secured two of those flags, the Buckeye regiment won the distinction of presenting all six to the commander of the Army of the Potomac.[39]

Throughout the next three months, the Sixth Corps remained in Virginia on occupation duty. On April 13, after remaining at Appomattox Court House for several days, the regiment moved to Burkeville Junction, and then ten days later, the regiment continued its movement to Danville, Virginia. After marching eighty-six miles in four days, the 110th arrived in Danville. During their occupation duty in the Old Dominion, the Ohioans associated with a variety of Southern citizens. In many instances, the soldiers commented on the structure of Southern society and how it perpetuated the slave system. Corporal Rhoades accused members of the Southern clergy of preaching to rationalize the peculiar institution. He also noticed that the agricultural system in Virginia was virtually nonexistent. Rhoades wrote that most Negroes had left and that the horses and mules appeared toil worn. He reported seeing only one Negro in the fields, and he was working the ground with a crude instrument.

Rhoades recorded that Confederate authorities spread many rumors about the invading Yankees. On April 27, he noted that rumors had informed Southerners that Union troops would kill them. On May 12, Rhoades wrote about a Southern couple who walked twenty-three miles to Danville to take the oath of allegiance and to get some food to eat. The couple informed him about rumors being spread that Yankee troops destroyed and plundered when they came into a region. In another instance, an elderly freedman horrified the Miami County corporal with a rumor of atrocities being committed by Union soldiers. Rhoades noted that the freedman was walking to Petersburg to inspect the fortifications there. When asked why, the elder man repeated a Confederate rumor that Yankee troops killed freedmen and used their corpses when constructing the fortifications at Petersburg.[40]

During the movement from Burkeville Junction to Danville, General Keifer talked with many local residents. He noted that the people of the region were anxious for a return to civil government. According to Keifer, the prominent citizens were quite eager to learn about the requirements needed for full acceptance back into the Union. Even while he camped upon the Flippin plantation near Danville and discussed the future with these former Confederates, he noted that he had little sympathy for the Southern whites.

The general discussed several times his belief that slavery was immoral. Although Keifer was an ardent Republican and abolitionist, he was still a product of his environment. In his April 27 letter to his wife, he announced his belief that the freedmen should remain in the South. He also believed that their labor was unsuitable for the Northern economy and furthermore that their inability to find work would force many black women and children into poorhouses. Keifer's comments confirm his support for the Southern proposal for leaving the freedmen in the South as a labor source.[41]

After occupying Danville for nineteen days, the 110th Ohio finally began their journey to Washington, D.C., to muster from the service. During the morning hours of May 15, 1865, many Buckeye boys embarked on rail cars. By May 21, the regiment arrived in Richmond. While in the former Confederate capital, the Union troops visited many notorious sites. Corporal Hill noted that he visited the city, while Keifer specified that he examined Castle Thunder, Belle Isle, and Libby Prisons.[42]

On May 24, the Sixth Corps marched for Washington, D.C. Four days later, Corporal Rhoades noted in a letter to his wife that many men died during this march. He blamed the deaths on the Virginia heat and over-zealous officers' desire to press forward to the capital. Rhoades thought it was a great tragedy for soldiers to survive so many battles only to die during the march home.[43]

On June 2, the Sixth Corps marched into Washington, D.C. For the next three weeks, the 110th remained in Washington. Six days later, the Sixth Corps marched in a grand review. Pres. Andrew Johnson, Secretary of the Treasury Hugh McCulloch, and Secretary of War Edwin Stanton were among the dignitaries that watched the Sixth Corps march down Pennsylvania Avenue. After the review, Keifer met President Johnson.[44]

During their stay in the nation's capital, mustering from service was the greatest concern of the officers and men of the regiment. On June 5, General Keifer visited General Meade and discussed the matter. During their meeting, Meade promised that Keifer's brigade would muster from service by the end of the month. Three days later, he gave Keifer official permission to apply for release from service. On June 10, Keifer met with Gov. William Dennison and impressed upon the Ohio governor the need to release that state's troops. Dennison agreed and said that he would visit Secretary of War Stanton on the following Monday, June 12.[45]

On June 21, the first regiment in the Second Brigade, Third Division, Sixth Corps, mustered from service. The soldiers of Keifer's brigade celebrated the dismissal of the 6th Maryland Infantry. After the Marylanders visited each regiment, brigade, and division headquarters to bid farewell, the soldiers of the brigade turned out for an informal, candlelight ceremony. After every man placed a candle in his bayonet, each regiment marched to the 6th Maryland's camp. Corporal Berry thought that "it mad[e] as grand a sight as ever I saw[.] We didn't get through until about 3 o'clock morning."[46]

On that same day, the War Department finally ordered the muster out of Ohio troops without exception. While General Keifer and his staff previously worked on brigade business in anticipation of this order, they now worked quickly to complete new muster rolls. On June 25, 1865, after completion of the necessary paperwork, the 110th Ohio Volunteer Infantry mustered from Federal service. The next morning, these Ohio veterans boarded rail cars bound for home. Three days later, they arrived in Columbus, and on June 30, the former soldiers started the last leg of their journey home.[47]

In the final months of the Civil War, the 110th Ohio played a significant role. After returning to the Federal lines besieging Petersburg, the 110th assaulted the Confederate fortifications and captured the outerworks of their defenses. On April 2, the regiment assaulted the main Confederate lines. After breaking through the Petersburg defenses, the 110th participated in the pursuit of the fleeing Confederate forces toward Appomattox Court House. During this operation, the unit engaged Rebel troops at Little Sayler's Creek. On April 9, the Ohioans encamped near Appomattox Court House and celebrated Lee's surrender. Shortly afterward, they lamented the loss of President Lincoln. After serving one month on occupation duty, these Buckeyes moved to Washington via Richmond. One month later, the men from Clark, Darke, Greene, and Miami Counties mustered from Federal military service and returned home.

During their nearly three years of service, the men of the 110th Ohio Volunteer Infantry endured many hardships. But through it they saw areas of their country that many would never get to see again or have seen otherwise. The Civil War experience also showed these men that their nation was real, and it created a personal, everlasting bond between the veterans. After the war, many of these men remained active in Grand Army of the Republic (GAR) posts and regularly attended regimental reunions. Several officers from the 110th entered politics at various levels: Quartermaster Albert Stark was a councilman in Xenia; Lt. Col. Aaron Spangler served several terms as mayor of Osborn (presently part of the city of Fairborn); Capt. William Shaw briefly served as superintendent of the Ohio Soldiers' and Sailors' Home in Xenia; Lt. Col. William Foster became a Miami County judge; and Col. Otho Binkley was an active Republican in Troy, Ohio.

Brig. Gen. J. Warren Keifer was the most celebrated individual from the regiment. While in the army, Keifer made many political connections. During his first fifteen months of service with the Army of the Ohio, he met Brig. Gen. James A. Garfield. Making additional contacts while serving in

Congressman J. Warren Keifer. Courtesy of USAMHI.

the Army of the Potomac, he twice met Ulysses Grant and Andrew Johnson. His Shenandoah Valley service allowed him the chance to meet Col. Rutherford B. Hayes and Maj. William McKinley. One unit in Keifer's brigade contained yet another political connection for him. Col. William H. Seward Jr., son of the secretary of state, commanded the 9th New York Heavy Artillery. After the Civil War, Keifer served several terms as commandant of the GAR's Ohio Commandery. He then served two terms in the Ohio Senate before being elected to the U.S. House of Representatives. While serving one of his seven terms as congressman, Keifer was Speaker of the House. In 1898, Pres. William McKinley recalled the then sixty-two-year-old Ohioan back to military service during the Spanish-American War. J. Warren Keifer died in 1932.

Other men in the unit were not nearly so celebrated. Pvt. Henry Kauffman returned to Harmony, Ohio, but he did not return to his blacksmith trade. Instead, Kauffman taught in a one-room schoolhouse. Cpl. Josiah Hill returned to Fletcher, Ohio, where he also became a schoolteacher. And Cpl. John Rhoades went back to his Brown Township farm near Fletcher.

In his letter of April 10, 1865, Rhoades summarized the soldiers' experience as viewed by the men of the 110th Ohio: "I am not sorry now that I have had a hand in helping to put down the rebellion. I now have a contry I can call my home. . . . I now feel that my children have for them a home in the land of the free and the home of the Brave."[48]

Appendix: The Official Roster

From 1886 to 1895, the State of Ohio's Adjutant General's Office compiled the rosters of all infantry, cavalry, and artillery regiments. The following is a reproduction of the roster of the 110th Ohio Volunteer Infantry.

Following the regimental staff, each compny is listed alphabetically. Within the staff and companies, the roster is further organized by commissioned and noncomissioned officers listed by rank. The enlisted men are then listed in roughly alphabetical order. There are errors of omission and commission within the roster, and many misspellings can be found. As casualties mounted throughout the war and discharges were granted for various reasons, many commissioned and noncommissioned officers were promoted or changed companies.

Note: The Publisher regrets the inconsistent appearance of the Roster pages. They represent the best images available at the time of publication.

110TH REGIMENT OHIO VOLUNTEER INFANTRY.

FIELD AND STAFF.

Mustered in Oct. 3, 1862, at Camp Piqua, O., by Alexander E. Drake, Captain 2d Infantry, U. S. A. Mustered out June 25, 1865, near Washington, D. C., by J. C. Robinson, Brevet Major and A. C. M. 3d Division, 6th Army Corps.

Names.	Rank.	Age.	Date of Entering the Service.	Period of Service.	Remarks.
J. Warren Kiefer........	Colonel.	26	June 12, 1861	3 yrs.	Promoted from Lieut. Colonel 3d O. V. I. Sept. 30, 1862; wounded June 13 and 14, 1863, in battle of Winchester, Va.; May 5, 1864, in battle of Wilderness, Va.; also Sept. 19, 1864, in battle of Opequan, Va.; brevet Brig. General Oct. 19, 1864, and assigned to 2d Brigade, 3d Division, 6th Army Corps; brevet Maj. General Volunteers to date April 9, 1865; mustered out June 27, 1865, by order of War Department; appointed Lieut. Colonel 26th Infantry, U. S. A., Oct. 18, 1866; declined.
William N. Foster.......	Lt. Col.	41	Sept. 13, 1862	3 yrs.	Resigned Dec. 24, 1863.
Otho H. Binkley..........	....do....	36	Sept. 1, 1862	3 yrs.	Promoted from Major Jan. 1, 1864; brevet Colonel Oct. 19, 1864; mustered out with regiment June 25, 1865.
William S. McElwain...	Major.	32	Aug. 15, 1862	3 yrs.	Promoted from Captain Co. D Jan. 1, 1864; killed May 5, 1864, in battle of the Wilderness, Va.
Aaron Spangler...........	....do....	26	Aug. 15, 1862	3 yrs.	Promoted from Captain Co. F June 25, 1864; brevet Lieut. Colonel Oct. 19, 1864; wounded March 25, 1865, in action near Petersburg, Va.; mustered out with regiment June 25, 1865.
Sumner Pixley..........	Surgeon.	46	Sept. 4, 1862	3 yrs.	Resigned May 1, 1863.
Robert R. McCandliss...	....do....	35	Aug. 25, 1862	3 yrs.	Promoted from Asst. Surgeon May 1, 1863; captured June 15, 1863, at battle of Winchester, Va.; exchanged Nov. 24, 1863; mustered out with regiment June 25, 1865.
Thomas C. Owen........	As. Surg.	31	Aug. 20, 1862	3 yrs.	Captured June 15, 1863, at battle of Winchester, Va.; escaped July 4, 1863; resigned April 20, 1864.
Alexander W. Pinkerton	....do....	43	April 1, 1864	3 yrs.	Discharged Aug. 20, 1864, by order of War Department.
William H. Park.........	....do....	32	July 13, 1864	3 yrs.	Mustered out with regiment June 25, 1865.
E. Pierson Ebersole.....	....do....	36	Sept. 5, 1864	3 yrs.	Mustered out with regiment June 25, 1865.
Joseph B. Van Eaton	Adjutant	25	Aug. 22, 1862	3 yrs.	Promoted from Sergeant Co. D Sept. 18, 1862; to Captain Co. B March 21, 1864.
Wesley Devenney.......	....do....	26	Aug. 11, 1862	3 yrs.	Promoted from 1st Sergeant Co. E April 12, 1864; to Captain Co. E, Aug. 8, 1864.
William H. Harry.......	....do....	26	Aug. 22, 1862	3 yrs.	Promoted to Sergt. Major from Sergeant Co. D Nov. 25, 1862; to 2d Lieutenant Co. B May 9, 1864; to 1st Lieutenant and Adjutant Aug. 8, 1864; brevet Captain April 2, 1865; promoted to Captain May 31, 1865, but not mustered; mustered out with regiment June 25, 1865.
Albert M. Stark..........	R. Q. M.	40	Aug. 13, 1862	3 yrs.	Captured June 15, 1863, at battle of Winchester, Va.; paroled Sept. 12, 1864; mustered out with regiment June 25, 1865.
James Harvey...........	Chaplain	45	Feb. 11, 1863	3 yrs.	Captured June 15, 1863, at battle of Winchester, Va.; released Oct. —, 1863; resigned Nov. 18, 1863, for physical disability.
Lucius W. Chapman.....	....do....	37	Feb. 18, 1864	3 yrs.	Resigned April 28, 1864.
Milton J. Miller..........	....do....	33	Aug. 8, 1864	3 yrs.	Mustered out with regiment June 25, 1865.
James A. Fox............	Ser. Maj.	32	Aug. 20, 1862	3 yrs.	Promoted from Sergeant Co. F Oct. 4, 1862; to 2d Lieutenant Co. D Nov. 25, 1862.
David S. French..........	....do....	18	Aug. 15, 1862	3 yrs.	Promoted from Sergeant Co. A June 8, 1864; to 2d Lieutenant Co. A Aug. 23, 1864.
Dock W. Richardson.....	....do....	26	Aug. 12, 1862	3 yrs.	Promoted from private Co. F Sept. 1, 1864; to 2d Lieutenant Co. G Dec. 24, 1864.
Francis M. McMillen....	....do....	30	Aug. 15, 1862	3 yrs.	Promoted from Sergeant Co. C May 2, 1865; mustered out with regiment June 25, 1865.

Names.	Rank.	Age.	Date of Entering the Service.	Period of Service.	Remarks.
J. Mills Conwell.........	Q. M. S.	24	Aug. 21, 1862	3 yrs.	Promoted to 2d Lieutenant Co. F April 12, 1864.
Robert W. Wiley........	....do....	25	Aug. 18, 1862	3 yrs.	Promoted from private Co. C April 19, 1864; to 2d Lieutenant Co. B July 22, 1864.
Joseph G. Dye.............	....do....	21	Aug. 15, 1862	3 yrs.	Promoted from Corporal Co. A Aug. 13, 1864; reduced to ranks and transferred to Co. A April 14, 1865.
Thomas J. Daugherty...	....do....	23	Aug. 22, 1862	3 yrs.	Promoted from Corporal Co. D April 14, 1865 ; mustered out with regiment June 25, 1865.
David J. Martin.........	Com. Ser.	33	Aug. 22, 1862	3 yrs.	Captured Aug. 16, 1864, at battle of Crooked Run, Va.; released Oct. 8, 1864; mustered out with regiment June 25, 1865.
William W. Locke.......	Hos. St'd.	32	Aug. 22, 1862	3 yrs.	Promoted from private Co. G Aug. 22, 1862; to 2d Lieutenant Co. E April 12, 1864.
Erastus Layton...........	....do....	19	Aug. 14, 1862	3 yrs.	Promoted from Sergeant Co. I April 23, 1864 ; to 2d Lieutenant Co. G Dec. 9, 1864.
William Lefever...........	....do....	20	Aug. 12, 1862	3 yrs.	Promoted from Corporal Co. A Sept. 1, 1864; mustered out with regiment June 25, 1865.
Lucius C. Cron..........	Prin. Mus	23	Aug. 7, 1862	3 yrs.	Promoted from Musician Co. A Oct. —, 1862; mustered out with regiment June 25, 1865.
William H. Morris......	....do....	29	Aug. 9, 1862	3 yrs.	Promoted from Musician Co. A Oct. —, 1862; captured June 15, 1863, at battle of Winchester, Va.; mustered out with regiment June 25, 1865.

COMPANY A.

Mustered in Oct. 2, 1862, at Camp Piqua, O., by Alexander E. Drake, Captain 2d Infantry, U. S. A. Mustered out June 25, 1865, near Washington, D. C., by J. C. Robinson, Brevet Major and A. C. M. 3d Division, 6th Army Corps.

Names.	Rank.	Age.	Date of Entering the Service.	Period of Service.	Remarks.
William D. Alexander..	Captain.	32	Aug. 7, 1862	3 yrs.	Discharged Dec. 15, 1863, on Surgeon's certificate of disability.
Elias A. Shepherd.......	....do....	25	Aug. 6, 1862	3 yrs.	Transferred from Co. B April 1, 1864; to Co. B Aug. 13, 1864.
William D.Shellenberger	....do....	21	Aug. 7, 1862	3 yrs.	Accidentally wounded at Winchester, Va.,——, 1863; promoted to 1st Lieutenant from 2d Lieutenant March 21, 1864; Captain July 22, 1864; wounded Oct. 19, 1864, in battle of Cedar Creek, Va.; also April 2, 1865, in action at Petersburg, Va.; mustered out with company June 25, 1865.
William L. Cron.........	1st Lieut.	35	Aug. 7, 1862	3 yrs.	Promoted to Captain March 21, 1864, but not mustered; resigned March 23, 1864.
John T. Sherer.............	....do....	27	Aug. 7, 1862	3 yrs.	Promoted to 2d Lieutenant from 1st Sergeant April 12, 1864; to 1st Lieutenant to date May 9, 1864; wounded July 9, 1864, in battle of Monocacy, Md.; promoted to Captain Co. C April 26, 1865.
Milton H. Myers	....do....	21	Nov. 13, 1862	3 yrs.	Promoted from 1st Sergeant Co. K May 31, 1865 ; mustered out with company June 25, 1865.
David S. French.........	2d Lieut.	18	Aug. 15, 1862	3 yrs.	Promoted to Sergt. Major from Sergeant June 8, 1864; 2d Lieutenant Aug. 23, 1864; 1st Lieutenant Co. B Jan. 31, 1865.
James W. McNair.......	1st Sergt.	21	Aug. 7, 1862	3 yrs.	Appointed from Sergeant April 20, 1864; killed Oct. 19, 1864, in battle of Cedar Creek, Va.
Samuel D. Frank..........	....do....	21	Aug. 18, 1862	3 yrs.	Appointed Sergeant from Corporal April 20, 1864; wounded July 9, 1864, in battle of Monocacy, Md.; appointed 1st Sergeant Oct. 20, 1864; discharged Dec. 24, 1864, on Surgeon's certificate of disability.
John W. Hays.............	....do....	20	Aug. 12, 1862	3 yrs.	Appointed Sergeant from Corporal Aug. 13, 1864; 1st Sergeant Dec. 24, 1864; mustered out with company June 25, 1865.
Joseph M. Patterson....	Sergeant.	32	Aug. 20, 1862	3 yrs.	Wounded and captured May 6, 1864, at battle of the Wilderness, Va.; discharged March 14, 1865, for wounds received in action ; arm amputated.
Robert Ainsworth........	....do....	32	Aug. 11, 1862	3 yrs.	Wounded Sept. 19, 1864, in battle of Opequan. Va.; appointed from Corporal Oct. 20, 1864; mustered out June 30, 1865, at Washington, D. C., by order of War Department.
William A. Shuler	....do....	27	Aug. 18, 1862	3 yrs.	Captured June 15, 1863, at battle of Winchester, Va.; wounded May 12, 1864, in battle of Spottsylvania C. H., Va.; appointed from Corporal Aug. 13, 1864; discharged May 13, 1865, for wounds received in action.
Leonidas Folckemmer..	....do....	18	Aug. 18, 1862	3 yrs.	Captured June 15, 1863, at battle of Winchester, Va.; appointed from Corporal Dec. 24, 1864; mustered out with company June 25, 1865.

Names.	Rank.	Age.	Date of Entering the Service.	Period of Service.	Remarks.
Le Roy S. Jordan........	Sergeant	21	Aug. 7, 1862	3 yrs.	Appointed Corporal ——; captured June 15, 1863, at battle of Winchester, Va.; wounded June 3, 1864, in battle of Cold Harbor, Va.; appointed Sergeant March 15, 1865; mustered out May 12, 1865, at Columbus, O., by order of War Department.
Jerry A. Lindley........	....do....	17	Aug. 8, 1862	3 yrs.	Appointed Corporal April 20, 1864; Sergeant May 13, 1865; mustered out with company June 25, 1865.
James E. Campbell......	Corporal.	27	Aug. 8, 1862	3 yrs.	Discharged Aug. 27, 1864, at Washington, D. C., on Surgeon's certificate of disability.
William Lefever........	....do....	20	Aug. 12, 1862	3 yrs.	Wounded June 3, 1864, in battle of Cold Harbor, Va.; appointed Corporal June 12, 1864; promoted to Hospital Steward Sept. 1, 1864.
Albert M. Blackmer.....	....do....	31	Aug. 12, 1862	3 yrs.	Appointed Aug. 13, 1864; mustered out with company June 25, 1865.
Conover Hall...........	....do....	20	Aug. 8, 1862	3 yrs.	Appointed Oct. 20, 1864; mustered out with company June 25, 1865.
Calvin M. Espy........	....do....	25	Aug. 8, 1862	3 yrs.	Captured June 15, 1863, at battle of Winchester, Va.; appointed Corporal Dec. 31, 1864; wounded April 2, 1865, in front of Petersburg, Va.; discharged June 21, 1865, at Cleveland, O., on Surgeon's certificate of disability.
Aaron W. Graham......	....do....	23	Aug. 16, 1862	3 yrs.	Captured June 15, 1863, in battle of Winchester, Va.; appointed Corporal Dec. 31, 1864; mustered out June 9, 1865, at Washington, D. C., by order of War Department.
Gustavus Hunt........	....do....	19	Aug. 7, 1862	3 yrs.	Appointed Aug. 27, 1864; wounded Sept. 19, 1864, in battle of Opequan, Va.; discharged May 3, 1865, for wounds received in action.
John L. Keifer........	....do....	18	Aug. 11, 1862	3 yrs.	Wounded June 3, 1864, in battle of Cold Harbor, Va.; appointed Corporal Sept. 1, 1864; mustered out with company June 25, 1865.
Noah Overmyer........	....do....	24	Aug. 9, 1862	3 yrs.	Captured June 15, 1863, at battle of Winchester, Va.; appointed Corporal May 3, 1865; mustered out with company June 25, 1865.
Edward A. Lines........	....do....	18	Aug. 8, 1862	3 yrs.	Wounded May 12, 1864, in battle of Spottsylvania C. H., Va.; appointed Corporal May 13, 1865; mustered out with company June 25, 1865.
Charles W. Deputee.....	....do....	20	Mch. 27, 1864	3 yrs.	Appointed June 9, 1865; mustered out with company June 25, 1865.
George F. Simons........	....do....	19	Aug. 18, 1862	3 yrs.	Appointed March 16, 1865; mustered out with company June 25, 1865.
William H. Morris......	Musician	29	Aug. 9, 1862	3 yrs.	Promoted to Principal Musician Oct. —, 1862.
Lucius C. Crop.........	....do....	23	Aug. 7, 1862	3 yrs.	Promoted to Principal Musician Oct. —, 1862.
Alexander, Melville W...	Private.	18	Aug. 18, 1862	3 yrs.	Captured June 15, 1863, at battle of Winchester, Va.; wounded Nov. 27, 1863, in battle of Mine Run, Va.; discharged April 28, 1864, for wounds received in action.
Amarine, Isaiah........	....do....	18	Aug. 13, 1862	3 yrs.	Captured June 15, 1863, at battle of Winchester, Va.; mustered out with company June 25, 1865.
Anderson, John T.......	....do....	21	Aug. 8, 1862	3 yrs.	Killed May 6, 1864, in battle of the Wilderness, Virginia.
Aspinall, William........	....do....	20	Aug. 11, 1862	3 yrs.	Discharged Feb. 21, 1863, at Winchester, Va., by order of War Department.
Baldock, Lafayette......	....do....	31	Aug. 8, 1862	3 yrs.	Wounded June 3, 1864, in battle of Cold Harbor, Va.; discharged April 17, 1865, for wounds received in action.
Barnes, Thompson......	....do....	19	Aug. 18, 1862	3 yrs.	Died Feb. 9, 1864, at his home in Ohio.
Bates, David S..........	....do....	21	Aug. 11, 1862	3 yrs.	Captured June 15, 1863, at battle of Winchester, Va.; mustered out with company June 25, 1865.
Burke, Michael F........	....do....	22	Sept. 8, 1862	3 yrs.	Captured June 15, 1863, at battle of Winchester, Va.
Bushnell, Oliver........	....do....	28	Aug. 8, 1862	3 yrs.	Mustered out with company June 25, 1865.
Byers, George W........	....do....	25	Aug. 8, 1862	3 yrs.	Mustered out with company June 25, 1865.
Byers, William H........	....do....	18	Aug. 9, 1862	3 yrs.	Killed Nov. 27, 1863, in battle of Mine Run, Virginia.
Carney, William........	....do....	19	June 18, 1864	3 yrs.	Substitute; captured July 9, 1864, at battle of Monocacy, Md. No further record found.
Carroll, William H......	....do....	18	Oct. 18, 1863	3 yrs.	
Chadwick, James........	....do....	19	June 18, 1864	3 yrs.	Substitute; captured July 9, 1864, at battle of Monocacy, Md. No further record found.
Chrowl, Daniel H.......	....do....	18	Aug. 11, 1862	3 yrs.	Died Feb. 11, 1863, in hospital at Winchester, Virginia.
Cline, Charles W........	....do....	20	Aug. 8, 1862	3 yrs.	Captured May 6, 1864, at battle of the Wilderness, Va.; paroled Nov. 30, 1864. No further record found.
Collins, William........	....do....	28	Oct. 23, 1863	3 yrs.	Mustered out with company June 25, 1865.
Compton, John W.......	....do....	19	Aug. 7, 1862	3 yrs.	Mustered out with company June 25, 1865.
Conkling, George A......	....do....	18	Aug. 9, 1862	3 yrs.	Reduced from Corporal ——; mustered out with company June 25, 1865.

Names.	Rank.	Age.	Date of Entering the Service.	Period of Service.	Remarks.
Cotterman, John H.....	Private..	26	Aug. 7, 1862	3 yrs.	Mustered in as Wagoner; captured Nov. 12, 1864, at battle of Cedar Springs, Va.; mustered out June 10, 1865, at Camp Chase, O., by order of War Department.
Crapsey, Jacob..........	....do....	20	Aug. 13, 1862	3 yrs.	Wounded Nov. 27, 1863, in battle of Mine Run, Va.; also May 6, 1864, in battle of the Wilderness, Va.; discharged April 17, 1865, for wounds received in action.
Crapsey, William H.....	....do....	18	Sept. 1, 1863	3 yrs.	Mustered out with company June 25, 1865.
Crawford, William......	....do....	17	Aug. 13, 1862	3 yrs.	Discharged Feb. 21, 1863, at Winchester, Va.
Cron, Henry.............	....do....	18	Aug. 22, 1862	3 yrs.	Captured June 15, 1863, at battle of Winchester, Va.; mustered out May 18, 1865, by order of War Department.
Crosby, Horace S........	....do....	21	Aug. 15, 1862	3 yrs.	Captured June 15, 1863, at battle of Winchester, Va.; mustered out with company June 25, 1865.
Cruse, George W........	....do....	23	Aug. 7, 1862	3 yrs.	Wounded Sept. 19, 1864, in battle of Opequan, Va.; mustered out with company June 25, 1865.
Davis, George N.........	....do....	17	Aug. 8, 1862	3 yrs.	Mustered out with company June 25, 1865.
Deckman, Edward J....	....do....	30	Aug. 19, 1862	3 yrs.	Wounded April 2, 1865, in front of Petersburg, Va.; mustered out with company June 25, 1865.
Deitrich, George F......	....do....	21	Aug. 9, 1862	3 yrs.	Wounded May 6, 1864, in battle of the Wilderness, Va.; also June 3, 1864, in battle of Cold Harbor, Va.; mustered out May 23, 1865, at Philadelphia, Pa., by order of War Department.
Denman, Joseph..........	....do....	24	Aug. 15, 1862	3 yrs.	Mustered out with company June 25, 1865.
Deweese, John............	....do....	21	Aug. 12, 1862	3 yrs.	Transferred to Veteran Reserve Corps Feb. 11, 1864.
Dowdy, George..........	....do....	19	June 18, 1864	3 yrs.	Substitute; captured July 9, 1864, at battle of Monocacy, Md. No further record found.
Dunning, John T........	....do....	17	Aug. 8, 1862	3 yrs.	Captured July 9, 1864, at battle of Monocacy, Md.; mustered out June 10, 1865, at Camp Chase, O., by order of War Department.
Dye, Joseph G............	....do....	21	Aug. 15, 1862	3 yrs.	Mustered in as Corporal; promoted to Q. M. Sergeant Aug. 13, 1864; reduced to ranks April 14, 1865; mustered out with company June 25, 1865.
Dye, Oliver H............	....do....	26	Aug. 9, 1862	3 yrs.	Transferred to Co. G, 24th Regiment, Veteran Reserve Corps. ——; mustered out July 18, 1865, at Washington, D. C., by order of War Department.
Edge, William W........	....do....	21	Aug. 15, 1862	3 yrs.	Transferred to Signal Corps, U. S. A., April 1, 1864.
Eichron, John............	....do....	18	Jan. 10, 1864	3 yrs.	Mustered out with company June 25, 1865.
Free, John................	....do....	20	Aug. 13, 1862	3 yrs.	Killed July 9, 1864, in battle of Monocacy, Maryland.
Freshour, George.........	....do....	17	Aug. 11, 1862	3 yrs.	Killed Nov. 27, 1863, in battle of Mine Run, Virginia.
Furrow, Alonzo J.......	....do....	19	Aug. 11, 1862	3 yrs.	Captured May 6, 1864, at battle of the Wilderness, Va.; mustered out June 10, 1865, at Camp Chase, O., by order of War Department.
Gale, Otho G.............	....do....	20	Aug. 13, 1862	3 yrs.	Captured June 15, 1863, at battle of Winchester, Va.; wounded Nov. 27, 1863, in battle of Mine Run, Va.; mustered out May 17, 1865, at Cincinnati, O., by order of War Department.
Grant, James A..........	....do....	20	Aug. 8, 1862	3 yrs.	Mustered out May 22, 1865, at Columbus, O., by order of War Department.
Grant, Joseph H.........	....do....	26	Aug. 7, 1862	3 yrs.	Mustered in as Corporal; appointed Sergeant June 12, 1864; reduced to Corporal Aug. 31, 1864; to ranks Nov. 1, 1864; mustered out June 13, 1865, near Washington, D. C., by order of War Department.
Green, Thomas W........	....do....	30	Aug. 8, 1862	3 yrs.	Wounded June 3, 1864, in battle of Cold Harbor, Va.; transferred to 2d Battalion, Veteran Reserve Corps, ——; mustered out Oct. 2, 1865, at Washington, D. C., on expiration of term of service.
Hasebrook, Albert......	....do....	18	Aug. 18, 1862	3 yrs.	Transferred to 42d Co., 2d Battalion, Veteran Reserve Corps, April 18, 1864; mustered out Aug. 24, 1865, by order of War Department.
Hays, William L.........	....do....	26	Aug. 8, 1862	3 yrs.	Died Sept. 27, 1863, in Rebel Prison at Richmond, Va.
Honsum, Charles P....	....do....	20	Aug. 13, 1862	3 yrs.	Transferred to 88th Co., 2d Battalion, Veteran Reserve Corps, April 6, 1865; mustered out June 30, 1865, at Cincinnati, O., by order of War Department.
Houser, Jacob C..........	....do....	27	Aug. 8, 1862	3 yrs.	Killed May 6, 1864, in battle of the Wilderness, Virginia.
Hughes, Hiram........ ...	....do....	17	Aug. 13, 1862	3 yrs.	Mustered out with company June 25, 1865.
Jeffries, George W........	....do....	22	Aug. 13, 1862	3 yrs.	Mustered out with company June 25, 1865.

Names.	Rank.	Age.	Date of Entering the Service.	Period of Service.	Remarks.
Jordan, Mark............	Private..	19	June 18, 1864	3 yrs.	Substitute ; captured July 9, 1864, at battle of Monocacy, Md. No further record found.
Jones, William H........	....do....	24	Sept. 25, 1863	3 yrs.	
Keyt, William J.........	....do....	29	Aug. 14, 1862	3 yrs.	Discharged Feb. 16, 1863, at Winchester, Va., on Surgeon's certificate of disability.
Lanpher, Oliver P.......	....do....	23	Jan. 14, 1864	3 yrs.	Mustered out with company June 25, 1865.
McClure, William S.....	....do....	18	Aug. 19, 1862	3 yrs.	Mustered out with company June 25, 1865.
McFarland, James B.....	....do....	21	Aug. 11, 1862	3 yrs.	Mustered out with company June 25, 1865.
Malosh, Joseph..........	....do....	20	Aug. 9, 1862	3 yrs.	Discharged March 6, 1863, at Winchester, Va., on Surgeon's certificate of disability.
Manson, James W........	....do....	22	Aug. 8, 1862	3 yrs.	Accidentally wounded May 16, 1864; mustered out with company June 25, 1865.
Matthews, John K.......	....do....	26	Aug. 11, 1862	3 yrs.	Killed Sept. 19, 1864, in battle of Opequan, Va.
Miller, Levi.............	....do....	26	Oct. 17, 1863	3 yrs.	Wounded May 6, 1864, in battle of the Wilderness, Va.; mustered out with company June 25th, 1865.
Miller, Thomas H.......	....do....	23	Sept. 22, 1863	3 yrs.	Killed July 9, 1864, in battle of Monocacy, Md.
Milhouse, Franklin......	....do....	23	Aug. 13, 1862	3 yrs.	Wounded May 12, 1864, in battle of Spottsylvania C. H., Va.; also April 2, 1865, in front of Petersburg, Va.; mustered out with company June 25, 1865.
Minich, Josiah..........	....do....	21	Aug. 9, 1862	3 yrs.	Wounded Oct. 19, 1864, in battle of Cedar Creek, Va.; mustered out with company June 25, 1865.
Minich, Valentine.......	....do....	21	Feb. 4, 1864	3 yrs.	Wounded June 4, 1864, in battle of Cold Harbor, Va.; mustered out June 9, 1865, at Washington, D. C., by order of War Department.
Mitchell, John J........	....do....	22	Sept. 4, 1862	3 yrs.	Mustered out July 9, 1865, at Washington, D. C., by order of War Department.
Nettleship, Isaac W.....	....do....	19	Aug. 8, 1862	3 yrs.	Mustered out with company June 25, 1865.
Niles, Ephraim.........	....do....	20	Aug. 8, 1862	3 yrs.	Discharged May 10, 1863, at Winchester, Va., on Surgeon's certificate of disability.
Raplyea, Nicholas.......	....do....	24	Aug. 15, 1862	3 yrs.	Captured June 15, 1863, at battle of Winchester, Va.; mustered out with company June 25, 1865.
Redinbaugh, Henry C...	....do....	24	Aug. 8, 1862	3 yrs.	Wounded Aug. 28, 1864, in action near Smithfield, Va.; killed April 2, 1865, in action at Petersburg, Va.
Riddle, William.........	....do....	19	Aug. 12, 1862	3 yrs.	Discharged March 6, 1863, at Winchester, Va., on Surgeon's certificate of disability.
Richeson, William C....	....do....	30	Aug. 18, 1862	3 yrs.	Captured June 15, 1863, at battle of Winchester, Va.; paroled ——; wounded Sept. 19, 1864, in battle of Opequan, Va.; also wounded Oct. 19, 1864, in battle of Cedar Creek, Va.; mustered out June 9, 1865, at Washington, D. C., by order of War Department.
Rockwood, Cephas A....	....do....	24	June 17, 1864	3 yrs.	Drafted ; mustered out with company June 25, 1865.
Rusk, John N...........	....do....	17	Aug. 11, 1862	3 yrs.	Killed June 3, 1864, in battle of Cold Harbor, Virginia.
Seiders, Henry.........	....do....	18	Feb. 4, 1864	3 yrs.	Mustered out June 19, 1865, at Washington, D. C., by order of War Department.
Shellabargar, Solomon..	....do....	27	Aug. 12, 1862	3 yrs.	Died May 20, 1863, in hospital at Winchester, Virginia.
Smith, William E.......	....do....	18	Jan. 2, 1864	3 yrs.	Transferred to Co. I, 2d Battalion, Veteran Reserve Corps, April 18, 1864; mustered out July 11, 1865, at Indianapolis, Ind., by order of War Department.
Stillwell, Morris J......	....do....	21	Aug. 12, 1862	3 yrs.	Wounded Sept. 19, 1864, in battle of Opequan, Va.; transferred to Co. D, 11th Regiment, Veteran Reserve Corps, ——; mustered out July 7, 1865, at Providence, R. I.
Stoker, David...........	....do....	18	Sept. 10, 1862	3 yrs.	Killed June 3, 1864, in battle of Cold Harbor, Virginia.
Thomas, Elmore A......	....do....	17	Aug. 3, 1862	3 yrs.	Captured June 15, 1863, at battle of Winchester, Va.; wounded Nov. 27, 1863, in battle of Mine Run, Va.; mustered out June 13, 1865, at Washington, D. C., by order of War Department.
Thompson, Charles.....	....do....	23	Aug. 12, 1862	3 yrs.	Mustered out with company June 25, 1865.
Thompson, James L....	....do....	27	Aug. 13, 1862	3 yrs.	Wounded June 3, 1864, in battle of Cold Harbor, Va.; mustered out with company June 25, 1865.
Weatherhead, James A.	....do....	18	Dec. 31, 1863	3 yrs.	Mustered out June 7, 1865, at Philadelphia, Pa., by order of War Department.
Whiteman, William M..	....do....	18	Jan. 19, 1864	3 yrs.	Wounded June 3, 1864, in battle of Cold Harbor, Va.; mustered out with company June 25, 1865.
Williamson, Edward J..	....do....	19	Aug. 18, 1862	3 yrs.	Transferred to U. S. Signal Corps April 1, 1864.
Wilson, George W.......	....do....	23	Aug. 15, 1862	3 yrs.	Captured June 15, 1863, at battle of Winchester, Va.; wounded Nov. 27, 1863, in battle of Mine Run, Va.
Wimer, Andrew C.......	....do....	25	Aug. 8, 1862	3 yrs.	Mustered out with company June 25, 1865.
Young, Henry..........	....do....	24	Aug. 17, 1862	3 yrs.	Transferred to Veteran Reserve Corps ——; mustered out Aug. 17, 1865, at Cumberland, Md., on expiration of term of service.

COMPANY B.

Mustered in Oct. 2, 1862, at Camp Piqua, O., by Alexander E. Drake, Captain 2d Infantry, U. S. A. Mustered out June 25, 1865, near Washington, D. C., by J. C. Robinson, Brevet Major and A. C. M. 3d Division, 6th Army Corps.

Names.	Rank.	Age.	Date of Entering the Service.	Period of Service.	Remarks.
Jason Young	Captain.	26	Aug. 7, 1862	3 yrs.	Resigned Dec. 18, 1862.
Elias A. Shepherd	....do....	25	Aug. 6, 1862	3 yrs.	Appointed 1st Lieutenant Aug. 7, 1862; promoted to Captain Dec. 18, 1862; captured June 15, 1863, at battle of Winchester, Va.; confined in Libby Prison, Va.; transferred to Co. A April 3, 1864; from Co. A Aug. 13, 1864; to Co. F ——; from Co. F Feb. 17, 1865; discharged March 13, 1865.
Joseph B. Van Eaton	....do....	25	Aug. 22, 1862	3 yrs.	Promoted from 1st Lieutenant and Adjutant to date March 21, 1864; wounded Sept. 19, 1864, in battle of Opequan, Va.; discharged Dec. 28, 1864, for wounds received in action.
Charles M. Gross	....do....	34	Aug. 16, 1862	3 yrs.	Mustered as Captain and transferred from Co. G May 9, 1865; mustered out with company June 25, 1865.
James A. Fox	1st Lieut.	32	Aug. 20, 1862	3 yrs.	Promoted from 2d Lieutenant Co. D Dec. 18, 1862; killed Nov. 27, 1863, in battle of Mine Run, Va.
Darius H. Moon	....do....	25	Aug. 6, 1862	3 yrs.	Promoted to 2d Lieutenant from 1st Sergeant Jan. 2, 1863; 1st Lieutenant March 21, 1864; discharged Nov. 27, 1864.
David S. French	....do....	18	Aug. 15, 1862	3 yrs.	Promoted from 2d Lieutenant Co. A Jan. 31, 1865; mustered out with company June 25, 1865.
David Langston	2d Lieut.	27	Aug. 18, 1862	3 yrs.	Promoted to 1st Lieutenant Dec. 18, 1862, but not mustered; resigned Jan. 2, 1863.
William H. Harry	....do....	26	Aug. 22, 1862	3 yrs.	Promoted from Sergt. Major May 9, 1864; to 1st Lieutenant and Adjutant Aug. 8, 1864.
Robert W. Wiley	....do....	25	Aug. 18, 1862	3 yrs.	Promoted from Q. M. Sergeant July 22, 1864; captured Oct. 19, 1864, at battle of Cedar Creek, Va.; promoted to 1st Lieutenant Dec. 9, 1864, but not mustered; mustered out May 12, 1865.
Harrison Bonham	1st Sergt.	22	Aug. 22, 1862	3 yrs.	Mustered as Corporal; wounded and captured June 15, 1863, in battle of Winchester, Va.; wounded May 5, 1864, in battle of the Wilderness, Va.; appointed 1st Sergeant June 1, 1864; mustered out May 16, 1865, at Philadelphia, Pa., by order of War Department.
John C. Lafever	Sergeant.	21	Aug. 6, 1862	3 yrs.	Wounded May 6, 1864, in battle of the Wilderness, Va.; also May 11, 1864, in battle of Spottsylvania C. H., Va.; died June 1, 1864, at Washington, D. C.
George W. Houk	....do....	37	Aug. 9, 1862	3 yrs.	Transferred to Co. B, 19th Regiment, Veteran Reserve Corps, Sept. 19, 1864; mustered out July 13, 1865, at Elmira, N. Y., by order of War Department.
Silas Morrison	....do....	24	Aug. 22, 1862	3 yrs.	Wounded and captured June 13, 1863, in battle of Winchester, Va.; transferred to Co. K, 3d Regiment, Veteran Reserve Corps, Nov. 21, 1864; mustered out July 10, 1865, at Hartford, Conn., by order of War Department.
Martin P. Baker	....do....	25	Aug. 6, 1862	3 yrs.	Mustered as private; appointed Sergeant Nov. 23, 1862; wounded Nov. 27, 1863, in battle of Mine Run, Va.; transferred to 37th Co., 2d Battalion, Vet. Reserve Corps, March 8, 1865.
William Trace	....do....	21	Aug. 11, 1862	3 yrs.	Appointed Corporal Aug. 1, 1864; Sergeant Nov. 21, 1864; mustered out with company June 25, 1865.
Courtland Corwin	....do....	18	June 9, 1863	3 yrs.	Appointed Corporal Aug. 1, 1864; Sergeant Dec. 1, 1864; mustered out with company June 25, 1865.
George F. Russ	....do....	21	Aug. 9, 1862	3 yrs.	Appointed Corporal Aug. 10, 1864; Sergeant Feb. 18, 1865; wounded April 2, 1865, in front of Petersburg, Va.; discharged July 21, 1865, at Columbus, O., on Surgeon's certificate of disability.
Silas Lappin	Corporal.	27	Aug. 11, 1862	3 yrs.	Discharged Feb. 26, 1863, at Winchester, Va., on Surgeon's certificate of disability.
George Martin	....do....	28	Aug. 11, 1862	3 yrs.	Died Aug. 10, 1864, in hospital at Alexandria, Virginia.
Perry J. Albright	....do....	18	Aug. 6, 1862	3 yrs.	Wounded and captured June 15, 1863, in battle of Winchester, Va.; also wounded July 9, 1864, in battle of Monocacy, Md.; discharged Feb. 10, 1865, at Camp Dennison, O., on Surgeon's certificate of disability.

Names.	Rank.	Age.	Date of Entering the Service.	Period of Service.	Remarks.
Philip S. Albright.......	Corporal.	25	Aug. 21, 1862	3 yrs.	Appointed March 1, 1863; wounded April 2, 1865, in front of Petersburg, Va.; mustered out with company June 25, 1865.
Jonathan Stager..........	....do....	27	Aug. 9, 1862	3 yrs.	Captured May 5, 1864, at battle of the Wilderness, Va.; appointed May 18, 1864; mustered out with company June 25, 1865.
William A. Slade..........	....do....	22	Aug. 7, 1862	3 yrs.	Wounded June 15, 1863, in battle of Winchester, Va.; appointed Corporal Aug. 1, 1864; died Oct. 21, 1864, of wounds received Oct. 19, 1864, in battle of Cedar Creek, Va.
Clark Baker..............	....do....	19	Aug. 13, 1862	3 yrs.	Appointed Oct. 24, 1864; mustered out with company June 25, 1865.
John W. Bernhizel......	....do....	19	Aug. 7, 1862	3 yrs.	Captured June 15, 1863, at battle of Winchester, Va.; wounded Nov. 27, 1863, in battle of Mine Run, Va.; appointed Corporal Feb. 18, 1865; mustered out with company June 25, 1865.
Adam Briney.............	....do....	19	Aug. 13, 1862	3 yrs.	Appointed Nov. 1, 1864; mustered out with company June 25, 1865.
John B. W. Dynes........	....do....	21	Aug. 6, 1862	3 yrs.	Appointed March 1, 1865; mustered out with company June 25, 1865.
Ephraim Pitman........	....do....	29	Aug. 6, 1862	3 yrs.	Captured June 15, 1863, at battle of Winchester, Va.; appointed Corporal Nov. 21, 1864; mustered out with company June 25, 1865.
Joseph Zerby.............	....do....	20	Aug. 20, 1862	3 yrs.	Appointed Dec. 1, 1864; mustered out with company June 25, 1865.
Isaac F. Branch.........	Wagoner.	27	Aug. 7, 1862	3 yrs.	Mustered out with company June 25, 1865.
Albright, William K....	Private.	25	July 9, 1863	3 yrs.	Mustered out with company June 25, 1865.
Aydlott, John............	....do....	22	Aug. 6, 1862	3 yrs.	
Barnhart, Harvey........	....do....	21	Aug. 13, 1862	3 yrs.	Captured June 15, 1863, at battle of Winchester, Va.; died April 30, 1864, at Brandy Station, Va.
Barnhart, Levi..........	....do....	19	Aug. 13, 1862	3 yrs.	Mustered out May 13, 1865, at Chester, Pa., by order of War Department.
Barnhart, Lorenzo D.....	....do....	20	Sept. 3, 1862	3 yrs.	Mustered out with company June 25, 1865.
Barkelow, Middleton.....	....do....	20	June 9, 1863	3 yrs.	Wounded Nov. 27, 1863, in battle of Mine Run, Va.; mustered out with company June 25, 1865.
Beam, John L..........	....do....	27	Sept. 6, 1862	3 yrs.	Mustered out with company June 25, 1865.
Bender, Elias	....do....	22	Aug. 6, 1862	3 yrs.	Reduced from Corporal Aug. 1, 1864; wounded Oct. 19, 1864, in battle of Cedar Creek, Va.; mustered out with company June 25, 1865.
Best, Joseph E..........	....do....	18	Oct. 19, 1863	3 yrs.	Wounded July 9, 1864, in battle of Monocacy, Md.; mustered out with company June 25, 1865.
Black, Samuel C..........	....do....	27	Aug. 21, 1862	3 yrs.	Captured June 15, 1863, at battle of Winchester, Va.; killed May 5, 1864, in battle of the Wilderness, Va.
Blackburn, Benjamin...	....do....	22	Aug. 6, 1862	3 yrs.	Captured June 15, 1863, at battle of Winchester, Va.; also July 9, 1864, in battle of Monocacy, Md.; died Jan. 14, 1865, in Rebel Prison at Danville, Va.
Bliss, Nathaniel.........	....do....	39	Aug. 9, 1862	3 yrs.	Captured June 15, 1863, at battle of Winchester, Va.; wounded May 5, 1864, in battle of the Wilderness, Va.; mustered out with company June 25, 1865.
Brace, Willis.............	....do....	20	Oct. 18, 1862	3 yrs.	Mustered out June 19, 1865, at Washington, D. C., by order of War Department
Brenbarger, Henry......	....do....	28	Aug. 13, 1862	3 yrs.	Captured June 15, 1863, at battle of Winchester, Va.; wounded March 25, 1865, in front of Petersburg, Va.; discharged Aug. 10, 1865, at Washington, D. C., on Surgeon's certificate of disability.
Briney, Daniel..........	....do....	21	Aug. 6, 1862	3 yrs.	Captured June 15, 1863, at battle of Winchester, Va.; mustered out with company June 25, 1865.
Brock, Isaac.............	....do....	27	Aug. 6, 1862	3 yrs.	Mustered out with company June 25, 1865.
Brock, William P.........	....do....	21	Aug. 7, 1862	3 yrs.	Wounded June 3, 1864, in battle of Cold Harbor, Va.; discharged Feb. 9, 1865, at Philadelphia, Pa., by order of War Department.
Brown, William N........	....do....	23	Aug. 6, 1862	3 yrs.	Discharged March 14, 1863, at Winchester, Va., on Surgeon's certificate of disability.
Cameron, George W......	....do....	20	May 29, 1863	3 yrs.	Mustered out with company June 25, 1865.
Caywood, Philemon	....do....	33	Aug. 13, 1862	3 yrs.	Wounded June 14, 1863, in battle of Winchester, Va.; discharged Aug. 26, 1863, at Baltimore, Md., on Surgeon's certificate of disability.
Childers, Daniel M......	....do....	23	Aug. 5, 1862	3 yrs.	Captured June 15, 1863, at battle of Winchester, Va.
Childers, Isaac B........	....do....	26	Aug. 6, 1862	3 yrs.	Mustered out with company June 25, 1865.
Clark, John W	....do....	23	Aug. 11, 1862	3 yrs.	Wounded June 14, 1863, in battle of Winchester, Va.; transferred to Co. H, 18th Regiment, Veteran Reserve Corps, April 18, 1864; mustered out July 25, 1865, at Washington, D. C., by order of War Department.

Names.	Rank.	Age.	Date of Entering the Service.	Period of Service.	Remarks.
Cromwell, Henry	Private..	18	Aug. 13, 1862	3 yrs.	Killed May 5, 1864, in battle of the Wilderness, Va.
Decker, Barnhart	....do....	19	Aug. 8, 1862	3 yrs.	Wounded and captured June 15, 1863, in battle of Winchester, Va.; mustered out with company June 25, 1865.
Doan, Sylvester B.	....do....	36	Aug. 21, 1862	3 yrs.	Captured May 5, 1864, at battle of the Wilderness, Va.; died Sept. 30, 1864, while a prisoner of war.
Fellers, George F.	....do....	21	Aug. 11, 1862	3 yrs.	Mustered out with company June 25, 1865.
Gates, Peter.	....do....	19	Aug. 21, 1862	3 yrs.	Mustered out with company June 25, 1865.
Gramm, Anthony	....do....	22	Aug. 7, 1862	3 yrs.	Appointed Sergeant from Corporal Aug. 1, 1864; reduced to ranks Dec. 1, 1864; mustered out with company June 25, 1865.
Hall, Francis M.	....do....	18	Feb. 24, 1864	3 yrs.	Mustered out with company June 25, 1865.
Hartman, Samuel B.	....do....	28	Aug. 17, 1862	3 yrs.	Killed Nov. 27, 1863, in battle of Mine Run, Virginia.
Hipple, Leonidas	....do....	22	Sept. 26, 1863	3 yrs.	Mustered out with company June 25, 1865.
Holdeman, Felix	....do....	22	Aug. 13, 1862	3 yrs.	Captured June 15, 1863, at battle of Winchester, Va.; wounded Oct. 19, 1864, in battle of Cedar Creek, Va.; mustered out July 7, 1865, at Washington, D. C., by order of War Department.
Holdeman, Henry	....do....	20	Aug. 13, 1862	3 yrs.	Died June 15, 1864, at Alexandria, Va., of wounds received May 5, 1864, in battle of the Wilderness, Va.
Homan, Ukle,	....do....	29	Aug. 15, 1862	3 yrs.	Wounded May 5, 1864, in battle of the Wilderness, Va.; discharged Jan 5, 1865, at Philadelphia, Pa., on Surgeon's certificate of disability.
Hood, William H. C.	....do....	20	Aug. 6, 1862	3 yrs.	Mustered in as Musician; captured June 15, 1863, at battle of Winchester, Va.; transferred to Co. K, 5th Regiment, Veteran Reserve Corps, ——; mustered out July 5, 1865, at Indianapolis, Ind., by order of War Department.
Hyre, Jesse	....do....	22	Aug. 20, 1862	3 yrs.	Wounded and captured June 15, 1863, in battle of Winchester, Va.; mustered out with company June 25, 1865.
Leach, Stephen	....do....	38	Sept. 8, 1862	3 yrs.	Killed July 9, 1864, in battle of Monocacy, Maryland.
Lighthizer, William	....do....	24	Aug. 11, 1862	3 yrs.	Discharged March 17, 1863, at Winchester, Va., on Surgeon's certificate of disability.
Lucas, Hamilton W	....do....	22	Aug. 9, 1862	3 yrs.	Mustered in as Sergeant; killed Sept. 19, 1864, in battle of Opequan, Va.
McCowen, William C.	....do....	17	Oct. 5, 1863	3 yrs.	Mustered out with company June 25, 1865.
McGriff, John V.	....do....	20	Aug. 9, 1862	3 yrs.	Killed Nov. 27, 1863, in battle of Mine Run, Virginia.
McQuay, Harvey	....do....	25	Aug. 6, 1862	3 yrs.	Mustered out with company June 25, 1865.
Miller, Thomas C.	....do....	22	Oct. 2, 1863	3 yrs.	Mustered out with company June 25, 1865.
Mote, Casville.	....do....	18	Aug. 7, 1862	3 yrs.	Wounded April 6, 1865, in battle of Sailors' Creek, Va.; discharged June 21, 1865, at Baltimore, Md., on Surgeon's certificate of disability.
Mote, Daniel	....do....	18	Aug. 8, 1862	3 yrs.	Mustered out with company June 25, 1865.
Mote, Nelson	....do....	20	Aug. 7, 1862	3 yrs.	Wounded June 1, 1864, in battle of Cold Harbor, Va.; also April 2, 1865, in front of Petersburg, Va.; discharged May 19, 1865, at Washington, D. C., on Surgeon's certificate of disability.
Mullenix, Abraham	....do....	21	Aug. 6, 1862	3 yrs.	Captured June 15, 1863, at battle of Winchester, Va.; wounded May 5, 1864, in battle of the Wilderness, Va.; discharged to date May 6, 1864, by order of War Department.
Myres, George	....do....	18	Aug. 22, 1862	3 yrs.	Captured June 15, 1863, at battle of Winchester, Va.; killed June 3, 1864, in battle of Cold Harbor, Va.
Niswonger, David W	....do....	21	Jan. 30, 1864	3 yrs.	Captured July 9, 1864, in battle of Monocacy, Md.; mustered out June 2, 1865, at Columbus, O., by order of War Department.
Nolder, Orrin	....do....	18	Feb. 23, 1864	3 yrs.	Wounded May 6, 1864, in battle of the Wilderness, Va.; mustered out June 6, 1865, at Washington, D. C., by order of War Department.
Olwine, Manasseh	....do....	19	Aug. 7, 1862	3 yrs.	Wounded and captured June 15, 1863, in battle of Winchester, Va.; killed Sept. 19, 1864, in battle of Opequan, Va.
Owen, John K.	....do....	23	Aug. 21, 1862	3 yrs.	Mustered out with company June 25, 1865.
Paramore, Samuel C.	....do....	18	Aug. 9, 1862	3 yrs.	Mustered in as Musician; discharged Nov. 4, 1863, at Columbus, O., on Surgeon's certificate of disability.
Paulus, Samuel	....do....	24	Aug. 14, 1862	3 yrs.	Mustered out with company June 25, 1865.
Reed, Joseph	....do....	27	Aug. 22, 1862	3 yrs.	Mustered out with company June 25, 1865.
Reed, William L	....do....	37	Sept. 4, 1862	3 yrs.	Reduced from Corporal ——; captured June 15, 1863, at battle of Winchester, Va.; mustered out with company June 25, 1865.

Names.	Rank.	Age	Date of Entering the Service.	Period of Service.	Remarks.
Robbins, Daniel.........	Private..	18	Sept. 3, 1862	3 yrs.	Wounded May 5, 1864, in battle of the Wilderness, Va.; transferred to Veteran Reserve Corps Sept. 2, 1864.
Rodgers, John...........	...do....	19	Aug. 11, 1862	3 yrs.	Captured June 15, 1863, at battle of Winchester, Va. No further record found.
Rodebaugh, Henry......	...do....	28	Aug. 9, 1862	3 yrs.	Captured May 5, 1864, at battle of the Wilderness, Va. No further record found.
Rodebaugh, Simon.......	...do....	25	Aug. 9, 1862	3 yrs.	Transferred to Co. E, 9th Regiment, Veteran Reserve Corps, April 8, 1864; mustered out July 12, 1865, at Washington, D. C., by order of War Department.
Roser, John F...........	...do....	41	Aug. 7, 1862	3 yrs.	Reduced from Sergeant ——; killed Oct. 19, 1864, in battle of Cedar Creek, Va.
Row, William....... ...	...do....	33	Dec. 3, 1863	3 yrs.	Killed May 5, 1864, in battle of the Wilderness, Va.
Ruch, John	...do....	25	Aug. 22, 1862	3 yrs.	Died ——, of wounds received May 5, 1864, in battle of the Wilderness, Va.
Rynearson, Isaiah.......	...do....	18	Aug. 13, 1862	3 yrs.	Wounded May 5, 1864, in battle of the Wilderness, Va.; discharged Nov. 3, 1864, at Camp Dennison, O., on Surgeon's certificate of disability.
Seas, Levi	...do....	18	Aug. 8, 1862	3 yrs.	Died Sept. 21, 1864, at Winchester, Va., of wounds received Sept. 19, 1864, in battle of Opequan, Va.
Shepherd, Asa B........	...do....	33	Aug. 6, 1862	3 yrs.	Discharged March 23, 1865, at Philadelphia, Pa., on Surgeon's certificate of disability.
Shepherd, Elmund T...	...do....	19	May 27, 1863	3 yrs.	Captured June 1, 1864, at battle of Cold Harbor, Va. No further record found.
Shields, Isaac..........	...do....	18	Aug. 6, 1862	3 yrs.	Mustered out with company June 25, 1865.
Shilt, Riley...........	...do....	27	Aug. 21, 1862	3 yrs.	Mustered out with company June 25, 1865.
Shover, John...........	...do....	29	Aug. 8, 1862	3 yrs.	Wounded June 15, 1863, in battle of Winchester, Va.; discharged May 18, 1865, at Covington, Ky., on Surgeon's certificate of disability.
Slade, Hamilton.........	...do....	27	Aug. 6, 1862	3 yrs.	Captured June 15, 1863, at battle of Winchester, Va.; wounded May 12, 1864, in battle of Spottsylvania C. H., Va.; discharged Jan. 20, 1865, at Philadelphia, Pa., by order of War Department.
Small, Elwood J	...do....	35	Aug. 18, 1862	3 yrs.	Captured July 9, 1864, in battle of Monocacy, Md.; discharged May 23, 1865, at Columbus, O., on Surgeon's certificate of disability.
Smith, Jesse...........	...do....	19	Oct. 2, 1863	3 yrs.	Mustered out with company June 25, 1865.
Sprecher, Henry S.......	...do....	18	Aug. 6, 1862	3 yrs.	Wounded May 5, 1864, in battle of the Wilderness, Va.; mustered out with company June 25, 1865.
Steinmetz, Abraham R..	...do....	20	Aug. 9, 1862	3 yrs.	Captured June 15, 1863, at battle of Winchester, Va.; mustered out with company June 25, 1865.
Strader, Levi...........	...do....	18	Aug. 9, 1862	3 yrs.	Mustered out with company June 25, 1865.
Terrell, Charles H.......	...do....	20	Aug. 6, 1862	3 yrs.	Captured June 15, 1863, at battle of Winchester, Va.; wounded May 12, 1864, in battle of Spottsylvania C. H., Va.; mustered out with company June 25, 1865.
Thatcher, Moses........	...do....	21	Aug. 22, 1862	3 yrs.	Discharged April 12, 1865, at Annapolis Junction, Md., on Surgeon's certificate of disability.
Thomas, Daniel E.......	...do....	20	Aug. 17, 1862	3 yrs.	Appointed Sergeant Aug. 1, 1864; reduced to ranks Feb. 18, 1865; mustered out with company June 25, 1865.
Trace, John	...do....	19	Aug. 7, 1862	3 yrs.	Transferred to Co. C, 9th Regiment, Veteran Reserve Corps, April 18, 1864; mustered out July 21, 1865, at Washington, D. C.
Turner, John	...do....	25	Aug. 6, 1862	3 yrs.	Captured June 15, 1863, at battle of Winchester, Va.; mustered out with company June 25, 1865.
Vance, Harrison.........	...do....	30	Aug. 6, 1862	3 yrs.	Appointed Corporal Jan. —, 1863; captured May 5, 1864, at battle of the Wilderness. No further record found.
Vines, George	...do....	23	Aug. 8, 1862	3 yrs.	Mustered out with company June 25, 1865.
Walker, Moses..........	...do....	18	Aug. 12, 1862	3 yrs.	Died Dec. 31, 1863, at Cumberland, Md.
Walker, Purnell........	...do....	20	Aug. 6, 1862	3 yrs.	Died Aug. 21, 1863, at Annapolis, Md.
Walters, Elias..........	...do....	37	Aug. 8, 1862	3 yrs.	Wounded May 5, 1864, in battle of the Wilderness, Va.; mustered out with company June 25, 1865.
Whittlesey, Hiram M.....	...do....	37	Aug. 7, 1862	3 yrs.	Captured June 15, 1863, at battle of Winchester, Va.; mustered out with company June 25, 1865.

COMPANY C.

Mustered in Oct. 2, 1862, at Camp Piqua, O., by Alexander E. Drake, Captain 2d Infantry, U. S. A. Mustered out June 25, 1865, near Washington, D. C., by J. C. Robinson, Brevet Major and A. C. M. 3d Division, 6th Army Corps.

Names.	Rank.	Age.	Date of Entering the Service.	Period of Service.	Remarks.
Nathan S. Smith	Captain.	34	Aug. 14, 1862	3 yrs.	Discharged Aug. 20, 1863, at Frederick, Md., on Surgeon's certificate of disability.
William A. Hathaway	....do....	26	July 15, 1862	3 yrs.	Promoted from 1st Lieutenant Co. I March 30, 1864; killed July 9, 1864, in battle of Monocacy, Md.
Henry H. Stevens	....do....	22	Aug. 5, 1862	3 yrs.	Promoted from 1st Lieutenant Co. I July 22, 1864; killed April 2, 1865, in action in front of Petersburg, Va.
John T. Sherer	....do....	27	Aug. 7, 1862	3 yrs.	Promoted from 1st Lieutenant Co. A April 26, 1865; mustered out with company June 25, 1865.
John Cannon	1st Lieut.	38	Aug. 25, 1862	3 yrs.	Discharged Feb. 5, 1864, at Washington, D. C., on Surgeon's certificate of disability.
Amos Shaul	....do....	35	Aug. 21, 1862	3 yrs.	Appointed 1st Sergeant from Sergeant April 20, 1864; promoted to 2d Lieutenant Co. K Dec. 9, 1864; from 2d Lieutenant Co. K April 8, 1865; mustered out with company June 25, 1865.
Paris Horney	2d Lieut.	32	Aug. 25, 1862	3 yrs.	Captured June 14, 1863, at battle of Winchester, Va.; promoted to 1st Lieutenant March 21, 1864, but not mustered; died Nov. 7, 1864, in Rebel Prison at Columbia, S. C.
George O. McMillen	....do....	32	Aug. 14, 1862	3 yrs.	Promoted from 1st Sergeant April 12, 1864; to 1st Lieutenant July 22, 1864, but not mustered; died Aug. 21, 1864, at Frederick, Md., of wounds received July 9, 1864, in battle of Monocacy, Md.
Russell B. McCollum	1st Sergt.	35	Aug. 15, 1862	3 yrs.	Captured July 9, 1864, at battle of Monocacy, Md.; appointed from Sergeant Jan. 5, 1865; mustered out with company June 25, 1865.
Francis M. McMillen	Sergeant.	30	Aug. 15, 1862	3 yrs.	Promoted to Sergt. Major May 2, 1865.
Darwin Pierce	....do....	21	Aug. 15, 1862	3 yrs.	Appointed from Corporal April 20, 1864; wounded June 3, 1864, in battle of Cold Harbor, Va.; also July 1, 1864, in battle of Monocacy, Md.; mustered out with company June 25, 1865.
Thomas J. Hicks	....do....	35	Aug. 21, 1862	3 yrs.	Appointed Corporal May 1, 1863; Sergeant Aug. 1, 1864; mustered out with company June 25, 1865.
Finley B. Newson	....do....	18	Aug. 18, 1862	3 yrs.	Appointed from Corporal Jan. 5, 1865; mustered out with company June 25, 1865.
Daniel J. C. Polly	....do....	25	Aug. 18, 1862	3 yrs.	Appointed Corporal Feb. 1, 1864; wounded May 6, 1864, in battle of the Wilderness, Va.; Sergeant May 2, 1865; mustered out with company June 25, 1865.
James T. McKinnon	Corporal.	24	Aug. 14, 1862	3 yrs.	Discharged Feb. 25, 1864, at Columbus, O., for wounds received June 15, 1863, in battle of Winchester, Va.
Jacob Lambing	....do....	29	Aug. 14, 1862	3 yrs.	Discharged May 3, 1863, at Winchester, Va., on Surgeon's certificate of disability.
George W. Little	....do....	28	Aug. 15, 1862	3 yrs.	Wounded May 5, 1864, in battle of the Wilderness, Va.; mustered out with company June 25, 1865.
George B. Hamilton	....do ...	22	Aug. 18, 1862	3 yrs.	Captured June 15, 1863, at battle of Winchester, Va.; wounded July 9, 1864, in battle of Monocacy, Md.; mustered out with company June 25, 1865.
William H. Sheets	....do....	32	Aug. 21, 1862	3 yrs.	Transferred to Co. F, 19th Regiment, Veteran Reserve Corps, Jan. 15, 1864; mustered out July 13, 1865, at Elmira, N. Y., by order of War Department.
Joseph H. McKinnon	....do....	22	Aug. 15, 1862	3 yrs.	Appointed Corporal Aug. 1, 1864; mustered out with company June 25, 1865.
Keran M. McKinney	....do....	18	Aug. 18, 1862	3 yrs.	Wounded and captured June 15, 1863, in battle of Winchester, Va.; appointed Corporal Sept. 1, 1864; wounded Oct. 19, 1864, in battle of Cedar Creek, Va.; mustered out with company June 25, 1865.
Henry L. Bennett	....do....	29	Aug. 20, 1862	3 yrs.	Appointed Jan. 5, 1865; mustered out with company June 25, 1865.
Bynner B. Sweet	....do....	22	Aug. 14, 1862	3 yrs.	Appointed March 1, 1865; mustered out with company June 25, 1865.
....ogast	....do....	27	Aug. 22, 1862	3 yrs.	Captured June 15, 1863, at battle of Winchester, Va.; appointed Corporal March 26, 1865; mustered out with company June 25, 1865.

Names.	Rank.	Age.	Date of Entering the Service.	Period of Service.	Remarks.
James W. Griffith	Corporal.	23	Aug. 14, 1862	3 yrs.	Captured June 15, 1863, at battle of Winchester, Va.; wounded Nov. 27, 1863, in battle of Mine Run, Va.; captured July 9, 1864, at battle of Monocacy, Md.; died Nov. 14, 1864, in Rebel Prison at Danville, Va.
Joseph F. Bennett	....do....	20	Aug. 14, 1862	3 yrs.	Appointed April 1, 1864; died March 26, 1865, at South Charleston, O.
Wilson M. D. Clemons	....do....	30	Aug. 14, 1862	3 yrs.	Wounded Nov. 27, 1863, in battle of Mine Run, Va.; also Oct. 19, 1864, in battle of Cedar Creek, Va.; appointed Corporal May 2, 1865; mustered out with company June 25, 1865.
John Hendrix	....do....	26	Aug. 20, 1862	3 yrs.	Appointed April 20, 1864; wounded July 9, 1864, in battle of Monocacy, Md.; died Aug. 11, 1864, in hospital at Frederick, Md.
Abbott, Newton	Private.	19	June 8, 1864	3 yrs.	Substitute.
Akers, George W	....do....	18	Aug. 18, 1862	3 yrs.	Wounded June 12, 1864, in action; mustered out with company June 25, 1865.
Anderson, Harmon	....do....	38	Aug. 15, 1862	3 yrs.	Captured June 6, 1864, at battle of the Wilderness, Va.; paroled June 5, 1865; mustered out June 23, 1865, at Camp Chase, O., by order of War Department.
Anderson, Isaac	....do....	41	Aug. 18, 1862	3 yrs.	Captured June 15, 1863, at battle of Winchester, Va.; wounded Sept. 19, 1864, in battle of Opequan, Va.; mustered out with company June 25, 1865.
Arbenz, Solomon	....do....	19	Aug. 15, 1862	3 yrs.	Captured June 15, 1863, at battle of Winchester, Va.; wounded Sept. 19, 1864, in battle of Opequan, Va.; mustered out with company June 25, 1865.
Anglebarger, David F.	....do....	23	Aug. 21, 1862	3 yrs.	Discharged March 25, 1863, at Cumberland, Md.; on Surgeon's certificate of disability.
Bennett, Enoch M	....do....	22	Aug. 14, 1862	3 yrs.	Captured July 9, 1864, at battle of Monocacy, Md.; mustered out with company June 25, 1865.
Bricker, Amon	....do....	23	Mch. 10, 1864	3 yrs.	Accidentally wounded while in camp April 26, 1864.
Bricker, Cornelius	....do....	19	Feb. 22, 1864	3 yrs.	
Brown, John	....do....	31	Aug. 18, 1862	3 yrs.	Captured June 15, 1863, at battle of Winchester, Va.; mustered out with company June 25, 1865.
Canaday, Samuel	....do....	47	Aug. 18, 1862	3 yrs.	Captured July 9, 1864, at battle of Monocacy, Md.; died Nov. 8, 1864, in hospital at Annapolis, Md.
Cavanaugh, John	....do....	29	Aug. 15, 1862	3 yrs.	Captured June 15, 1863, at battle of Winchester; Va.; wounded May 5, 1864, in battle of the Wilderness, Va.; mustered out Aug. 18, 1865, at Cincinnati, O., by order of War Department.
Chancellor, James M	....do....	18	Aug. 18, 1862	3 yrs.	Captured June 15, 1863, at battle of Winchester, Va.; wounded Sept. 19, 1864, in battle of Opequan, Va.; mustered out with company June 25, 1865.
Cheney, William	....do....	20	Aug. 15, 1862	3 yrs.	Mustered out June 5, 1865, at Washington, D. C., by order of War Department.
Clancey, John	....do....	27	June 8, 1864	3 yrs.	Substitute; wounded July 9, 1864, in battle of Monocacy, Md.; mustered out with company June 25, 1865.
Clark, Joseph P	....do....	21	Aug. 26, 1862	3 yrs.	Mustered out with company June 25, 1865.
Conway, Patrick	....do....	34	Aug. 19, 1862	3 yrs.	Transferred to Co. B, 10th Regiment, Veteran Reserve Corps, ——; discharged Oct. 17, 1864, at Washington, D. C., on Surgeon's cerificate of disability.
Cooper, Joseph	....do....	21	Dec. 28, 1863	3 yrs.	Mustered out with company June 25, 1865.
Cory, Joseph N	....do....	23	Aug. 18, 1862	3 yrs.	Captured June 15, 1863, at battle of Winchester, Va.; mustered out with company June 25, 1865.
Coss, David	....do....	33	Feb. 25, 1864	3 yrs.	Died April 2, 1864, at Cumberland, Md.
Coss, John	....do....	21	Aug. 15, 1862	3 yrs.	Wounded June 3, 1864, in battle of Cold Harbor, Va.; mustered out with company June 25, 1865.
Curl, John	....do....	40	Aug. 22, 1862	3 yrs.	Discharged May 15, 1865, at Danville, Va., on Surgeon's certificate of disability.
Cyster, John I	....do....	35	Aug. 18, 1862	3 yrs.	Reduced from Sergeant ——; discharged March 25, 1863, at Cumberland, Md., on Surgeon's certificate of disability.
Daily, Harrison H	....do....	23	Aug. 18, 1862	3 yrs.	Mustered out with company June 25, 1865.
Day, William	....do....	18	Aug. 18, 1862	3 yrs.	Mustered out with company June 25, 1865.
Defendau, Thomas	....do....	30	Aug. 16, 1862	3 yrs.	Captured June 15, 1863, at battle of Winchester, Va.; wounded July 9, 1864, in battle of Monocacy, Md.; mustered out June 17, 1865, at Washington, D. C., by order of War Department.
DeHaven, Jesse	....do....	23	Jan. 30, 1864	3 yrs.	Mustered out with company June 25, 1865.
Dwyer, Michael	....do....	18	Aug. 18, 1862	3 yrs.	Wounded May 5, 1864, in battle of the Wilderness, Va.; killed March 25, 1865, in action near Petersburg, Va.

Names.	Rank.	Age.	Date of Entering the Service.	Period of Service.	Remarks.
Edwards, Robert H......	Private..	18	Aug. 16, 1862	3 yrs.	Discharged Aug. 12, 1863, at Columbus, O., on Surgeon's certificate of disability.
Eppinger, Oliver.........	....do....	21	June 8, 1864	3 yrs.	Substitute.
Forbes, George W.........	....do....	23	Mch. 31, 1864	3 yrs.	Captured May 6, 1864, in battle of the Wilderness, Va.; mustered out with company June 25, 1865.
Griffith, John T.......	....do....	20	Aug. 14, 1862	3 yrs.	Killed June 15, 1863, in battle of Winchester, Virginia.
Hamilton, William	....do....	29	Aug. 18, 1862	3 yrs.	Mustered out with company June 25, 1865.
Hankins, Charles.........	....do....	34	June 9, 1864	3 yrs.	Substitute; captured July 9, 1864, at battle of Monocacy, Md.; mustered out with company June 25, 1865.
Hill, William.............	....do....	21	June 9, 1864	3 yrs.	Substitute; mustered out with company June 25, 1865.
Hope, Christopher	....do....	18	Aug. 15, 1862	3 yrs.	Captured May 6, 1864, at battle of the Wilderness, Va.; paroled June 6, 1865; mustered out June 23, 1865, at Camp Chase, O., by order of War Department.
Hope, James	....do....	21	Aug. 15, 1862	3 yrs.	Captured June 15, 1863, at battle of Winchester, Va.; wounded Oct. 19, 1864, in battle of Cedar Creek, Va.; mustered out with company June 25, 1865.
Hope, Luke...............	....do....	44	Jan. 20, 1864	3 yrs.	Discharged Jan. 5, 1865, at David's Island, New York Harbor, on Surgeon's certificate of disability.
Huffman, George.........	....do....	16	Aug. 16, 1862	3 yrs.	Died Oct. 15, 1864, in hospital at Cincinnati, O.
Huffman, William M....	....do....	22	Aug. 22, 1862	3 yrs.	Wounded May 6, 1864, in battle of the Wilderness, Va.; died July 12, 1864, in hospital at Washington, D. C.
Irwin, Amos.............	....do....	21	Dec. 31, 1863	3 yrs.	Died March 15, 1864, in hospital at Brandy Station, Va.
Johnson, David L.........	....do....	35	Aug. 20, 1862	3 yrs.	Transferred to Co. F, 18th Regiment, Veteran Reserve Corps, Feb. 15, 1864; discharged May 6, 1865, at Washington, D. C., on Surgeon's certificate of disability.
Kennedy, John............	....do....	27	June 9, 1864	3 yrs.	Substitute.
King, Spencer............	....do....	32	Aug. 21, 1862	3 yrs.	Captured June 15, 1863, at battle of Winchester, Va.; mustered out June 19, 1865, at Baltimore, Md., by order of War Department.
Kinert, William E.......	....do....	25	Aug. 18, 1862	3 yrs.	Discharged March 15, 1864, at Alexandria, Va., on Surgeon's certificate of disability.
Long, John T.............	....do....	21	Aug. 22, 1862	3 yrs.	Mustered out with company June 25, 1865.
Longshore, John.........	....do....	32	June 4, 1864	3 yrs.	Substitute; mustered out with company June 25, 1865.
McCormick, Patrick.....	....do....	45	Aug. 14, 1862	3 yrs.	Wounded and captured June 15, 1863, at battle of Winchester, Va.; also July 9, 1864, at battle of Monocacy, Md.; mustered out July 6, 1865, at Columbus, O., by order of War Department.
Marsh, Milton	....do....	28	Feb. 12, 1864	3 yrs.	Wounded Sept. 19, 1864, in battle of Opequan, Va.; mustered out with company June 25, 1865.
Marshall, Freeman.......	....do....	36	Aug. 18, 1862	3 yrs.	Transferred to 110th Co., 2d Battalion, Veteran Reserve Corps, April 8, 1864.
May, Christian............	....do....	31	May 25, 1864	3 yrs.	Wounded and captured Oct. 19, 1864, in battle of Cedar Creek, Va.; mustered out May 29, 1865, at Philadelphia, Pa., by order of War Department.
Maywood, Walter S	....do....	25	Aug. 18, 1862	3 yrs.	Transferred to Co. C, 6th Regiment, Veteran Reserve Corps, April 18, 1864; mustered out July 5, 1865, at Cincinnati, O., by order of War Department.
Morgan, George W.......	....do....	22	June 7, 1864	3 yrs.	Substitute.
Mull, George L...........	....do....	22	Aug. 18, 1862	3 yrs.	Mustered in as Musician; captured June 15, 1863, at battle of Winchester, Va.; discharged March 15, 1864, at Mt. Pleasant Hospital, on Surgeon's certificate of disability.
Neer, Joseph F..........	....do....	43	Aug. 22, 1862	3 yrs.	Discharged Nov. 23, 1863, at Columbus, O., on Surgeon's certificate of disability.
Newton, Franklin.......	....do....	23	June 5, 1864	3 yrs.	Substitute.
Obenchain, Samuel......	....do....	29	Aug. 18, 1862	3 yrs.	Appointed Sergeant May 1, 1863; wounded Nov. 27, 1863, in battle of Mine Run, Va.; reduced to ranks ——; mustered out with company June 25, 1865.
Osborn, Jacob R..........	....do....	32	Aug. 22, 1862	3 yrs.	Discharged March 25, 1863, at Cumberland, Md., on Surgeon's certificate of disability.
Paullin, Charles..........	....do....	21	Aug. 19, 1862	3 yrs.	Discharged Feb. 21, 1863, at Winchester, Va., on Surgeon's certificate of disability.
Peters, Samuel J	....do....	41	Aug. 21, 1862	3 yrs.	Captured June 15, 1863, at battle of Winchester, Va.; mustered out with company June 25, 1865.
Pierce, John L	....do....	18	Aug. 15, 1862	3 yrs.	Captured June 15, 1863, at battle of Winchester, Va.; mustered out with company June 25, 1865.
Powell, William..........	....do....	22	Feb. 28, 1864	3 yrs.	Mustered out with company June 25, 1865.

Names.	Rank.	Age.	Date of Entering the Service.	Period of Service.	Remarks.
Reeder, Lewis J.........	Private..	28	Aug. 14, 1862	3 yrs.	Wounded June 15, 1863, in battle of Winchester, Va.; also July 9, 1864, at battle of Monocacy, Md.; died Aug. 3, 1864, in hospital at Frederick, Md.
Robinson, Samuel T....	....do....	33	Aug. 26, 1862	3 yrs.	Appointed Sergeant ——; reduced to ranks ——; wounded and captured June 15, 1863, in battle of Winchester, Va.; discharged June 20, 1864, at Columbus, O., on Surgeon's certificate of disability.
Ross, David	....do....	21	Aug. 18, 1862	3 yrs.	Mustered out with company June 25, 1865.
Schickendantz, Joseph..	....do....	20	Aug. 14, 1862	3 yrs.	Mustered out with company June 25, 1865.
Scorce, Alcetus J........	....do....	18	Aug. 18, 1862	3 yrs.	Captured June 15, 1863, in battle of Winchester, Va.; discharged Dec. 24, 1863, at Alexandria, Va., on Surgeon's certificate of disability.
Scott, Leonard	....do....	33	Sept. 1, 1862	3 yrs.	Captured May 6, 1864, at battle of the Wilderness, Va.; died Oct. 30, 1864, in Rebel Prison at Florence, S. C.
Sheetz, Francis...........	....do....	24	Aug. 13, 1862	3 yrs.	Captured June 15, 1863, at battle of Winchester, Va.; mustered out with company June 25, 1865.
Sheetz, James H..........	....do....	30	Aug. 18, 1862	3 yrs.	Captured June 15, 1863, at battle of Winchester, Va.; mustered out with company June 25, 1865.
Smith, Benjamin G	....do....	17	Aug. 18, 1862	3 yrs.	Wounded Nov. 27, 1863, in battle of Mine Run, Va.; mustered out with company June 25, 1865.
Smith, Thomas...........	....do....	26	Aug. 15, 1862	3 yrs.	Captured June 15, 1863, at battle of Winchester, Va.; wounded June 1, 1864, in battle of Cold Harbor, Va.; sent to hospital June 2, 1864. No further record found.
Stewart, William.........	....do....	31	Aug. 14, 1862	3 yrs.	Discharged Aug. 18, 1863, at Columbus, O., on Surgeon's certificate of disability.
Suman, Eli J.............	....do....	36	June 10, 1864	3 yrs.	Substitute; mustered out with company June 25, 1865.
Taylor, Morrison.........	....do....	19	Aug. 18, 1862	3 yrs.	Mustered out with company June 25, 1865.
Tharp, Wilbur B.........	....do....	18	Aug. 18, 1862	3 yrs.	Captured June 15, 1863, in battle of Winchester, Va.; died Aug. 21, 1863, at Dayton, O.
Thomas, Noah	....do....	28	Dec. 28, 1863	3 yrs.	Discharged Sept. 27, 1864, at Columbus, O., for wounds received June 2, 1864, in battle of Cold Harbor, Va.
Thomas, William R	....do....	25	Dec. 25, 1863	3 yrs.	Wounded March 25, 1865, in action near Petersburg, Va.; mustered out June 16, 1865, at Washington, D. C., by order of War Department.
Truett, George P.........	....do....	21	Aug. 14, 1862	3 yrs.	Captured June 15, 1863, at battle of Winchester, Va.; wounded July 9, 1864, in battle of Monocacy, Md.; died July 27, 1864, in hospital at Annapolis, Md.
Trumbo, Levi M	....do....	18	Aug. 18, 1862	3 yrs.	Died Dec. 24, 1862, at Moorefield, Va.
Vance, Thomas...........	....do....	18	Aug. 14, 1862	3 yrs.	Captured June 15, 1863, at battle of Winchester, Va.; wounded May 6, 1864, in battle of the Wilderness, Va.; discharged Oct. 25, 1864, at Columbus, O.
Warrington, John W....	....do....	18	Aug. 21, 1862	3 yrs.	Wounded April 2, 1865, in action near Petersburg, Va.; discharged July 24, 1865, at Douglass Hospital, Washington, D. C., on Surgeon's certificate of disability.
Watson, Charles..........	....do....	23	June 8, 1864	3 yrs.	Substitute.
Welch, Patrick...........	....do....	32	Aug. 14, 1862	3 yrs.	Wounded April 2, 1865, in action near Petersburg, Va.; discharged Aug. 15, 1865, at Columbus, O., on Surgeon's certificate of disability.
Wheatley, Charles K....	....do...	38	Feb. 18, 1864	3 yrs.	Mustered out with company June 25, 1865.
Wheatley, Joseph H.....	....do....	44	Feb. 18, 1864	3 yrs.	Wounded July 9, 1864, in battle of Monocacy, Md.; died July 24, 1864, in hospital at Annapolis, Md.
Whiteman, John.........	....do....	18	Dec. 31, 1863	3 yrs.	Wounded May 5, 1864, in battle of the Wilderness, Va.; died June 15, 1864, in hospital at Philadelphia, Pa.
Wiley, Robert W	....do....	25	Aug. 18, 1862	3 yrs.	Promoted to Q. M. Sergeant April 19, 1864.
Wilhide, Thomas C.....	....do....	21	Aug. 14, 1862	3 yrs.	Captured June 15, 1863, at battle of Winchester, Va.; also July 9, 1864, at battle of Monocacy, Md.; mustered out June 25, 1865, at Camp Chase, O., by order of War Department.

COMPANY D.

Mustered in Oct. 3, 1862, at Camp Piqua, O., by Alexander E. Drake, Captain 2d Infantry, U. S. A. Mustered out June 25, 1865, near Washington, D. C., by J. C. Robinson, Brevet Major and A. C. M. 3d Division, 6th Army Corps.

Names.	Rank.	Age.	Date of Entering the Service.	Period of Service.	Remarks.
William S. McElwain....	Captain.	32	Aug. 15, 1862	3 yrs.	Promoted to Major Jan. 1, 1864.
Alexander Trimble	....do....	32	Aug. 15, 1862	3 yrs.	Promoted to 1st Lieutenant from 2d Lieutenant Nov. 25, 1862; Captain Jan. 1, 1864; died Oct. 6, 1864, of wounds received Sept. 19, 1864, in battle of Opequan, Va.
George P. Boyer.........	....do....	23	Aug. 5, 1862	3 yrs.	Promoted from 1st Lieutenant Co. H to date Nov. 3, 1864; mustered out with company June 25, 1865.
Daniel D. Moore.........	1st.Lieut.	30	Aug. 15, 1862	3 yrs.	Resigned Nov. 25, 1862.
Thomas J. Weakley......	....do....	24	July 15, 1862	3 yrs.	Transferred from Co. I April 15, 1864; to Co. K Aug 25, 1864.
Charles M. Gross.........	....do....	34	Aug. 16, 1862	3 yrs.	Transferred from Co. G Aug. 25, 1864; to Co. G Feb. 17, 1865.
Jacob M. Conwell	....do....	24	Aug. 21, 1862	3 yrs.	Transferred from Co. E Feb. 17, 1865; mustered out with company June 25, 1865.
James A. Fox	2d Lieut.	32	Aug. 20, 1862	3 yrs.	Promoted from Sergt. Major Nov. 25, 1862; to 1st Lieutenant Co. B Dec. 18, 1862.
Thomas S. Clark	....do....	25	Aug. 16, 1862	3 yrs.	Promoted from 1st Sergeant Dec. 18, 1862; to 1st Lieutenant March 30, 1864, but not mustered; discharged March 22, 1864.
William A. Jones.........	....do....	25	Aug. 20, 1862	3 yrs.	Appointed 1st Sergeant from Sergeant April 20, 1863; promoted to 2d Lieutenant to date July 22, 1864; 1st Lieutenant Nov. 3, 1864, but not mustered; transferred to Co. F Nov. 20, 1864.
William H. Byrd........	1st Sergt.	25	Aug. 16, 1862	3 yrs.	Appointed from Sergeant Aug. 22, 1864; killed Sept. 19, 1864, in battle of Opequan, Va.
John A. Fichthorn......	....do....	21	Aug. 15, 1862	3 yrs.	Appointed Sergeant from Corporal May 1, 1863; wounded May 5, 1864, in battle of the Wilderness; appointed 1st Sergeant Sept. 19, 1864; mustered out with company June 25, 1865.
Joseph B. Van Eaton....	Sergeant.	25	Aug. 22, 1862	3 yrs.	Promoted to 1st Lieutenant and Adjutant Sept. 18, 1862.
William H. Harry........	....do....	26	Aug. 22, 1862	3 yrs.	Promoted to Sergt. Major Nov. 25, 1862.
Lewis H. Beall	....do....	23	Aug. 22, 1862	3 yrs.	Appointed from Corporal Aug. 22, 1862; mustered out June 30, 1865, at Columbus, O., by order of War Department.
Frank H. McDaniel......	....do....	23	Aug. 15, 1862	3 yrs.	Appointed from Corporal Nov. 25, 1862; wounded July 9, 1864, in battle of Monocacy, Md.; mustered out with company June 25, 1865.
Thomas Goe.............	....do....	21	Aug. 22, 1862	3 yrs.	Appointed from Corporal Sept. 19, 1864; mustered out with company June 25, 1865.
Abraham Sheeley........	....do....	24	Aug. 21, 1862	3 yrs.	Wounded May 5, 1864, in battle of the Wilderness, Va.; appointed from Corporal Aug. 22, 1864; transferred to 2d Co., 2d Battalion, Veteran Reserve Corps, April 25, 1865; mustered out July 10, 1865, at Washington, D. C., by order of War Department.
Thomas J. Daugherty...	Corporal.	23	Aug. 22, 1862	3 yrs.	Wounded June 15, 1863, in battle of Winchester, Va.; promoted to Q. M. Sergeant April 14, 1865.
William V. Luce	....do....	19	Aug. 16, 1862	3 yrs.	Wounded Sept. 19, 1864, in battle of Opequan, Va.; also Oct. 19, 1864, in battle of Cedar Creek, Va.; mustered out with company June 25, 1865.
Frederick La Rue........	....do....	39	Aug. 22, 1862	3 yrs.	Captured July 9, 1864, at battle of Monocacy, Md.; mustered out with company June 25, 1865.
James C. Bratton.........	....do....	24	Aug. 22, 1862	3 yrs.	Appointed Aug. 22, 1862; mustered out with company June 25, 1865.
Patrick H. Maley........	....do....	20	Aug. 22, 1862	3 yrs.	Appointed May 6, 1864; mustered out with company June 25, 1865.
Jonas Peterson, Jr........	....do....	24	Aug. 29, 1862	3 yrs.	Appointed July 28, 1864; mustered out with company June 25, 1865.
Robert K. Stevenson......	....do....	19	Aug. 22, 1862	3 yrs.	Appointed Aug. 22, 1864; wounded Sept. 19, 1864, in battle of Opequan, Va.; mustered out with company June 25, 1865.
Amos W. Files.............	....do....	25	Aug. 22, 1862	3 yrs.	Appointed Sept. 19, 1864; mustered out with company June 25, 1865.
James F. Hartsook........	....do....	31	Aug. 21, 1862	3 yrs.	Wounded Sept. 19, 1864, in battle of Opequan, Va.; appointed Corporal April 15, 1865; mustered out with company June 25, 1865.

Names.	Rank.	Age.	Date of Entering the Service.	Period of Service.	Remarks.
Hiram W. Crumley	Corporal.	19	Aug. 16, 1862	3 yrs.	Appointed Nov. 27, 1863; died July 28, 1864, of wounds received July 18, 1864, in action at Snicker's Gap, Va.
George F. Watts	....do....	38	Aug. 22, 1862	3 yrs.	Appointed Nov. 25, 1862; discharged Nov. 27. 1863, at Camp Dennison, O., on Surgeon's certificate of disability.
Joseph H. Patterson	....do....	30	Aug. 22, 1862	3 yrs.	Appointed April 30, 1863; killed May 5, 1864, in battle of the Wilderness, Va.
Adams, Nelson G	Private..	24	Aug. 20, 1862	3 yrs.	Wounded May 5, 1864, in battle of the Wilderness, Va.; mustered out with company June 25, 1865.
Adams, Samuel N	....do....	21	Aug. 16, 1862	3 yrs.	Wounded Oct. 19, 1864, in battle of Cedar Creek, Va.; also April 2, 1865, in action near Petersburg, Va.; discharged Sept. 11, 1865, at Washington, D. C., on Surgeon's certificate of disability.
Anderson, Harmon	....do....	18	Aug. 27, 1862	3 yrs.	Mustered out with company June 25, 1865.
Anderson, James W	....do....	20	July 4, 1863	3 yrs.	Wounded June 23, 1864, in action near Petersburg, Va.; mustered out with company June 25, 1865.
Anderson, Preston	....do....	22	Aug. 22, 1862	3 yrs.	Mustered out with company June 25, 1865.
Baker, Barney S	....do....	29	Oct. 4, 1862	3 yrs.	Discharged Nov. 5, 1863, at Bealton Station, Va., on Surgeon's certificate of disability.
Barber, Oren E	....do....	18	June 2, 1864	3 yrs.	Substitute; mustered out with company June 25, 1865.
Bodmer, Marcus	....do....	39	May 10, 1864	3 yrs.	Drafted; captured July 9, 1864, at battle of Monocacy, Md.; mustered out with company June 25, 1865.
Bricely, Albert	....do....	37	May 27, 1864	3 yrs.	Drafted; wounded Sept. 19, 1864, in battle of Opequan, Va.; mustered out June 27, 1865. at Tripler Hospital, Columbus, O., by order of War Department.
Clemons, James H	....do....	23	Aug. 20, 1862	3 yrs.	Killed June 3, 1864, in battle of Cold Harbor, Virginia.
Clemons, Jesse C	....do....	18	Aug. 22, 1862	3 yrs.	Captured June 15, 1863, at battle of Winchester, Va.; paroled ——; died Aug. 10, 1863, at Annapolis, Md.
Clevell, Dolphus	....do....	18	Oct. 6, 1862	3 yrs.	Mustered out with company June 25, 1865.
Collins, Thomas	....do....	19	May 26, 1864	3 yrs.	Drafted; mustered out with company June 25, 1865.
Crawford, David	....do....	32	Aug. 22, 1862	3 yrs.	Wounded Oct. 19, 1864, in battle of Cedar Creek, Va.; discharged June 16, 1865, at York, Pa., on Surgeon's certificate of disability.
Crites, John	....do....	20	Aug. 22, 1862	3 yrs.	Captured June 15, 1863, at battle of Winchester, Va.; wounded April 2, 1865, in action near Petersburg, Va.; mustered out May 23, 1865, at Philadelphia, Pa., by order of War Department.
Crites, Nimrod	....do....	19	Sept. 7, 1864	1 yr.	Mustered out with company June 25, 1865.
Curl, David A	....do....	34	Aug. 16, 1862	3 yrs.	Mustered out with company June 25, 1865.
Day, Joseph	....do....	45	Oct. 6, 1862	3 yrs.	Substitute; discharged May 15, 1863, at Winchester, Va, on Surgeon's certificate of disability.
Day, William R	....do....	19	Aug. 17, 1862	3 yrs.	Wounded Nov. 27, 1863, in battle of Mine Run. Va., wounded and captured May 6, 1864, at battle of the Wilderness, Va.; mustered out with company June 25, 1865.
Daughters, Henry	....do....	26	June 29, 1863	3 yrs.	Mustered out July 7, 1865, at Washington. D. C., by order of War Department.
Dungan, Jehiel G	....do....	24	Nov. 23, 1863	3 yrs.	Transferred to 2d Brigade Band, 3d Division, 6th Army Corps, Jan. 4, 1865, from which mustered out June 25, 1865, near Washington, D. C.
Dungan, Martin W	....do....	19	Nov. 23, 1863	3 yrs.	Transferred to 2d Brigade Band, 3d Division, 6th Army Corps, Jan. 4, 1865, from which mustered out June 25, 1865, near Washington, D. C.
Dunn, Stephen	....do....	19	Aug. 20, 1862	3 yrs.	Wounded June 3, 1864, in battle of Cold Harbor, Va.; mustered out with company June 25, 1865.
Durkin, James	....do....	22	Aug. 18, 1862	3 yrs.	Wounded Sept. 19, 1864, in battle of Opequan. Va.; mustered out with company June 25, 1865.
Elam, John B	....do....	18	Mch. 31, 1864	3 yrs.	Wounded June 3, 1864, in battle of Cold Harbor, Va.; mustered out with company June 25, 1865.
Flecther, George W	....do....	25	Aug. 22, 1862	3 yrs.	Transferred to Veteran Reserve Corps March 13, 1865.
Foreman, James C	....do....	39	Aug. 17, 1862	3 yrs.	Mustered out with company June 25, 1865.
Gano, George W	....do....	23	Aug. 22, 1862	3 yrs.	Discharged March 5, 1863, at Winchester, Va., on Surgeon's certificate of disability.
Gaylor, John	....do....	21	Aug. 22, 1862	3 yrs.	Captured June 15, 1863, at battle of Winchester, Va.; mustered out with company June 25, 1865.
Gaylor, William	....do....	22	Aug. 22, 1862	3 yrs.	Mustered out with company June 25, 1865.
Harshman, James H.	....do....	20	Aug. 22, 1862	3 yrs.	Mustered out with company June 25, 1865.

9

Names.	Rank.	Age.	Date of Entering the Service.	Period of Service.	Remarks.
Hawkins, Henry C......	Private..	34	Nov. 23, 1863	3 yrs.	Transferred to 2d Brigade Band, 3d Division. 6th Army Corps, Jan. 4, 1865, from which mustered out June 25, 1865, near Washington, D. C.
Hawkins, Joseph G......	....do....	19	Aug. 16, 1862.	3 yrs.	Killed May 5, 1864, in battle of the Wilderness, Virginia.
Heaton, Toliver P.	....do....	19	Aug. 20, 1862	3 yrs.	Mustered out July 12, 1865, at Columbus, O., by order of War Department.
Hersher, Frederick......	....do....	31	Aug. 16, 1862	3 yrs.	Wounded July 9, 1864, in battle of Monocacy, Md.; mustered out with company June 25, 1865.
Holt, James	....do....	29	Sept. 4, 1862	3 yrs.	Wounded May 12, 1864, in battle of Spottsylvania C. H., Va.; also March 25, 1865, in action near Petersburg, Va.; discharged May 25, 1865, at Washington, D. C., on Surgeon's certificate of disability.
Honecker, Peter..........	....do....	32	Aug. 21, 1862	3 yrs.	Wounded June 6, 1864, in battle of Cold Harbor, Va.; mustered out with company June 25, 1865.
Hoover, John H..........	....do....	25	Aug. 22, 1862	3 yrs.	Discharged March 5, 1863, at Winchester, Va., on Surgeon's certificate of disability.
Hopping, David R.......	....do....	20	Aug. 29, 1862	3 yrs.	Captured June 15, 1863, at battle of Winchester, Va.; wounded May 12, 1864, in battle of Spottsylvania C. H., Va.; mustered out with company June 26, 1865.
Hornick, Christopher....	....do....	23	Aug. 19, 1862	3 yrs.	Captured May 6, 1864, at battle of the Wilderness, Va.; died Nov. 26, 1864, in Rebel Prison at Andersonville, Ga.
Hubbard, Anson J. C....	....do....	33	Aug. 22, 1862	3 yrs.	Discharged Sept. 9, 1864, at Columbus, O., on Surgeon's certificate of disability.
Humston, John A........	....do....	18	April 13, 1865	1 yr.	Mustered out with company June 25, 1865.
Hutchinson, John F.....	....do....	39	June 17, 1864	3 yrs.	Substitute.
Irwin, William H.......	....do....	24	Dec. 10, 1863	3 yrs.	Transferred to 2d Brigade Band, 3d Division. 6th Army Corps, Jan. 4, 1865, from which mustered out June 25, 1865, near Washington, D. C.
James, John F...........	....do....	36	Aug. 22, 1862	3 yrs.	Captured June 15, 1863, at battle of Winchester, Va.; mustered out with company June 25, 1865.
Jenkins, Peter...........	....do....	18	June 18, 1864	3 yrs.	Substitute.
Kinney, Andrew J.......	....do....	29	June 20, 1863	3 yrs.	Mustered out with company June 25, 1865.
Klanke, Henry..........	....do....	31	June 17, 1864	3 yrs.	Drafted; killed Oct. 19, 1864, in battle of Cedar Creek, Va.
Long, Francis M.........	....do....	18	Mch. 31, 1864	3 yrs.	Killed Oct. 19, 1864, in battle of Cedar Creek, Virginia.
Losty, James.............	....do....	23	Aug. 19, 1862	3 yrs.	Captured June 15, 1863, at battle of Winchester, Va.; also May 6, 1864, at battle of the Wilderness, Va.; died Nov. 25, 1864, in Rebel Prison at Andersonville, Ga.
Luce, Charles B..........	....do....	18	June 16, 1864	3 yrs.	Substitute; mustered out with company June 25, 1865.
Lumley, John...........	....do....	22	June 10, 1864	3 yrs.	Substitute.
McBride, James..........	....do....	19	June 18, 1864	3 yrs.	Substitute; mustered out with company June 25, 1865.
McIntosh, Adolph B.....	....do....	18	Jan. 28, 1864	3 yrs.	Mustered out with company June 25, 1865.
McIntyre, Samuel C.....	....do....	18	Nov. 23, 1863	3 yrs.	Transferred to 2d Brigade Band, 3d Division. 6th Army Corps, Jan. 4, 1865, from which mustered out June 25, 1865, near Washington, D. C.
McLaughlin, William R.	....do....	20	Aug. 20, 1862	3 yrs.	Wounded June 3, 1864, in battle of Cold Harbor, Va.; discharged May 20, 1865, at Columbus, O., on Surgeon's certificate of disability.
McMillan, Samuel H....	....do....	26	Aug. 22, 1862	3 yrs.	Wounded July 9, 1864, in battle of Monocacy, Md.; mustered out with company June 25, 1865.
McNamee, John..........	....do....	55	Oct. 5, 1862	3 yrs.	Substitute; captured June 15, 1863, at battle of Winchester, Va.; transferred to Veteran Reserve Corps April 15, 1864.
Matthews, William D. F.	....do....	43	May 26, 1864	3 yrs.	Drafted; mustered out June 26, 1865, at Baltimore, Md.
Mendenhall, Samuel.....	....do....	24	Sept. 1, 1862	3 yrs.	Mustered out with company June 25, 1865.
Mendenhall, Smith......	....do....	18	Aug. 22, 1862	3 yrs.	Died Dec. 25, 1862, at Spring Valley, O.
Miller, Albert McH.....	....do....	21	Aug. 22, 1862	3 yrs.	Mustered out with company June 25, 1865.
Morris, William J.......	....do....	22	Sept. 28, 1864	1 yr.	Mustered out with company June 25, 1865.
Nickolas, John..........	....do....	32	Oct. 6, 1862	3 yrs.	
Noble, John W..........	....do....	29	Aug. 20, 1862	3 yrs.	
Norton, Addison.........	....do....	24	June 8, 1864	3 yrs.	Substitute; mustered out July 15, 1865, at Columbus, O.
O'Donnel, Martin.......	....do....	26	Aug. 22, 1862	3 yrs.	Captured June 15, 1863, at battle of Winchester, Va.
Peterson, Abel F........	....do....	21	Aug. 22, 1862	3 yrs.	Transferred to 2d Co., 2d Battalion, Veteran Reserve Corps, ——; mustered out Oct. 2, 1865, at Washington, D. C., on expiration of term of service.

Names.	Rank.	Age.	Date of Entering the Service.	Period of Service.	Remarks.
Peterson, Christopher C.	Private..	22	Aug. 22, 1862	3 yrs.	Discharged April 18, 1863, at Winchester, Va., on Surgeon's certificate of disability.
Peterson, Lewis............	....do....	26	Aug. 22, 1862	3 yrs.	Wounded July 9, 1864, in battle of Monocacy, Md.; discharged Feb. 9, 1865, at Columbus, O., on Surgeon's certificate of disability.
Peterson, Wilbur..........	....do....	22	Aug. 22, 1862	3 yrs.	Mustered out with company June 25, 1865.
Quinn, James M...........	....do....	24	Aug. 16, 1862	3 yrs.	Mustered out with company June 25, 1865.
Reid, James R.............	....do....	34	Aug. 17, 1862	3 yrs.	Discharged May 7, 1863, at Columbus, O., on Surgeon's certificate of disability.
Reid, Thomas.............	....do....	21	Aug. 14, 1862	3 yrs.	Mustered out with company June 25, 1865.
Roby, Henry H............	....do....	35	May 26, 1864	3 yrs.	Drafted; discharged Feb. 20, 1865, for wounds received July 9, 1864, in battle of Monocacy, Maryland.
Russell, Anthony C......	....do....	19	Aug. 22, 1862	3 yrs.	Discharged May 15, 1865, for wounds received July 9, 1864, in battle of Monocacy, Md.
Schmidt, Jacob M........	....do....	21	June 15, 1864	3 yrs.	Substitute; killed March 25, 1865, in action near Petersburg, Va.
Shindledecker, Calvin..	....do....	18	Oct. 6, 1862	3 yrs.	Substitute; discharged May 5, 1863, at Winchester, Va., on Surgeon's certificate of disability.
Shook William H........	....do....	23	Aug. 22, 1862	3 yrs.	Died May 31, 1864, of wounds received May 5, 1864, in battle of the Wilderness, Va.
Short, Benjamin..........	....do....	32	Aug. 22, 1862	3 yrs.	Died Feb. 12, 1863, at Winchester, Va.
Smith, James M..........	....do....	24	Aug. 22, 1862	3 yrs.	Discharged Dec. 2, 1864, for wounds received Nov. 27, 1863, in battle of Mine Run, Va.
Squires, Fenton..........	....do....	24	Aug. 22, 1862	3 yrs.	Captured June 15, 1863, at battle of Winchester, Va.; wounded Sept. 19, 1864, in battle of Opequan, Va.; mustered out with company June 25, 1865.
Starr, James M...........	....do....	22	Aug. 22, 1862	3 yrs.	Captured July 9, 1864, at battle of Monocacy, Md.; paroled ——. No further record found.
Stewart, John D. M......	....do....	19	Aug. 17, 1862	3 yrs.	Mustered out with company June 25, 1865.
Stienaker, Henry.........	....do....	21	May 31, 1864	3 yrs.	Drafted; mustered out with company June 25, 1865.
Stratton, Alfred..........	....do....	19	Aug. 22, 1862	3 yrs.	Captured June 15, 1863, at battle of Winchester, Va.; died June 29, 1864, of wounds received May 5, 1864, in battle of the Wilderness, Va.
Street, William H........	....do....	20	Aug. 18, 1862	3 yrs.	Discharged June 2, 1865, at Camp Dennison, O., for wounds received May 5, 1864, in battle of the Wilderness, Va.
Sutton, Jacob M..........	....do....	28	Sept. 4, 1862	3 yrs.	Died Nov. 17, 1863, at Brandy Station, Va.
Tannyhill, John K........	....do....	20	Aug. 22, 1862	3 yrs.	Mustered out with company June 25, 1865.
Thompson, John C.......	....do....	35	Aug. 22, 1862	3 yrs.	Killed Nov. 27, 1863, in battle of Mine Run, Virginia.
Thompson, Samuel.......	....do....	28	Aug. 19, 1862	3 yrs.	Died June 4, 1863, at Winchester, Va.
Walton, William M.......	....do....	19	Aug. 22, 1862	3 yrs.	Wounded Sept. 19, 1864, in battle of Opequan, Va.; mustered out with company June 25, 1865.
Ward, Albert.............	....do....	17	June 8, 1864	3 yrs.	Substitute.
Way, Charles E...........	....do....	19	Aug. 22, 1862	3 yrs.	Captured June 15, 1863, at battle of Winchester, Va.; died Aug. 5, 1863, in Rebel Prison at Winchester, Va.
Welch, James A..........	....do....	36	Aug. 17, 1862	3 yrs.	Captured June 15, 1863, at battle of Winchester, Va.; mustered out May 30, 1865, at Columbus, O., by order of War Department.
Williams, Rensellaer J..	....do....	25	Nov. 26, 1863	3 yrs.	Transferred to 2d Brigade Band, 3d Division, 6th Army Corps, Jan. 4, 1865, from which mustered out June 25, 1865, near Washington, D. C.
Womble, Mahlon..........	....do....	39	Aug. 22, 1862	3 yrs.	Mustered out with company June 25, 1865.
Wright, Joseph H........	....do....	33	Aug. 22, 1862	3 yrs.	Captured June 15, 1863, at battle of Winchester, Va.; mustered out with company June 25, 1865.

COMPANY E.

Mustered in Oct. 3, 1862, at Camp Piqua, O., by Alexander E. Drake, Captain 2d Infantry, U. S. A. Mustered out June 25, 1865, near Washington, D. C., by J. C. Robinson, Brevet Major and A. C. M. 3d Division, 6th Army Corps.

Names.	Rank.	Age.	Date of Entering the Service.	Period of Service.	Remarks.
William R. Moore	Captain.	28	Aug. 15, 1862	3 yrs.	Detached as Act. Asst. Inspector General 2d Brigade, 3d Division, 3d Army Corps, Dec. 5, 1863; died Feb. 27, 1864, at Brandy Station, Virginia.
Wesley Devenney	....do....	26	Aug. 11, 1862	3 yrs.	Promoted to 1st Lieutenant and Adjutant from 1st Sergeant April 12, 1864; to Captain Aug. 8, 1864; died Oct. 23, 1864, of wounds received Oct. 19, 1864, in battle of Cedar Creek, Virginia.
William L. Shaw	....do....	30	Aug. 4, 1862	3 yrs.	Promoted from 1st Lieutenant Co. F Dec. 9, 1864; brevet Major April 2, 1865; mustered out June 26, 1865, by order of War Department.
Henry Y. Rush	1st Lieut.	26	Aug. 15, 1862	3 yrs.	Appointed Aug. 16, 1862; resigned Oct. 6, 1863, on account of physical disability.
Joseph McKnight	....do....	39	Aug. 8, 1862	3 yrs.	Promoted from 2d Lieutenant Nov. 25, 1863; to Captain ——, but not mustered; died May 25, 1864, of wounds received May 5, 1864, in battle of the Wilderness, Va.
Jacob M. Conwell	....do....	24	Aug. 21, 1862	3 yrs.	Promoted from 2d Lieutenant Co. F July 22, 1864; was Act. Regt. Quartermaster; transferred to Co. D Feb. 17, 1865.
Edward S. Dukeshier	....do....	42	Aug. 15, 1862	3 yrs.	Appointed Sergeant from private Nov. 3, 1862; wounded and captured June 15, 1863, in battle of Winchester, Va.; paroled July 8, 1863; returned to company Nov. 16, 1863; appointed 1st Sergeant April 20, 1864; wounded May 5, 1864, in battle of the Wilderness, Va.; promoted to 2d Lieutenant Co. H Aug. 8, 1864, to date Jan. 31, 1865; mustered out with company June 25, 1865.
William W. Locke	2d Lieut.	32	Aug. 22, 1862	3 yrs.	Promoted from Hospital Steward April 12, 1864; discharged Jan. 4, 1865.
James W. Bailey	1st Sergt.	24	Aug. 21, 1862	3 yrs.	Accidentally wounded Jan. 18, 1864, near Culpepper, Va.; appointed Sergeant from private July 12, 1864; 1st Sergeant Nov. 3, 1864; mustered out with company June 25, 1865.
Matthias McAnally	Sergeant.	43	Aug. 21, 1862	3 yrs.	Captured June 14, 1863, at battle of Winchester, Va.; died Nov. 2, 1864, at Jeffersonville, Indiana.
James Howell	....do....	34	Aug. 13, 1862	3 yrs.	Died July 11, 1864, at Frederick, Md., of wounds received July 9, 1864, in battle of Monocacy, Md.
John C. Class	....do....	36	Aug. 22, 1862	3 yrs.	Discharged March 20, 1863, at Columbus, O., on Surgeon's certificate of disability.
Samuel C. Calvert	....do....	30	Aug. 17, 1862	3 yrs.	Appointed from Corporal May 5, 1863; wounded July 9, 1864, in battle of Monocacy, Md.; mustered out May 31, 1865, at Columbus, O., by order of War Department.
Charles C. Jones	....do....	23	Aug. 21, 1862	3 yrs.	Appointed from Corporal April 20, 1864; mustered out with company June 25, 1865.
James Crampton	....do....	26	Aug. 21, 1862	3 yrs.	Appointed Corporal Sept. 15, 1864; Sergeant Nov. 4, 1864; mustered out with company June 25, 1865.
Isaiah Hays	....do....	28	Aug. 9, 1862	3 yrs.	Appointed Corporal March 1, 1864; Sergeant Nov. 4, 1864; mustered out with company June 25, 1865.
Ennis E. Sherwood	Corporal.	27	Aug. 9, 1862	3 yrs.	Wounded Oct. 19, 1864, in battle of Cedar Creek, Va.; mustered out May 13, 1865, at Cumberland, Md., by order of War Department.
Alpheus Line	....do....	43	Aug. 15, 1862	3 yrs.	Transferred to Veteran Reserve Corps Sept. 22, 1862.
John R. Rhoades	....do....	43	Aug. 15, 1862	3 yrs.	Captured June 14, 1863, at battle of Winchester, Va.; paroled July 26, 1863; mustered out with company June 25, 1865.
William P. Smith	....do....	40	Aug. 16, 1862	3 yrs.	Appointed Sept. 15, 1864; wounded March 25, 1865, in action near Petersburg, Va.; discharged July 1, 1865, at Columbus, O., on Surgeon's certificate of disability.
Palestine Miller	....do....	22	Aug. 20, 1862	3 yrs.	Appointed April 20, 1864; wounded July 9, 1864, in battle of Monocacy, Md.; mustered out June 22, 1865, at Chester, Pa., by order of War Department.

Names.	Rank.	Age.	Date of Entering the Service.	Period of Service.	Remarks.
William E. Starry	Corporal.	20	Aug. 21, 1862	3 yrs.	Wounded June 3, 1864, in battle of Cold Harbor, Va.; appointed Corporal Sept. 15, 1864; mustered out with company June 25, 1865.
George W. Search	do...	18	Aug. 12, 1862	3 yrs.	Appointed Nov. 5, 1864; mustered out with company June 25, 1865.
Samuel W. Helvie	do...	18	Aug. 21, 1862	3 yrs.	Appointed Dec. 1, 1864; mustered out with company June 25, 1865.
Martin Smith	do...	20	Aug. 18, 1862	3 yrs.	Appointed Nov. 1, 1864; mustered out with company June 25, 1865.
Frank Herring	do...	31	Aug. 22, 1862	3 yrs.	Appointed ——; died May 16, 1864, at Fredericksburg, Va., of wounds received May 5, 1864, in battle of the Wilderness, Va.
Andrews, Charles	Private..	38	May 23, 1864	3 yrs.	Drafted; mustered out with company June 25, 1865.
Armor, Andrew	do...	26	June 10, 1864	3 yrs.	Drafted; mustered out with company June 25, 1865.
Baker, Conrad	do...	23	Aug. 21, 1862	3 yrs.	Discharged Oct. 23, 1863, on Surgeon's certificate of disability.
Basaker, John	do...	18	Feb. 17, 1864	3 yrs.	Wounded July 9, 1864, in battle of Monocacy, Md.; mustered out with company June 25, 1865.
Beckner, George	do...	25	Aug. 21, 1862	3 yrs.	Mustered out with company June 25, 1865.
Benham, Aaron	do...	32	Aug. 14, 1862	3 yrs.	Wounded July 9, 1864, in battle of Monocacy, Md.; mustered out with company June 25, 1865.
Biser, Daniel	do...	40	Aug. 18, 1862	3 yrs.	Reduced from Corporal Sept. 14, 1864; discharged to date March 4, 1864, by order of War Department.
Bond, William	do...	19	June 14, 1864	3 yrs.	Substitute; wounded Sept. 19, 1864, in battle of Opequan, Va.; mustered out with company June 25, 1865.
Bowers, John H	do...	27	Aug. 21, 1862	3 yrs.	Died Feb. 22, 1863, at Winchester, Va.
Bowers, Uriah	do...	23	Aug. 21, 1862	3 yrs.	Captured June 15, 1863, at battle of Winchester, Va.; paroled July 26, 1863; captured May 5, 1864, at battle of the Wilderness, Va.; mustered out with company June 25, 1865.
Bowles, John H	do...	21	June 8, 1864	3 yrs.	Drafted; wounded July 9, 1864, in battle of Monocacy, Md.; mustered out with company June 25, 1865.
Bradford, Sebren	do...	18	Jan. 2, 1864	3 yrs.	Mustered out with company June 25, 1865.
Brokaw, Henry	do...	18	Oct. 7, 1862	3 yrs.	Captured June 15, 1863, at battle of Winchester, Va.; paroled July 26, 1863; mustered out with company June 25, 1865.
Brokaw, James	do...	42	Aug. 12, 1862	3 yrs.	Transferred to Veteran Reserve Corps March 7, 1864.
Brown, John C	do...	24	Jan. 16, 1864	3 yrs.	Died Oct. 19, 1864, in hospital at Baltimore, Maryland.
Burch, Joseph H	do...	29	Jan. 25, 1864	3 yrs.	Mustered out June 13, 1865, at Philadelphia, Pa., by order of War Department.
Camp, William	do...	23	Aug. 21, 1862	3 yrs.	Discharged Jan. 1, 1863, on Surgeon's certificate of disability.
Carpenter, James H	do...	39	Dec. 24, 1863	3 yrs.	Died July 16, 1864, at Washington, D. C., of wounds received June 22, 1864, in action.
Cavenaugh, David	do...	23	Aug. 21, 1862	3 yrs.	Mustered out with company June 25, 1865.
Clark, James B	do...	24	Aug. 11, 1863	3 yrs.	Captured June 15, 1863, at battle of Winchester, Va.; paroled July 26, 1863; wounded July 9, 1864, in battle of Monocacy, Md.; mustered out with company June 25, 1865.
Coburn, David J	do...	22	Mch. 9, 1864	3 yrs.	Wounded and captured May 5, 1864, in battle of the Wilderness, Va.; mustered out July 10, 1865, at Camp Chase, O., by order of War Department.
Coburn, John A	do...	40	Jan. 28, 1864	3 yrs.	Died May 16, 1864, at Fredericksburg, Va., of wounds received May 5, 1864, in battle of the Wilderness, Va.
Combs, Thomas B	do...	37	Aug. 15, 1862	3 yrs.	Mustered out May 23, 1865, at Philadelphia, Pa., by order of War Department.
Cotterman, Henry	do...	24	Aug. 14, 1862	3 yrs.	Wounded May 5, 1864, in battle of the Wilderness, Va.; mustered out with company June 25, 1865.
Cotterman, Isaac	do...	21	Aug. 21, 1862	3 yrs.	Captured June 15, 1863, at battle of Winchester, Va.; paroled June 30, 1863; died May 29, 1865, in hospital at Baltimore, Md.
Cotterman, John J	do...	27	Feb. 26, 1864	3 yrs.	Wounded Sept. 19, 1864, in battle of Opequan, Va.; mustered out with company June 25, 1865.
Cotterman, Seymour	do...	20	Sept. 19, 1863	3 yrs.	Wounded Nov. 27, 1863, in battle of Mine Run, Va.; also June 3, 1864, in battle of Cold Harbor, Va.; mustered out with company June 25, 1865.
Counts, Lewis F	do...	18	Aug. 16, 1862	3 yrs.	Transferred to Veteran Reserve Corps Nov. 28, 1863; mustered out July 31, 1865, at Rochester, N. Y., by order of War Department.
Crabtree, Thomas E	do...	18	Jan. 11, 1864	3 yrs.	Wounded Sept. 19, 1864, in battle of Opequan, Va.; died June 10, 1865, at Houston, O.

Names.	Rank.	Age.	Date of Entering the Service.	Period of Service.	Remarks.
Cunningham, Ross	Private..	18	Jan. 12, 1864	3 yrs.	Mustered out with company June 25, 1865.
Darling, Roice	....do....	18	Feb. 19, 1864	3 yrs.	Killed May 5, 1864, in battle of the Wilderness, Va.
Dukeshier, Charles	....do....	28	Aug. 14, 1862	3 yrs.	Captured June 14, 1863, at battle of Winchester, Va.; paroled July 26, 1863; wounded May 5, 1864, in battle of the Wilderness, Va.; also March 25, 1865, in action near Petersburg, Va.; mustered out May 30, 1865, at Washington, D. C., by order of War Department.
Dukeshier, Wintworth..	....do....	26	Aug. 15, 1862	3 yrs.	Mustered in as Wagoner; captured June 15, 1863, at battle of Winchester, Va.; wounded May 5, 1864, in battle of the Wilderness, Va.; transferred to Co. K, 8th Regiment, Veteran Reserve Corps, Dec. 3, 1864.
Forbes, Lewis	....do....	18	Aug. 21, 1862	3 yrs.	Discharged Feb. 16, 1864, at Fairfax Seminary Hospital, Va., on Surgeon's certificate of disability.
Fowler, Luther	....do....	34	May 14, 1864	3 yrs.	Drafted; mustered out with company June 25, 1865.
French, David M	....do....	29	Dec. 1, 1863	3 yrs.	Wounded April 2, 1865, in action near Petersburg, Va.; mustered out June 13, 1865, at Philadelphia, Pa., by order of War Department.
Garrell, Abraham	....do....	35	Aug. 16, 1862	3 yrs.	Discharged April 6, 1863, at Winchester, Va., on Surgeon's certificate of disability.
Gearhart, Silas	....do....	23	Aug. 21, 1862	3 yrs.	Captured June 15, 1863, at battle of Winchester, Va.; paroled Sept. 23, 1863; mustered out with company June 25, 1865.
Gray, William H	....do....	18	Aug. 20, 1862	3 yrs.	Killed Sept. 19, 1864, in battle of Opequan, Virginia.
Hamilton, Samuel	....do....	18	Aug. 16, 1862	3 yrs.	Captured June 15, 1863, at battle of Winchester, Va.; paroled July 26, 1863; wounded May 5, 1864, in battle of the Wilderness, Va.; mustered out June 10, 1865, at Washington, D. C., by order of War Department.
Hammond, Richard P ..	....do....	30	Aug. 21, 1862	3 yrs.	Captured June 15, 1863, at battle of Winchester, Va.; recaptured Aug. 5, 1863, by Averill's Cavalry; returned to company Nov. 16, 1863; reduced from Sergeant at his own request ——; wounded April 2, 1865, in action near Petersburg, Va.; discharged June 19, 1865, at Philadelphia, Pa., on Surgeon's certificate of disability.
Haney, Isaac R	....do....	22	Aug. 22, 1862	3 yrs.	Died June 27, 1863, at Winchester, Va., of wounds received June 14, 1863, in battle of Winchester, Va.
Hanse, Seymour	....do....	19	Sept. 14, 1862	3 yrs.	Wounded May 5, 1864, in battle of the Wilderness, Va.; transferred to Veteran Reserve Corps April 1, 1865.
Harter, George W	....do....	20	Aug. 20, 1862	3 yrs.	Discharged March 18, 1863, at Winchester, Va., on Surgeon's certificate of disability.
Heath, Joseph	....do....	22	Aug. 16, 1862	3 yrs.	Mustered in as Musician; mustered out with company June 25, 1865.
Hess, Theodore	....do....	22	May 15, 1864	3 yrs.	Drafted; captured July 9, 1864, at battle of Monocacy, Md.; mustered out with company June 25, 1865.
Hetzler, George	....do....	19	Aug. 15, 1862	3 yrs.	Discharged Jan. 1, 1863, at Cumberland, Md., on Surgeon's certificate of disability.
Hicksenhiser, John J....	....do....	18	Aug. 19, 1862.	3 yrs.	Wounded Oct. 19, 1863, in battle of Cedar Creek, Va.; mustered out with company June 25, 1865.
Hill, Josiah L.	....do....	27	Aug. 12, 1862	3 yrs.	Reduced from Corporal ——; wounded Nov. 27, 1863, in battle of Mine Run, Va.; also July 9, 1864, in battle of Monocacy, Md.; mustered out with company June 25, 1865.
Hoesh, George	....do....	39	June 18, 1864	3 yrs.	Substitute; died Aug. 8, 1864, at Frederick, Md., of wounds received July 9, 1864, in battle of Monocacy, Md.
Holden, John	....do....	31	Feb. 25, 1864	3 yrs.	Wounded July 9, 1864, in battle of Monocacy, Md.; transferred to Co. E, 10th Regiment, Veteran Reserve Corps, Nov. 15, 1864; mustered out July 20, 1865, at Washington, D. C., by order of War Department.
Hume, John R	....do....	30	Feb. 5, 1864	3 yrs.	Mustered out with company June 25, 1865.
Hume, Robert	....do....	22	Feb. 4, 1864	3 yrs.	Died July 9, 1864, on the field, of wounds received the same day in battle of Monocacy, Md.
Johns, Jacob	....do....	24	Aug. 22, 1862	3 yrs.	
Kauftman, Philip	....do....	38	May 10, 1864	3 yrs.	Drafted; wounded April 2, 1865, in action near Petersburg, Va.; mustered out June 14, 1865, by order of War Department.
Kennedy, George	....do....	22	Aug. 21, 1862	3 yrs.	Mustered out with company June 25, 1865.
Kester, Henry L	....do....	23	Aug. 21, 1862.	3 yrs.	Captured June 15, 1863, at battle of Winchester, Va.; paroled July 8, 1863.
Kiser, Joseph	....do....	18	Jan. 11, 1864	3 yrs.	Mustered out with company June 25, 1865.

Names.	Rank.	Age.	Date of Entering the Service.	Period of Service.	Remarks.
Kiser, William I.	Private..	18	Oct. 21, 1862	3 yrs.	Wounded and captured June 15, 1863, in battle of Winchester, Va.; mustered out with company June 25, 1865.
Kiser, William T.	..do....	18	Feb. 18, 1864	3 yrs.	Mustered out with company June 25, 1865.
Knoop, John	..do....	18	Aug. 11, 1862	3 yrs.	Captured June 15, 1863, at battle of Winchester, Va.; paroled July 26, 1863; wounded April —, 1865, in action near Petersburg, Va.; mustered out July 12, 1865, at Columbus, O., by order of War Department.
Kreysig, Alexander	..do....	27	June 16, 1864	3 yrs.	Substitute; captured July 9, 1864, at battle of Monocacy, Md.; paroled ——; died Oct. 20, 1864, on board steamer.
Landis, James	..do....	21	Aug. 13, 1862	3 yrs.	Mustered out with company July 25, 1865.
Main, John F	..do...:	28	Aug. 20, 1862	3 yrs.	Mustered in as Corporal; transferred to Co. G, 1st Regiment, Veteran Reserve Corps, Jan. 24, 1865; mustered out July 19, 1865, at Elmira, N. Y.
Manson, Mahlon P	..do....	18	Aug. 15, 1862	3 yrs.	Wounded May 5, 1864, in battle of the Wilderness, Va.; transferred to Co. G, 6th Regiment, Veteran Reserve Corps, Jan. 12, 1865; mustered out July 14, 1865, at Cleveland, O., by order of War Department.
Mills, Elias	..do....	22	Aug. 15, 1862	3 yrs.	Captured June 15, 1863, at battle of Winchester, Va.; paroled July 8, 1863; wounded May 5, 1864, in battle of the Wilderness, Va.; mustered out with company June 25, 1865.
Miller, Dallas	..do....	18	Aug. 14, 1862	3 yrs.	Mustered in as Musician; mustered out with company June 25, 1865.
Morrow, Jeremiah	..do....	25	Aug. 9, 1862	3 yrs.	Mustered out with company June 25, 1865.
Morrow, John C	..do....	28	Aug. 9, 1862	3 yrs.	Died Nov. 27, 1863, in hospital at Washington, D. C.
Mosier, Francis M	..do....	18	Feb. 24, 1864	3 yrs.	Mustered out with company June 25, 1865.
Motter, Tillman	..do....	27	Aug. 16, 1862	3 yrs.	Died Aug. 7, 1863, in hospital at Baltimore, Maryland.
Murray, John	..do....	19	Aug. 20, 1862	3 yrs.	Discharged Jan. 1, 1863, at Cumberland, Md., on Surgeon's certificate of disability.
Norris, Charles C	..do....	27	May 14, 1864	3 yrs.	Drafted; wounded July 9, 1864, in battle of Monocacy, Md.; mustered out June 3, 1865, at New York, by order of War Department, as Carlos C. Norris.
O'Neil, James	..do....	26	June 4, 1864	3 yrs.	Substitute; captured July 9, 1864, at battle of Monocacy, Md. No further record found.
Orchard, James	..do....	27	June 4, 1864	3 yrs.	Substitute; captured July 9, 1864, at battle of Monocacy, Md. No further record found.
Pearson, William	..do....	34	Aug. 21, 1862	3 yrs.	Died Feb. 28, 1863, at his home in Miami County, O.
Pinkerton, Frederick	..do....	16	Aug. 16, 1862	3 yrs.	Captured June 15, 1863, at battle of Winchester, Va.; paroled July 26, 1863; mustered out with company June 25, 1865.
Pogue, Joseph	..do. ..	20	Aug. 15, 1862	3 yrs.	Wounded Oct. 4, 1864, in action; mustered out May 18, 1865, by order of War Department.
Potorph, George	..do....	32	Aug. 13, 1862	3 yrs.	Transferred to Co. K, 12th Regiment, Veteran Reserve Corps, Dec. 28, 1864.
Potts, Harrison M	..do....	17	Aug. 15, 1862	3 yrs.	Captured June 15, 1863, at battle of Winchester, Va.; paroled July 26, 1863; mustered out with company June 25, 1865.
Proctor, John	..do....	31	Aug. 12, 1862	3 yrs.	Died June 2, 1864, in hospital, 2d Division, 18th Army Corps, of wounds received June 1, 1864, in battle of Cold Harbor, Va.
Rallston, Andrew	..do....	23	Aug. 15, 1862	3 yrs.	Mustered out with company June 25, 1865.
Rapp, Benjamin F	..do....	28	Aug. 21, 1862	3 yrs.	Discharged Sept. 4, 1863, at Columbus, O., on Surgeon's certificate of disability.
Reiss, Paul	..do....	24	June 16, 1864	3 yrs.	Substitute; mustered out May 20, 1865, at Baltimore, Md., by order of War Department.
Richter, Rudolph	..do....	25	Feb. 6, 1865	1 yr.	Mustered out with company June 25, 1865.
Roller, Levi	..do....	30	Aug. 21, 1862	3 yrs.	Discharged March 18, 1863, at Winchester, Va., on Surgeon's certificate of disability.
Simmons, Philip	..do....	29	Feb. 26, 1864	3 yrs.	Killed May 5, 1864, in battle of the Wilderness, Virginia.
Smith, John	..do....	22	Feb. 1, 1864	3 yrs.	Mustered out with company June 25, 1865.
Snyder, Frederick W	..do....	44	June 8, 1864	3 yrs.	Drafted; wounded and captured July 9, 1864, in battle of Monocacy, Md.; mustered out to date June 25, 1865, at Columbus, O., by order of War Department.
Spangler, Peter	..do....	26	Aug. 21, 1862	3 yrs.	Discharged Feb. 13, 1864, at Camp Dennison, O., for wounds received June 15, 1863, in battle of Winchester, Va.
Spicer, Samuel	..do....	21	Aug. 18, 1862	3 yrs.	Transferred to Veteran Reserve Corps March 16, 1864.
Stafford, James C	..do....	20	Aug. 21, 1862	3 yrs.	Mustered out June 5, 1865, at Washington, D. C., by order of War Department.
Stichler, William	..do....	18	Aug. 20, 1862	3 yrs.	Mustered out with company June 25, 1865.
Summit, Caleb	..do....	25	May 26, 1864	3 yrs.	Drafted; captured July 9, 1864, in battle of Monocacy, Md.; released Feb. 19, 1865; mustered out with company June 25, 1865.

Names.	Rank.	Age.	Date of Entering the Service.	Period of Service.	Remarks.
Taylor, William.........	Private..	18	Aug. 21, 1862	3 yrs.	Captured June 15, 1863, at battle of Winchester, Va.; paroled Sept. 23, 1863; wounded Sept. 19, 1864, in battle of Opequan, Va.; mustered out with company June 25, 1865.
Thorn, Joseph.............	....do....	18	Aug. 21, 1862	3 yrs.	Mustered out with company June 25, 1865.
Truman, Levi	....do....	36	Feb. 5, 1864.	3 yrs.	Wounded May 18, 1864, in action; transferred to 37th Co., 2d Battalion, Veteran Reserve Corps, March 7, 1865.
Uhrich, Philip	....do....	40	Aug. 22, 1862	3 yrs.	Wounded May 5, 1864, in battle of the Wilderness, Va.; mustered out with company June 25, 1865.
Vandiver, Robert........	....do....	18	Aug. 21, 1862	3 yrs.	Wounded Nov. 27, 1863, in battle of Mine Run, Va.; transferred to Co. A. 12th Regiment, Veteran Reserve Corps, Dec. 31, 1864.
Weatherhead, Thomas J	....do....	18	Jan. 8, 1864	3 yrs.	Died March 27, 1864, in hospital at Brandy Station, Va.
Welsh, Patrick............	....do....	36	Aug. 22, 1863	3 yrs.	Died Dec. 18, 1864, at Frederick, Md.
White, Yardly S	....do....	19	Jan. 4, 1864	3 yrs.	Mustered out with company June 25, 1865.
Whitney, Cyrus W......	....do....	25	Aug. 20, 1862	3 yrs.	Transferred to 12th Regiment, Veteran Reserve Corps, April 1, 1865; mustered out July 12, 1865, at Washington, D. C., by order of War Department.
Winans, Benjamin F....	....do....	30	Aug. 17, 1862	3 yrs.	Transferred to Veteran Reserve Corps Nov. 20, 1863.
Zipple, Rudolph..........	....do....	24	June 16, 1864	3 yrs.	Substitute; captured July 9, 1864, at battle of Monocacy, Md.; mustered out June 2, 1865, at Camp Dennison, O., by order of War Department.
Zuelch, Conrad...........	....do....	37	June 16, 1864	3 yrs.	Drafted; mustered out with company June 25, 1865.

COMPANY F.

Mustered in Oct. 2, 1862, at Camp Piqua, O., by Alexander E. Drake, Captain 2d Infantry, U. S. A. Mustered out June 25, 1865, near Washington, D. C., by J. C. Robinson, Brevet Major and A. C. M. 3d Division, 6th Army Corps.

Names.	Rank.	Age.	Date of Entering the Service.	Period of Service.	Remarks.
Aaron Spangler..........	Captain.	26	Aug. 15, 1862	3 yrs.	Wounded May 12, 1864, in battle of Spottsylvania C. H., Va.; promoted to Major June 25, 1864.
Elias A. Shepherd.......	....do....	25	Aug. 6, 1862	3 yrs.	Transferred from Co. B ——; to Co. B Feb. 17, 1865.
Elam Harter..............	....do....	30	Aug. 8, 1862	3 yrs.	Promoted to 2d Lieutenant from 1st Sergeant July 22, 1864; 1st Lieutenant Co. H Dec. 9, 1864; from 1st Lieutenant Co. H to date Jan. 31, 1865; wounded March 25, 1864, in front of Petersburg, Va.; discharged May 15, 1865.
William L. Shaw........	1st Lieut.	30	Aug. 4, 1862	3 yrs.	Appointed Aug. 7, 1862; detailed as A. D. C. on General Elliott's Staff, 3d Division, 3d promoted to Army Corps, Nov. 14, 1863; Captain Co. E Dec. 9, 1864.
Jonn E. Miller............	....do....	28	Aug. 18, 1862	3 yrs.	Appointed 1st Sergeant from Sergeant Jan. 1, 1864; captured May 6, 1864, in battle of the Wilderness, Va.; promoted to 2d Lieutenant July 22, 1864; 1st Lieutenant Nov. 3, 1864; mustered out with company June 25, 1865.
Henry F. De Haven.....	2d Lieut.	31	Aug. 15, 1862	3 yrs.	
Jacob M. Conwell........	....do....	24	Aug. 21, 1862	3 yrs.	Promoted from Q. M. Sergeant April 12, 1864; to 1st Lieutenant Co. E July 22, 1864.
William A. Jones........	....do....	25	Aug. 20, 1862	3 yrs.	Transferred from Co. D Nov. 20, 1864; discharged Jan. 31, 1865.
William Harner.........	1st Sergt.	23	Aug. 18, 1862	3 yrs.	Appointed Sergeant from Corporal Oct. 4, 1862; captured June 15, 1863, at battle of Winchester, Va.; appointed 1st Sergeant April 13, 1865; mustered out with company June 25, 1865.
James A. Fox............	Sergeant.	22	Aug. 20, 1862	3 yrs.	Promoted to Sergt. Major Oct. 4, 1862.
Eli C. Beall..............	....do....	21	Aug. 21, 1862	3 yrs.	Appointed from Corporal Aug. 1, 1864; mustered out with company June 25, 1865.
Christian Kauffman.....	....do....	36	Aug. 22, 1862	3 yrs.	Appointed from Corporal May 12, 1864; wounded July 9, 1864, in battle of Monocacy, Md.; mustered out June 12, 1865, at Washington, D. C., by order of War Department.
Jonathan Harner.........	....do....	21	Aug. 18, 1862	3 yrs.	Appointed Corporal May 12, 1864, Sergeant Sept. 1, 1864; mustered out with company 25, 1865.
Dock W. Richardson....	....do....	26	Aug. 12, 1862	3 yrs.	Appointed Corporal Oct. 16, 1862; Sergeant Jan. 1, 1863; promoted to Sergt. Major Sept. 1, 1864.

Names.	Rank.	Age.	Date of Entering the Service.	Period of Service.	Remarks.
William H. Routzahn ...	Sergeant.	22	Aug. 22, 1862	3 yrs.	Appointed from Corporal Jan. 1, 1864; killed May 12, 1864, in battle of Spottsylvania C. H., Virginia.
Andrew J. Furay.........	....do....	28	Aug. 18, 1862	3 yrs.	Reduced to ranks from Corporal Aug. 18, 1864; appointed Sergeant April 13, 1865; mustered out June 17, 1865, at Washington, D. C., by order of War Department.
Joshua M. Whiteman...	....do....	32	Aug. 7, 1862	3 yrs.	Appointed Corporal July 13, 1864; Sergeant June 13, 1865; mustered out with company June 25, 1865.
David C. Stafford........	Corporal.	24	Aug. 22, 1862	3 yrs.	Discharged March 23, 1863, at Winchester, Va., on Surgeon's certificate of disability.
Matthew Brown..........	....do....	36	Aug. 18, 1862	3 yrs.	Appointed March 1, 1863; captured May 17, 1864, at battle of Spottsylvania C. H., Va.; died Sept. 4, 1864, in Rebel Prison at Andersonville, Ga.
Charles H. Winter........	....do....	29	Aug. 22, 1862	3 yrs.	Appointed Jan. 1, 1864; discharged Dec. 13, 1864, for wounds received May 12, 1864, in battle of Spottsylvania C. H., Va.
Charles E. Brewer........	....do....	30	Aug. 14, 1862	3 yrs.	Appointed Aug. 16, 1864; mustered out with company June 25, 1865.
Charles E. Garlinger	....do....	22	Aug. 22, 1862	3 yrs.	Appointed Sept. 1, 1864; mustered out with company June 25, 1865.
John Linnscott..........	....do....	22	Aug. 22, 1862	3 yrs.	Wounded June 3, 1864, in battle of Cold Harbor, Va.; appointed Sept. 1, 1864; mustered out with company June 25, 1865.
Patrick Doolan	....do....	38	Aug. 15, 1862	3 yrs.	Captured June 15, 1863, at battle of Winchester, Va.; wounded May 5, 1864, in battle of the Wilderness, Va.; appointed Corporal Sept. 1, 1864; mustered out with company June 25, 1865.
Elwood Middleton.......	....do....	18	Aug. 20, 1862	3 yrs.	Appointed Sept. 15, 1864; wounded March 25, 1865, in action near Petersburg, Va.; mustered out May 31, 1865, at Columbus, O., by order of War Department.
William P. Harner......	...do....	22	Aug. 19, 1862	3 yrs.	Appointed Jan. 1, 1864; killed May 9, 1864, in battle of Spottsylvania C. H., Va.
John W. Carson..........	....do....	28	Aug. 22, 1862	3 yrs.	Appointed Jan. 1, 1864; discharged Sept. 15, 1864, for wounds received May 10, 1864, in action.
David F. Baker..........	....do....	23	Sept. 2, 1862	3 yrs.	Appointed Corporal Dec. 14, 1864; mustered out with company June 25 1865.
Daniel Sidenstick	....do....	18	Sept. 15, 1863	3 yrs.	Appointed Jan. 1, 1865; mustered out with company June 25, 1865.
John Quinn.............	....do....	38	Aug. 21, 1862	3 yrs.	Captured June 15, 1863, at battle of Winchester, Va.; appointed Corporal May 30, 1865; mustered out with company June 25, 1865.
William A. Cowan	....do....	21	June 7, 1864	3 yrs.	Substitute; appointed Corporal June 13, 1865; mustered out with company June 25, 1865.
Harrison Miller..........	....do....	22	Aug. 22, 1862	3 yrs.	Appointed May 9, 1864; died July 13, 1864, of wounds received July 9, 1864, in battle of Monocacy, Md.
Elias Musselman........	Wagoner.	28	Aug. 18, 1862	3 yrs.	Captured June 15, 1863, at battle of Winchester, Va.; mustered out with company June 25, 1865.
Baker, Otho W..........	Private..	27	Sept. 3, 1862	3 yrs.	Captured June 15, 1863, at battle of Winchester, Va.; mustered out with company June 25, 1865.
Ball, James I	....do....	20	Aug. 22, 1862	3 yrs.	Captured June 15, 1863, at battle of Winchester, Va.; wounded June 3, 1864, in battle of Cold Harbor, Va.; mustered out with company June 25, 1865.
Barnett, John A	....do....	38	Aug. 19, 1862	3 yrs.	Died April 26, 1863, in hospital at Winchester, Virginia.
Barr, Henry..............	....do....	34	Aug. 21, 1862	3 yrs.	Captured June 15, 1863, at battle of Winchester, Va.; mustered out May, 17, 1865, at Wilmington, Del., by order of War Department.
Barrs, Cornelius.........	....do....	30	Aug. 18, 1862	3 yrs.	Discharged Feb. 23, 1863, at Winchester, Va.
Beck, Jesse	....do....	36	Aug. 22, 1862	3 yrs.	Captured June 15, 1863, at battle of Winchester, Va.; died July 25, 1863, at Annapolis, Maryland.
Bell, Lewis L.............	....do....	27	Aug. 18, 1862	3 yrs.	Reduced from Sergeant Dec. 31, 1863; mustered out with company June 25, 1865.
Bellew, John.............	....do....	26	Sept. 16, 1862	3 yrs.	Captured June 15, 1863, at battle of Winchester, Va.; absent, sick in Ohio since Dec. 1, 1863. No further record found.
Bisine, Andrew..........	....do....	42	Aug. 16, 1862	3 yrs.	Discharged Nov. 5, 1863, at Alexandria, Va., on Surgeon's certificate of disability.
Blinn, Henry............	....do....	26	Aug. 21, 1862	3 yrs.	Captured June 15, 1863, at battle of Winchester, Va. Mustered out with company June 25, 1865.
Boyle, James M..........	....do....	18	Dec 16, 1863	3 yrs.	Mustered out with company June 25, 1865.
Brosey, Benjamin........	....do....	26	Sept. 14, 1862	3 yrs.	Captured June 15, 1863, at battle of Winchester, Va.; mustered out with company June 25, 1865.

Names.	Rank.	Age.	Date of Entering the Service.	Period of Service.	Remarks.
Butler, William A.......	Private..	27	Oct. 14, 1863	3 yrs.	Captured May 6, 1864, at battle of the Wilderness, Va.; died Feb. 1, 1865, in Rebel Prison at Florence, S. C.
Byle, Solomon...........	....do....	32	Aug. 22, 1862	3 yrs.	Captured June 15, 1863, at battle of Winchester, Va.; reduced from Corporal Sept. 1, 1864; mustered out May 30, 1865, at Cleveland, O., by order of War Department.
Christie, Robert V. B....	....do....	26	Nov. 23, 1863	3 yrs.	Transferred to 2d Brigade Band, 3d Division, 6th Army Corps, Jan. 4, 1865, from which mustered out June 25, 1865, near Washington, D. C.
Clayton, John	....do....	18	Jan. 2, 1864	3 yrs.	Died March 31, 1864, in hospital at Brandy Station, Va.
Coines, George T........	....do....	18	Aug. 20, 1862	3 yrs.	Captured June 15, 1863, at Winchester, Va.; wounded May 7, 1864, in battle of the Wilderness, Va.; mustered out with company June 25, 1865.
Craig, Samuel...........	....do....	22	June 8, 1864	3 yrs.	Substitute; captured July 9, 1864, at battle of Monocacy, Md.; died Jan. 1, 1865, in Rebel Prison at Salisbury, N. C.
Davis, John	....do....	25	Aug. 21, 1862	3 yrs.	Wounded May 6, 1864, in battle of the Wilderness, Va.; mustered out with company June 25, 1865.
Dear, Israel S	....do....	24	Aug. 20, 1862	3 yrs.	Wounded June 15, 1863, in battle of Winchester, Va.; also May 12, 1864, in battle of Spottsylvania C. H., Va.; mustered out with company June 25, 1865.
Dehart, John D	....do....	18	Aug. 22, 1862	3 yrs.	Captured June 15, 1863, at battle of Winchester, Va.; mustered out with company June 25, 1865.
Dehart, Winant	....do....	34	Sept. 23, 1864	1 yr.	Mustered out June 6, 1865, at Columbus, O., by order of War Department.
Downey, Lewis..........	....do....	27	Aug. 20, 1862	3 yrs.	Wounded May 5, 1864, in battle of the Wilderness, Va.; mustered out with company June 25, 1865.
Fiste, Samuel...........	....do....	21	Sept. 6, 1862	3 yrs.	Wounded Oct. 19, 1864, in battle of Cedar Creek, Va.; mustered out June 17, 1865, at Washington, D. C., by order of War Department.
Folkerth, Luman A. P...	....do....	19	Aug. 22, 1862	3 yrs.	Discharged March 17, 1863, at Winchester, Va., on Surgeon's certificate of disability.
Frantz, Frederick........	....do....	25	June 26, 1864	3 yrs.	Substitute; mustered out with company June 25, 1865.
Funderburg, Benjamin F	....do....	19	Oct. 16, 1863	3 yrs.	Mustered out with company June 25, 1865.
Gallispie, James.........	....do....	18	June 5, 1864	3 yrs.	Substitute; mustered out with company June 25, 1865.
Gogerty, Patrick.........	....do....	18	Aug. 22, 1862	3 yrs.	Captured June 15, 1863, at battle of Winchester, Va.; wounded May —, 1864, in action; mustered out with company June 25, 1865.
Haines, George W.......	....do....	22	Sept. 4, 1862	3 yrs.	Captured May 6, 1864, at battle of the Wilderness, Va.; mustered out June 17, 1865, at Camp Chase, O., by order of War Department.
Havens, John J..........	....do....	27	Aug. 19, 1862	3 yrs.	Wounded June 15, 1863, in battle of Winchester, Va.; also Sept. 19, 1864, in battle of Opequan, Va.; mustered out with company June 25, 1865.
Heiser, John H..........	....do....	29	Aug. 22, 1862	3 yrs.	Captured June 15, 1863, at battle of Winchester, Va.; also May 6, 1864, at battle of the Wilderness, Va.; died Feb. 1, 1865, in Rebel Prison at Florence, S. C.
Hoy, Levi...............	....do....	40	May 25, 1864	3 yrs.	Drafted; mustered out with company June 25, 1865.
Johnson, Jacob..........	....do....	45	Sept. 4, 1862	3 yrs.	Died Dec. 3, 1862, in hospital at New Creek, Virginia.
Kauffman, Henry E.....	....do....	21	Aug. 22, 1862	3 yrs.	Mustered out with company June 25, 1865.
Kiler, Jacob P.....	....do....	19	Aug. 22, 1862	3 yrs.	Wounded June 3, 1864, in battle of Cold Harbor, Va.; discharged June 14, 1865, at Philadelphia, Pa., on Surgeon's certificate of disability.
Kirkwood, Wm. A. J....	....do....	33	Sept. 6, 1862	3 yrs.	Captured June 15, 1863, at battle of Winchester, Va.; discharged March 21, 1865, for wounds received May 5, 1864, in battle of the Wilderness, Va.
Kissinger, William......	....do....	31	Sept. 4, 1862	3 yrs.	
Kline, John S............	....do....	24	Aug. 16, 1862	3 yrs.	Discharged March 25, 1863, at Columbus, O., on Surgeon's certificate of disability.
Kooglar, Jacob H........	....do....	22	Aug. 18, 1862	3 yrs.	Died Feb. 22, 1863, at his home in Greene County, O.
Kooglar, John..........	....do....	21	Oct. 8, 1862	3 yrs.	Discharged Feb. 16, 1865, for wounds received July 22, 1864, in action.
Lamb, Jackson..........	....do....	24	Aug. 20, 1862	3 yrs.	
Lewis, William C........	....do....	30	June 4, 1864	3 yrs.	Substitute; captured July 9, 1864, at battle of Monocacy, Md.; paroled Feb. 22, 1865; furloughed March 6, 1865, from Camp Chase, O. No further record found.

Names.	Rank.	Age.	Date of Entering the Service.	Period of Service.	Remarks.
Lindamood, Moses	Private..	36	Aug. 21, 1862	3 yrs.	Mustered out with company June 25, 1865.
Luckey, Joseph	....do....	20	Aug. 21, 1862	3 yrs.	Captured May 6, 1864, at battle of the Wilderness, Va.; died Dec. 10, 1864, in Rebel Prison at Florence, S. C.
Martin, Erastus B.	....do....	44	Aug. 20, 1862	3 yrs.	Captured June 15, 1863, at battle of Winchester, Va.; mustered out June 17, 1865, at Washington, D. C., by order of War Department.
Middleton, John L.	....do....	26	Aug. 18, 1862	3 yrs.	Transferred to Veteran Reserve Corps Jan. —, 1864.
Middleton, Robert W.	....do....	18	Aug. 22, 1862	3 yrs.	Mustered out with company June 25, 1865.
Miller, William	....do....	20	Aug. 16, 1862	3 yrs.	Wounded Oct. 9, 1864, in battle of Cedar Creek, Va.; mustered out with company June 25, 1865.
Motz, William J.	....do....	18	Dec. 16, 1863	3 yrs.	Mustered out June 13, 1865, at Philadelphia, Pa.; by order of War Department.
Musselman, Michael	....do....	39	Aug. 19, 1862	3 yrs.	Reduced from Corporal ——; mustered out June 22, 1865, at Chester, Pa., by order of War Department.
Myers, James	....do....	45	Aug. 8, 1862	3 yrs.	Captured June 15, 1863, at battle of Winchester, Va.; wounded June 3, 1864, in battle of Cold Harbor, Va.; mustered out with company June 25, 1865.
Protzman, Silas	....do....	20	Aug. 18, 1862	3 yrs.	Reduced from Sergeant Dec. 31, 1864; mustered out with company June 25, 1865.
Ransom, Stephen	....do....	40	Aug. 22, 1862	3 yrs.	Discharged May 21, 1863, at Winchester, Va., on Surgeon's certificate of disability.
Raynor, William S	....do....	19	Aug. 19, 1862	3 yrs.	Wounded Nov. 27, 1863, in battle of Mine Run. Va.; captured May 5, 1864, in battle of the Wilderness, Va.; mustered out with company June 25, 1865.
Rike, Jonathan L.	....do....	28	Sept. 16, 1862	3 yrs.	Died Dec. 16, 1863, at Alexandria, Va., of wounds received Nov. 27, 1863, in battle of Mine Run, Va.
Roberts, Oliver A.	....do....	26	Feb. 14, 1865	1 yr.	Mustered out with company June 25, 1865.
Seldomridge, George W.	....do....	23	Aug. 9, 1862	3 yrs.	Mustered out with company June 25, 1865.
Serface, Reuben P.	....do....	23	Aug. 18, 1862	3 yrs.	Reduced from 1st Sergeant Jan. 1, 1863; mustered out with company June 25, 1865.
Serface, William H	....do....	25	Aug. 18, 1862	3 yrs.	Mustered out with company June 25, 1865.
Shaffer, John W	....do....	42	Sept. 4, 1862	3 yrs.	Captured May 6, 1864, at battle of the Wilderness, Va.; paroled Nov. 25, 1864; mustered out June 17, 1865, at Camp Chase, O., by order of War Department.
Shindledecker, Miles	....do....	18	Aug. 4, 1862	3 yrs.	Wounded June 14 and captured June 15, 1863, in battle of Winchester, Va.; discharged Feb. 10, 1865, for wounds received June 3, 1864, in battle of Cold Harbor, Va.
Sinsabaugh, James	....do....	44	Feb. 3, 1864	3 yrs.	
Smith, Andrew J	....do....	31	Sept. 26, 1864	1 yr.	Mustered out with company June 25, 1865.
Smith, William	....do....	25	Oct. 14, 1862	3 yrs.	Captured June 15, 1863, at battle of Winchester, Va.; wounded May 9, 1864, in battle of Spottsylvania C. H., Va.; mustered out with company June 25, 1865.
Stratton, Henry	....do....	17	Aug. 22, 1862	3 yrs.	Mustered out with company June 25, 1865.
Strome, Josephus	....do....	18	Feb. 24, 1864	3 yrs.	Mustered out with company June 25, 1865.
Swadner, William H	....do....	19	Aug. 20, 1862	3 yrs.	Discharged Dec. 17, 1863, at Columbus, O., on Surgeon's certificate of disability.
Taylor, Charles	....do....	23	Aug. 22, 1862	3 yrs.	Appointed Corporal March —, 1863; reduced Sept. 1, 1864; discharged June 26, 1865, at Camp Dennison, O., on Surgeon's certificate of disability.
Thomas, Robert G	....do....	17	Aug. 5, 1862	3 yrs.	Mustered as Musician; mustered out June 13, 1865, at Philadelphia, Pa., by order of War Department.
Tracy, John A.	....do....	25	Aug. 17, 1862	3 yrs.	Transferred to Co. D, 1st Regiment, Veteran Reserve Corps, June 15, 1864; mustered out July 14, 1865, at Elmira, N. Y., by order of War Department.
Turner, James	....do....	50	Aug. 21, 1862	3 yrs.	Transferred to Veteran Reserve Corps Jan. 18, 1864.
Underwood, James	....do....	48	Aug. 20, 1862	3 yrs.	Captured June 15, 1863, at battle of Winchester, Va.
Underwood, John	....do....	24	Aug. 19, 1862	3 yrs.	Mustered out with company June 25, 1865.
Wallace, Charles W	....do....	29	Aug. 22, 1862	3 yrs.	Captured July 9, 1864, at battle of Monocacy, Md.; paroled Feb. 25, 1865; mustered out June 10, 1865, at Camp Chase, O., by order of War Department.
Watts, James	....do....	21	Aug. 20, 1862	3 yrs.	Captured June 15, 1863, at battle of Winchester, Va.; wounded June 3, 1864, in battle of Cold Harbor, Va.; also Sept. 19, 1864, in battle of Opequan, Va.; mustered out May 13, 1865, at Chester, Pa., by order of War Department.
Watts, John M	....do....	17	Aug. 22, 1862	3 yrs.	Wounded Sept. 19, 1864, in battle of Opequan, Va.; mustered out with company June 25, 1865.

Names.	Rank.	Age	Date of Entering the Service.	Period of Service.	Remarks.
Watts, William	Private	..	Aug. 20, 1862	3 yrs.	Discharged April 18, 1863, at Columbus, O., on Surgeon's certificate of disability.
Wheeler, Charles W	....do	27	June 18, 1864	3 yrs.	Substitute; captured July 9, 1864, at battle of Monocacy, Md. No further record found.
Wilson, Daniel	....do	44	Sept. 26, 1864	1 yr.	Died April 10, 1865, of wounds received March 25, 1865, in action near Petersburg, Va.
Wilson, Jacob	....do	22	Aug. 20, 1862	3 yrs.	Captured June 15, 1863, at battle of Winchester, Va.; mustered out with company June 25, 1865.
Wintrich, Alexander	....do	18	Oct. 14, 1862	3 yrs.	Captured June 15, 1863, at battle of Winchester, Va.: wounded May 6, 1864, in battle of the Wilderness, Va.; mustered out with company June 25, 1865.
Wood, Paul	....do	25	June 14, 1864	3 yrs.	Substitute; captured July 9, 1864, at battle of Monocacy, Md.; paroled Nov. 19, 1864; transferred to Camp Chase, O., Jan. 19, 1865. No further record found.
Wooley, William	....do	18	Sept. 18, 1863	3 yrs.	Captured June 15, 1863, at battle of Winchester, Va.; mustered out with company June 25, 1865.

COMPANY G.

Mustered in Oct. 3, 1862, at Camp Piqua, O., by Alexander E. Drake, Captain 2d Infantry, U. S. A. Mustered out June 25, 1865, near Washington, D. C., by J. C. Robinson, Brevet Major and A. C. M. 3d Division, 6th Army Corps.

Names.	Rank.	Age	Date of Entering the Service.	Period of Service.	Remarks.
Joseph C. Ullery	Captain	32	Aug. 16, 1862	3 yrs.	Mustered out July 1, 1865, at Columbus, O., by order of War Department.
Charles M. Gross	1st Lieut.	34	Aug. 15, 1862	3 yrs.	Captured June 14, 1863, at battle of Winchester, Va.; appointed Captain March 21, 1864, but not mustered until May 9, 1865; transferred to Co. D as 1st Lieutenant Aug. 25, 1864; from Co. D Feb. 17, 1865; mustered as Captain and transferred to Co. B May 9, 1865.
Joshua S. Deeter	....do	22	Aug. 18, 1862	3 yrs.	Promoted to 2d Lieutenant from 1st Sergeant to date April 12, 1864; 1st Lieutenant to date June 14, 1864; died Sept. 22, 1864, of wounds received Sept. 19, 1864, in battle of Opequan, Va.
Edward D. Simes	....do	22	Aug. 19, 1862	3 yrs.	Promoted to 2d Lieutenant from 1st Sergeant July 22, 1864; wounded Sept. 19, 1864, in battle of Opequan, Va.; promoted to 1st Lieutenant Dec. 19, 1864; discharged Jan. 4, 1865, by order of War Department.
Dock W. Richardson	....do	26	Aug. 12, 1862	3 yrs.	Promoted to 2d Lieutenant from Sergt. Major Dec. 24, 1864; 1st Lieutenant May 31, 1865; mustered out with company June 25, 1865.
George W. Miller	2d Lieut.	34	Aug. 16, 1862	1 yr.	Captured June 14, 1863, at battle of Winchester, Va.; promoted to 1st Lieutenant March 21, 1864, but not mustered; resigned April 18, 1864.
Erastus, Layton	....do	19	Aug. 14, 1862	3 yrs.	Promoted from Hospital Steward to date Dec. 9, 1864; to 1st Lieutenant Co. H April 8, 1865.
Jacob Holsinger	1st Sergt.	37	Aug. 22, 1862	3 yrs.	Appointed from Sergeant Aug. 13, 1864; wounded Oct. 19, 1864, in battle of Cedar Creek, Va.; mustered out June 20, 1865, at Columbus, O., by order of War Department.
Peter Nikloi	Sergeant.	40	Aug. 19, 1862	3 yrs.	Discharged Oct. 3, 1863, at Camp Dennison, O., on Surgeon's certificate of disability.
Jeremiah W. Teeter	....do	23	Aug. 18, 1862	3 yrs.	Appointed from Corporal Sept. 23, 1863; captured July 9, 1864, at battle of Monocacy, Md.: died Dec. 20, 1864, in Rebel Prison at Danville, Va.
David Longnecker	....do	25	Aug. 19, 1862	3 yrs.	Captured July 9, 1864, at battle of Monocacy, Md.; appointed from Corporal Nov. 1, 1864: mustered out with company June 25, 1865.
Harvey Brown	....do	27	Aug. 22, 1862	3 yrs.	Appointed Corporal April 22, 1864; Sergeant Jan. 1, 1865; mustered out with company June 25, 1865.
Samuel W. Ullery	....do	26	Aug. 22, 1862	3 yrs.	Appointed from Corporal Nov. 1, 1863; captured May 5, 1864, at battle of the Wilderness, Va.; mustered out June 17, 1865, at Camp Chase, O., by order of War Department.
Richards Pearson	....do	25	Aug. 22, 1862	3 yrs.	Wounded and captured June 15, 1863, at battle of Winchester, Va.; appointed from Corporal April 20, 1864; wounded May 5, 1864, in battle of the Wilderness, Va.; also April 2, 1865, in action near Petersburg, Va.; mustered out June 5, 1865, at Philadelphia, Pa.; by order of War Department.

Names.	Rank.	Age	Date of Entering the Service.	Period of Service.	Remarks.
Charles Fink............	Corporal.	24	Aug. 18, 1862	3 yrs.	
Jacob U. Baumgardner.	....do....	28	Aug. 22, 1862	3 yrs.	Discharged April 22, 1863, at Winchester, Va., on Surgeon's certificate of disability.
Levi Childers.........	...do....	24	Aug. 22, 1862	3 yrs.	Captured June 15, 1863, at battle of Winchester, Va.; died July 23, 1864, at David's Island, New York Harbor, of wounds received June 1, 1864, in battle of Cold Harbor, Va.
Aaron, Stanfield..........	...do....	19	Aug. 19, 1862	3 yrs.	Appointed Sept. 1, 1864; mustered out with company June 15, 1865.
James Mott..............	...do....	26	Aug. 20, 1862	3 yrs.	Captured April 12, 1863, in action near Winchester, Va.; appointed Corporal Nov. 1, 1864; mustered out with company June 25, 1865.
Mark C. Jones.............	...do....	21	Aug. 22, 1862	3 yrs.	Appointed Jan. 1, 1865; mustered out with company June 25, 1865.
Albert M. Rontson.......	...do....	21	Aug. 22, 1862	3 yrs.	Appointed Jan. 1, 1865; mustered out with company June 25, 1865.
George W. Walker........	...do....	20	Aug. 22, 1862	3 yrs.	Wounded June 15, 1863, in battle of Winchester, Va.; appointed Corporal Jan. 1, 1864; wounded May 5, 1864, in battle of the Wilderness, Va.; mustered out June 6, 1865, at Washington, D. C., by order of War Department.
Frank Gulick..............	...do....	22	Aug. 22, 1862	3 yrs.	Captured June 15, 1863, at battle of Winchester, Va.; appointed Corporal Jan. 1, 1864; wounded July 9, 1864, in battle of Monocacy, Md.; mustered out July 1, 1865, at Columbus, O., by order of War Department.
Benjamin Hollopeter...	...do....	30	Aug. 22, 1862	3 yrs.	Appointed Nov. 1, 1864; wounded May 5, 1864, in battle of the Wilderness, Va.; mustered out June 6, 1865, at Columbus, O., by order of War Department.
Daniel W. Debra.........	...do....	18	Aug. 18, 1862	3 yrs.	Appointed April 20, 1864; wounded May 5, 1864, in battle of the Wilderness, Va.; discharged Feb. 6, 1865, at Toledo, O., on Surgeon's certificate of disability.
Isaac A. Landis..........	...do....	21	Aug. 18, 1862	3 yrs.	Appointed Jan. 1, 1864; wounded July 9, 1864, in battle of Monocacy, Md.; transferred to 105th Co., 2d Battalion, Veteran Reserve Corps, Oct. —, 1864; mustered out Sept. 1, 1865, at Philadelphia, Pa., by order of War Department.
Jackson Shade..........	Wagoner.	33	Aug. 19, 1862	3 yrs.	Captured June 15, 1863, at battle of Winchester, Va.; mustered out with company June 25, 1865.
Allers, August..........	Private..	22	Nov. 23, 1863	3 yrs.	Transferred to 2d Brigade Band, 3d Division, 6th Army Corps, Jan. 4, 1865, from which mustered out June 25, 1865, near Washington, D. C.
Babylon, Jeremiah.......	...do....	24	Aug. 22, 1862	3 yrs.	Captured April 12, 1863, in action near Winchester, Va.; died July 23, 1864, at David's Island, New York Harbor.
Babylon, Lewis L........	...do....	18	Aug. 20, 1862	3 yrs.	Mustered out with company June 25, 1865.
Barnhart, Henry.........	...do....	19	Aug. 20, 1862	3 yrs.	Mustered out with company June 25, 1865.
Bartmess, James.........	...do....	17	Aug. 22, 1862	3 yrs.	Captured June 14, 1863, at battle of Winchester, Va.; mustered out with company June 25, 1865.
Baumgardner, Martin...	...do....	20	Sept. 20, 1864	1 yr.	Mustered out with company June 25, 1865.
Benshepper, Henry......	...do....	38	Sept. 4, 1862	3 yrs.	Captured June 14, 1863, at battle of Winchester, Va.; wounded May 5, 1864, in battle of the Wilderness, Va.; also April 2, 1865, in action near Petersburg, Va.; mustered out June 17, 1865, at Washington, D. C., by order of War Department.
Book, John A............	...do....	22	Aug. 18, 1862	3 yrs.	Died June 21, 1863, at Harper's Ferry, Va.
Brady, James..........	...do....	25	Jan. 11, 1865	1 yr.	Mustered out with company June 25, 1865.
Brown, Ahijah..........	...do....	24	Aug. 22, 1862	3 yrs.	Mustered out with company June 25, 1865.
Brown, George..........	...do....	18	June 21, 1864	3 yrs.	Substitute; mustered out with company June 25, 1865.
Brown, James............	...do....	25	Aug. 22, 1862	3 yrs.	Wounded May 5, 1864, in battle of the Wilderness, Va.; discharged May 13, 1865, at Danville, Va., on Surgeon's certificate of disability.
Brown, Messer..........	...do....	34	Oct. 6, 1862	3 yrs.	Mustered out with company June 25, 1865.
Bushnell, Collins........	...do....	23	May 25, 1864	3 yrs.	Drafted.
Butt, Lewis...............	...do....	21	Sept. 5, 1862	3 yrs.	Killed July 9, 1864, in battle of Monocacy, Md.
Clark, Thomas...........	...do....	29	Aug. 22, 1862	3 yrs.	Captured June 7, 1863, in action near Pughtown, Va.; died May 19, 1864, at Fredericksburg, Va., of wounds received May 5, 1864, in battle of the Wilderness, Va.
Clegg, Harrison	...do....	19	May 22, 1863	3 yrs.	Died Nov. 27, 1863, at Fort Schuler, New York Harbor.
Coate, Daniel M.........	...do....	20	Sept. 8, 1863	3 yrs.	Wounded May 5, 1864, in battle of the Wilderness, Va.; mustered out with company June 25, 1865.
Coate, Elias B...........	...do....	32	Sept. 5, 1862	3 yrs.	Mustered out July 7, 1865, at Philadelphia, Pa., by order of War Department.

Names.	Rank.	Age.	Date of Entering the Service.	Period of Service.	Remarks.
Conner, John W.........	Private..	28	May 25, 1864	3 yrs.	Drafted; died Aug. 13, 1864, at David's Island, New York Harbor, of wounds received July 9, 1864, in battle of Monocacy, Md.
Cooper, Luther J........	....do....	24	Aug. 18, 1862	3 yrs.	Mustered out with company June 25, 1865.
Coppock, David C.......	....do....	30	Aug. 22, 1862	3 yrs.	Wounded Oct. 19, 1864, in battle of Cedar Creek, Va.; mustered out with company June 25, 1865.
Coppock, Henry.........	....do....	20	Aug. 22, 1862	3 yrs.	Did May 10, 1863, at Winchester, Va.
Cottrell, Thomas J.....	....do....	22	Nov. 26, 1863	3 yrs.	Transferred to 2d Brigade Band, 3d Division, 6th Army Corps, Jan. 4, 1865, from which mustered out June 25, 1865, near Washington, D. C.
Crawford, Thomas	....do....	27	May 25, 1864	3 yrs.	Drafted; died Aug. 12, 1864, at David's Island, New York Harbor.
Croft, James.:........	....do....	30	Aug. 22, 1862	3 yrs.	Wounded Oct. 19, 1864, in battle of Cedar Creek, Va.; transferred to Veteran Reserve Corps Jan. 1, 1865; mustered out July 11, 1865, at Albany, N. Y., by order of War Department.
Croghan, Edward........	....do....	24	Nov. 25, 1864	3 yrs.	Drafted; died Aug. 6, 1864.
Cruea, Joseph S. ...:..	....do....	27	Aug. 22, 1862	3 yrs.	Discharged March 17, 1863, at Winchester, Va., on Surgeon's certificate of disability.
Cushman, James L......	....do....	26	Nov. 23, 1863	3 yrs.	Transferred to 2d Brigade Band, 3d Division, 6th Army Corps, Jan. 4, 1865, from which mustered out June 25, 1865, near Washington, D. C.
Dalie, James H..........	....do....	21	Dec. 15, 1863	3 yrs.	Transferred to 2d Brigade Band, 3d Division, 6th Army Corps, Jan. 4, 1865, from which mustered out June 25, 1865, near Washington, D. C.
Eggerman, Conrad......	....do....	42	May 25, 1864	3 yrs.	Drafted; died Aug. 21, 1864, at Annapolis, Md.
Fisher, Harrison........	....do....	21	Aug. 20, 1862	3 yrs.	Discharged Jan. 18, 1864, at Camp Dennison, O., on Surgeon's certificate of disability.
Fletcher, William........	....do....	23	June 21, 1864	3 yrs.	Substitute; captured July 9, 1864, at battle of Monocacy, Md.; died Feb. 28, 1865, in Rebel Prison at Danville, Va.
Floummer, Barnhart ...	....do....	37	Aug. 22, 1862	3 yrs.	Wounded June 3, 1864, in battle of Cold Harbor, Va.; mustered out June 7, 1865, at Camp Dennison, O., by order of War Department.
Freeman, Alexander C..	....do....	29	Jan. 11, 1865	1 yr.	Mustered out June 9, 1865, at Baltimore, Md., by order of War Department.
Fullerton, Melanchthon	....do....	18	Sept. 18, 1863	3 yrs.	Discharged Feb. 20, 1864, at Washington, D. C., on Surgeon's certificate of disability.
Furnace, Isaac W........	....do....	18	Aug. 18, 1862	3 yrs.	Killed Oct. 19, 1864, in battle of Cedar Creek, Virginia.
Furnace, Joshua........	....do....	24	Dec. 11, 1863	3 yrs.	Wounded May 5, 1864, in battle of the Wilderness, Va.; mustered out June 12, 1865, by order of War Department.
Gill, W. Josiah. ....:	....do....	25	Aug. 19, 1862	3 yrs.	Captured June 13, 1863, at battle of Winchester, Va.; reduced from Sergeant April 20, 1864; mustered out with company June 25, 1865.
Green, John............	....do....	18	Sept. 18, 1863	3 yrs.	Captured July 9, 1864, at battle of Monocacy, Md.; died March 2, 1865, at Annapolis, Md.
Gindle, Benjamin........	....do....	25	Aug. 22, 1862	3 yrs.	Mustered out with company June 25, 1865.
Hall, Isaac N.............	....do....	18	Sept. 20, 1864	1 yr.	Mustered out with company June 25, 1865.
Hanks, Columbus M....	....do....	18	Sept. 22, 1863	3 yrs.	Discharged March 14, 1864, at Washington, D. C., on Surgeon's certificate of disability.
Harrison, William H....	....do....	21	Nov. 29, 1863	3 yrs.	Transferred to 2d Brigade Band, 3d Division, 6th Army Corps, Jan. 4, 1865, from which mustered out June 25, 1865, near Washington, D. C.
Hart, John..............	....do....	30	Aug. 20, 1862	3 yrs.	Mustered out with company June 25, 1865.
Hickman, Isaac D.......	....do....	18	Aug. 22, 1862	3 yrs.	Mustered out with company June 25, 1865.
Hoyworth, Alfred........	....do....	21	Aug. 22, 1862	3 yrs.	Died May 5, 1864, at the Wilderness, Va.
Hurley, Peter J.........	....do....	20	Sept. 5, 1863	3 yrs.	Mustered out with company June 25, 1865.
Iddings, Jefferson D...♦	....do....	18	Oct. 4, 1863	3 yrs.	Wounded May 5, 1864, in battle of the Wilderness, Va.; discharged Dec. 29, 1864, as minor, by order of War Department.
Ketchman, William....:.	....do....	27	Aug. 19, 1862	3 yrs.	Captured June 15, 1863, at battle of Winchester, Va.; wounded June 3, 1864, in battle of Cold Harbor, Va.; discharged Jan. 12, 1865, on Surgeon's certificate of disability.
King, John C..............	....do....	26	Nov. 23, 1863	3 yrs.	Transferred to 2d Brigade Band, 3d Division, 6th Army Corps, Jan. 4, 1865, from which mustered out June 25, 1865, near Washington, D. C.
Koons, John.............	....do....	20	Sept. 5, 1862	3 yrs.	Died March 1, 1863, at Cumberland, Md.
Langston, Jesse..........	....do....	18	Aug. 22, 1862	3 yrs.	Mustered out with company June 25, 1865.
Lasure, Samuel G........	....do....	22	May 25, 1864	3 yrs.	Drafted; wounded July 9, 1864, in battle of Monocacy, Md.; discharged June 10, 1865, at Frederick, Md., on Surgeon's certificate of disability.
Locke, William W.......	....do....	32	Aug. 22, 1862	3 yrs.	Promoted to Hospital Steward Aug. 22, 1862.
Long, Abraham P.......	....do....	19	Sept. 5, 1862	3 yrs.	Wounded May 5, 1864, in battle of the Wilderness, Va.; discharged May 11, 1865, at Washington, D. C., on Surgeon's certificate of disability.

Names.	Rank.	Age.	Date of Entering the Service.	Period of Service.	Remarks.
Long, Daniel E..........	Private..	18	Aug. 19, 1862	3 yrs.	Captured June 15, 1863, at battle of Winchester, Va.; mustered out with company June 25, 1865.
Long, Henry	....do....	20	Aug. 22, 1862	3 yrs.	Killed June 15, 1863, in battle of Winchester, Virginia.
McGee, John.............	....do....	28	Aug. 22, 1862	3 yrs.	Died Dec. 10, 1862, at Cumberland, Md.
Mader, David	....do....	20	Aug. 20, 1862	3 yrs.	Died Aug. 23, 1863, at Alexandria, Va.
Martin, David J.	....do....	33	Aug. 22, 1862	3 yrs.	Promoted to Com. Sergeant Aug. 22, 1862.
Mathers, John...........	....do....	34	Jan. 25, 1864	3 yrs.	Killed May 5, 1864, in battle of the Wilderness, Virginia.
Miles, Henry W..........	....do....	18	Aug. 22, 1862	3 yrs.	Captured June 14, 1863, at battle of Winchester, Va.; mustered out with company June 25, 1865.
Myres, Henry	....do....	18	Aug. 18, 1862	3 yrs.	Wounded April 2, 1865, in action at Petersburg, Va.; mustered out with company June 25, 1865.
Oaks, Peter..............	....do....	27	May 25, 1864	3 yrs.	Drafted; captured July 9, 1864, at battle of Monocacy, Md. No further record found.
O'Benour, Adam.........	....do....	33	May 25, 1864	3 yrs.	Drafted; mustered out with company June 25, 1865.
O'Conner, John,.........	....do....	18	Sept. 5, 1862	3 yrs.	Captured June 15, 1863, at battle of Winchester, Va.; mustered out with company June 25, 1865.
Patterson, Samuel........	....do....	25	Sept. 7, 1862	3 yrs.	Died Jan. 26, 1863, at Winchester, Va.
Pearson, Job	....do....	21	Aug. 22, 1862	3 yrs.	Killed June 3, 1864, in battle of Cold Harbor, Virginia.
Pearson, Levi	....do....	18	Oct. 13, 1863	3 yrs.	Discharged April 26, 1864, at Washington, D. C., on Surgeon's certificate of disability.
Pemberton, Moses........	....do....	20	Aug. 22, 1862	3 yrs.	Died Dec. 22, 1863, at Cumberland, Md.
Penny, John W...........	....do....	25	Sept. 6, 1862	3 yrs.	Mustered out with company June 25, 1865.
Randall, Eugene.........	....do....	25	May 25, 1864	3 yrs.	Drafted; wounded and captured July 9, 1864, at battle of Monocacy, Md.; died March 8, 1865, at Annapolis, Md.
Reibes, Benjamin.........	....do....	18	Feb. 4, 1864	3 yrs.	Died Feb. 29, 1864, at Brandy Station, Va.
Reiber, Jacob	....do....	27	Oct. 5, 1863	3 yrs.	Wounded May 5, 1864, in battle of the Wilderness, Va.; mustered out June 2, 1865, at Columbus, O., by order of War Department.
Reiber, Philip H.........	....do....	21	Aug. 22, 1862	3 yrs.	Wounded and captured May 5, 1864, at battle of the Wilderness, Va.; died Oct. 1, 1864, in Rebel Prison at Andersonville, Ga.
Reichman, John C.......	....do....	35	Aug. 22, 1862	3 yrs.	Mustered out with company June 25, 1865.
Reynolds, Melville C.....	....do....	21	Oct. 22, 1863	3 yrs.	Mustered out with company June 25, 1865.
Rhine, John..............	....do....	28	Sept. 5, 1862	3 yrs.	
Rhoades, Henry..........	....do....	19	Aug. 22, 1862	3 yrs.	Died Aug. 9, 1863, at Annapolis, Md.
Rideout, Alexander C....	....do....	20	Sept. 5, 1864	1 yr.	Mustered out May 13, 1865, at Cumberland, Md., by order of War Department.
Routson, Elias W.........	....do....	19	Aug. 22, 1862	3 yrs.	Mustered out with company June 25, 1865.
Shell, Henry	....do....	18	Aug. 20, 1862	3 yrs.	Wounded May 5, 1864, in battle of the Wilderness, Va.; mustered out with company June 25, 1865.
Shertzer, Henry N.......	....do....	18	Sept. 8, 1863	3 yrs.	Killed Sept. 19, 1864, in battle of Opequan, Virginia.
Shoe, David.	....do....	24	Aug. 18, 1862	3 yrs.	Reduced from Corporal ——; died Feb. 3, 1864, at Brandy Station. Va.
Shoup, Martin	....do....	23	Aug. 19, 1862	3 yrs.	Discharged March 13, 1863, at Winchester, Va., on Surgeon's certificate of disability.
Simpson, Samuel.........	....do....	16	Oct. 3, 1862	3 yrs.	Discharged Sept. 6, 1863, at Convalescent Camp, Va., on Surgeon's certificate of disability.
Stanfield, Horatio C.....	....do....	21	Nov. 6, 1863	3 yrs.	Mustered out with company June 25, 1865.
Streib, Barnhart	....do....	24	Aug. 21, 1862	3 yrs.	Mustered out with company June 25, 1865.
Taylor, Joseph...........	....do....	20	Aug. 22, 1862	3 yrs.	Mustered out with company June 25, 1865.
Torrence, Aaron W.......	....do....	29	Dec. 7, 1863	3 yrs.	Transferred to 2d Brigade Band, 3d Division, 6th Army Corps, Jan. 4, 1865, from which discharged April 12, 1865, at Annapolis, Md., on Surgeon's certificate of disability.
Tucker, Francis C........	....do....	20	Aug. 22, 1862	3 yrs.	Captured June 14, 1863, at battle of Winchester, Va.; mustered out with company June 25, 1865.
Van Kirk, John	....do....	22	Aug. 22, 1862	3 yrs.	Captured June 15, 1863, near Charlestown, Va.
Walker, Henry C.........	....do....	30	Aug. 20, 1862	3 yrs.	Captured June 15, 1863, at battle of Winchester, Va.; wounded Sept. 19, 1864, in battle of Opequan, Va.; discharged May 6, 1865, at Philadelphia, Pa., on Surgeon's certificate of disability.
Weddle, William H.......	....do....	21	Aug. 18, 1862	3 yrs.	Appointed Corporal ——; reduced ——; captured June 15, 1863, at battle of Winchester, Va.; discharged May 13, 1865, at Danville, Va., on Surgeon's certificate of disability.
Weisman, John	....do....	22	Sept. 5, 1862	3 yrs.	Captured June 15, 1863, at battle of Winchester, Va.; killed May 5, 1864, in battle of the Wilderness, Va.
Whitmer, George W......	....do....	20	Aug. 18, 1862	3 yrs.	Wounded May 5, 1864, in battle of the Wilderness, Va.; mustered out June 13, 1865, at Columbus, O.

Names.	Rank.	Age.	Date of Entering the Service.	Period of Service.	Remarks.
Worthington, John N...	Private..	27	Nov. 23, 1863	3 yrs.	Transferred to 2d Brigade Band, 3d Division, 6th Army Corps, Jan. 4, 1865, from which mustered out June 25, 1865, near Washington, D. C.
Wright, Alexander......	....do....	26	Aug. 22, 1862	3 yrs.	Captured June 7, 1863, in action near Pughtown, Va.; mustered out with company June 25, 1865.
Young, Nelson...........	....do....	21	June 21, 1864	3 yrs.	Substitute : mustered out with company June 25, 1865.

COMPANY H.

Mustered in Oct. 2, 1862, at Camp Piqua, O., by Alexander E. Drake, Captain 2d Infantry, U. S. A. Mustered out June 25, 1865, near Washington, D. C., by J. C. Robinson, Brevet Major and A. C. M. 3d Division, 6th Army Corps.

Names.	Rank.	Age.	Date of Entering the Service.	Period of Service.	Remarks.
Joseph G. Snodgrass.....	Captain.	32	Aug. 5, 1862	3 yrs.	Appointed Sept. 1, 1862; wounded June 14, 1863, in battle of the Wilderness, Va.; captured July 9, 1864, at battle of Monocacy, Md.; mustered out with company June 25, 1865.
William A. Orr..........	1st Lieut.	26	Aug. 8, 1862	3 yrs.	Resigned Feb. 22, 1864.
George P. Boyer.........	....do....	23	Aug. 5, 1862	3 yrs.	Promoted from 2d Lieutenant March 21, 1864 ; to Captain Co. D Nov. 3, 1864.
Elam Harter	....do....	30	Aug. 8, 1862	3 yrs.	Appointed 1st Sergeant from Sergeant ——; promoted to 2d Lieutenant Co. F July 22, 1864; from 2d Lieutenant Co. F to date Dec. 9, 1864 ; to Captain Co. F Jan. 31, 1865.
Erastus Layton...........	....do....	19	Aug. 14, 1862	3 yrs.	Promoted from 2d Lieutenant Co. G April 8, 1865; mustered out with company June 25, 1865.
William L. Robertson...	2d Lieut.	27	Aug. 8, 1862	3 yrs.	Promoted from 1st Sergeant April 12, 1864 ; to 1st Lieutenant Sept. 8, 1864, but not mustered ; discharged Nov. 2, 1864, for wounds received June 3, 1864, in battle of Cold Harbor, Va.
Edward S. Dukeshier....	....do....	42	Aug. 15, 1862	3 yrs.	Promoted from 1st Sergeant Co. E to date Aug. 8, 1864; to 1st Lieutenant Co. E Jan. 31, 1865.
Henry L. R. Biddle......	1st Sergt.	23	Aug. 8, 1862	3 yrs.	Wounded and captured June 15, 1863, at battle of Winchester, Va.; wounded June 12, 1864, in action; appointed 1st Sergeant from Sergeant Aug. 13, 1864 ; wounded Sept. 19, 1864, in battle of Opequan, Va.; mustered out with company June 25, 1865.
John B. Mitchell........	Sergeant.	20	Aug. 8, 1862	3 yrs.	Captured June 15, 1863, at battle of Winchester, Va.; mustered out with company June 25, 1865.
William B. Page..........	....do....	36	Aug. 8, 1862	3 yrs.	Mustered out with company June 25, 1865.
William Noggle..........	....do....	25	Aug. 9, 1862	3 yrs.	Captured June 15, 1863, at battle of Winchester, Va.; appointed from Corporal April 20, 1864 ; mustered out with company June 25, 1865.
William R. Moyer........	....do....	21	Aug. 4, 1862	3 yrs.	Appointed Corporal ——; Sergeant Aug. 13, 1864 ; mustered out with company June 25, 1865.
Daniel Dowlar	Corporal.	23	Aug. 9, 1862	3 yrs.	Mustered out with company June 25, 1865.
David N. Hamilton......	....do....	22	Aug. 9, 1862	3 yrs.	Captured June 15, 1863, at battle of Winchester, Va.; died May 15, 1864, at Washington, D. C., of wounds received May 5, 1864, in battle of the Wilderness, Va.
Randolph F. Hageman .	....do....	23	Aug. 10, 1862	3 yrs.	Mustered out June 30, 1865, at Columbus, O., by order of War Department.
George Hamilton........	....do....	33	Aug. 8, 1862	3 yrs.	Discharged March 5, 1863, at Winchester, Va., on Surgeon's certificate of disability.
George S. Harter........	....do....	18	Aug. 9, 1862	3 yrs.	Appointed Sept. 21, 1863; captured May 6, 1864, at battle of the Wilderness, Va.; mustered out with company June 25, 1865.
Adam Horine...........	....do....	18	Aug. 18, 1862	3 yrs.	Appointed March 20, 1863; mustered out with company June 25, 1865.
Levi Hart....:..........	....do....	21	Aug 8, 1862	3 yrs.	Wounded June 15, 1863, in battle of Winchester, Va.; also July 9, 1864, in battle of Monocacy, Md.; appointed Corporal April 20, 1864; mustered out with company June 25, 1865.
James W. Ludy..........	....do....	18	Aug. 9, 1862	3 yrs.	Appointed Aug. 13, 1864; mustered out with company June 25, 1865.
Henry C. Schriver.......	....do....	18	Aug. 8, 1862	3 yrs.	Appointed Corporal Aug. 13, 1864; mustered out with company June 25, 1865.
William R. Hoeg........	....do....	33	May 24, 1864	3 yrs.	Drafted ; mustered out Oct. 11, 1865, at Columbus, O., by order of War Department.

Names.	Rank.	Age.	Date of Entering the Service.	Period of Service.	Remarks.
John Smith............	Corporal.	19	Aug. 8, 1862	3 yrs.	Wounded May 5. 1864, in battle of the Wilderness, Va.; killed Sept. 19, 1864, in battle of Opequan, Va.
Levi W. Pearce..........	....do....	20	Aug. 9, 1862	3 yrs.	Captured June 15, 1863, at battle of Winchester, Va.; wounded June 3, 1864, in battle of Cold Harbor, Va.; appointed Corporal Sept. 28, 1864; mustered out with company June 25, 1865.
Adkins, Riley	Private..	20	Aug. 10, 1862	3 yrs.	Discharged Feb. 26, 1863, at Columbus, O., on Surgeon's certificate of disability.
Armstrong, John H	....do....	22	Aug. 8, 1862	3 yrs.	Captured June 15, 1863, at battle of Winchester, Va.: wounded May 5, 1864, in battle of the Wilderness, Va.; killed March 31, 1865, in action near Petersburg, Va.
Ballenger, John.....	....do....	27	Aug. 21, 1862	3 yrs.	Reduced from Corporal July 30, 1864; mustered out with company June 25 1865.
Bingham, William H....	....do....	18	Sept. 19, 1862	3 yrs.	Discharged Dec. 22, 1863, at Washington, D. C., on Surgeon's certificate of disability.
Birge, Robert W........	....do....	21	Aug. 8, 1862	3 yrs.	Captured June 15, 1863, at battle of Winchester, Va.; also May 5, 1864, at battle of the Wilderness, Va.; supposed killed. No further record found.
Bradley, James..........	....do....	27	June 9, 1864	3 yrs.	Substitute; captured July 9, 1864, at battle of Monocacy. Md.; died Dec. 25, 1864, in Rebel Prison at Salisbury, N. C.
Bricker, Joseph L........	....do....	29	Aug. 9, 1862	3 yrs.	Wounded May 6, 1864, in battle of the Wilderness, Va.; mustered out with company June 25, 1865.
Buck, Samuel W........	....do....	18	Aug. 21, 1862	3 yrs.	Captured June 15, 1863, at battle of Winchester, Va.; discharged April 3, 1865, at Columbus, O., for wounds received July 9, 1864, in battle of Monocacy, Md.
Buckingham, Harvey...	....do....	18	Aug. 8, 1862	3 yrs.	Captured June 15, 1863, at battle of Winchester, Va.; wounded Sept. 19, 1864, in battle of Opequan, Va.; mustered out May 23, 1865, at Philadelphia, Pa., by order of War Department.
Buell, George M..........	....do....	34	Sept. 1, 1862	3 yrs.	Discharged Feb. 3, 1863, at Winchester, Va., on Surgeon's certificate of disability.
Camp, George..........	....do....	20	Aug. 10, 1862	3 yrs.	Captured June 15, 1863, at battle of Winchester, Va.
Camp, James..............	....do....	24	Aug. 10, 1862	3 yrs.	Died July 25, 1863, at Alexandria, Va.
Chapman, Thomas C ...	....do....	19	June 7, 1864	3 yrs.	Substitute; mustered out with company June 25, 1865.
Clark, James..............	....do....	18	Aug. 9, 1862	3 yrs.	Mustered out with company June 25, 1865.
Conkright, John S	....do....	18	Aug. 9, 1862	3 yrs.	
Conover, John	....do....	22	Aug. 8, 1862	3 yrs.	Wounded June 6. 1864, in battle of Cold Harbor, Va.; mustered out with company June 25, 1865.
Cook, James..............	....do....	20	June 20, 1864	3 yrs.	Substitute.
Crowell, Jacob..........	....do....	28	Aug. 10, 1862	3 yrs.	Mustered out with company June 25. 1865.
Davis, Asa W..........	....do....	34	Aug. 8, 1862	3 yrs.	Reduced from Corporal Sept. 21, 1863; discharged Nov. 14, 1863, at Cumberland, Md., on Surgeon's certificate of disability.
Dill, Calvin H..........	....do....	21	Aug. 8, 1862	3 yrs.	Captured June 15, 1863, at battle of Winchester, Va.; died Feb. 15, 1865, at Baltimore, Maryland.
Dowlar, Uriah..........	....do....	20	Aug. 9, 1862	3 yrs.	Captured June 15, 1863, at battle of Winchester, Va.; reduced from Corporal Dec. 8, 1863; discharged April 5, 1865, at Columbus, O., for wounds received May 5, 1864, in battle of the Wilderness, Va.
Daly, George..............	....do....	42	June 8, 1864	3 yrs.	Substitute; mustered out with company June 25, 1865.
Ebling, George..........	....do....	25	Aug. 9, 1862	3 yrs.	Captured June 15, 1863, at battle of Winchester, Va ; discharged April 25, 1864, at Camp Dennison, O., on Surgeon's certificate of disability.
Ennis, Michael..........	,...do....	40	May 20, 1864	3 yrs.	Drafted; mustered out with company June 25, 1865.
Eubank, Hezekiah......	....do....	23	Aug. 10, 1862	3 yrs.	Mustered out with company June 25, 1865.
Fisher, John	....do....	27	Aug. 8. 1862	3 yrs.	Mustered out with company June 25, 1865.
Foulk, Christopher......	....do....	22	Aug. 10, 1862	3 yrs.	Transferred to Co. I, 18th Regiment. Veteran Reserve Corps, April 20. 1864; mustered out July 25. 1865, at Washington, D. C., by order of War Department.
Foulk, Frederick..........	....do....	20	Aug. 10, 1862	3 yrs.	Wounded June 1, 1864, in battle of Cold Harbor, Va.; mustered out with company June 25, 1865.
Funk, Joseph F..........	....do....	22	Aug. 17, 1862	3 yrs.	Wounded June 3, 1864, in battle of Cold Harbor, Va.; mustered out with company June 25, 1865.
Fye, Benjamin..........	....do....	22	Aug. 13, 1862	3 yrs.	Wounded May 5, 1864, in battle of the Wilderness, Va.; mustered out with company June 25, 1865.
Geeting, Daniel W	....do....	19	Aug. 9, 1862	3 yrs.	Died Aug. 16. 1863, at Alexandria, Va.

Names.	Rank.	Age.	Date of Entering the Service.	Period of Service.	Remarks.
Geeting, John H	Private..	21	Aug. 8, 1862	3 yrs.	Wounded ——; captured June 15, 1863, at battle of Winchester. Va.; mustered out with company June 25, 1865.
Greene, Hartwell........	....do....	22	Aug. 9, 1862	3 yrs.	Wounded May 5, 1864, in battle of the Wilderness, Va.; mustered out with company June 25, 1865.
Greene, James R........	....do....	28	Aug. 8, 1862	3 .yrs.	Captured June 15. 1863, at battle of Winchester, Va.; mustered out with company June 25, 1865.
Harless, James F........	....do....	20	Aug. 10, 1862	3 yrs.	Mustered out with company June 25, 1865.
Harless, Johnson........	....do....	21	Aug. 10, 1862	3 yrs.	Died May 3, 1865, at Danville, Va.
Harless, Powell..........	....do....	20	Aug. 8, 1862	3 yrs.	Mustered out with company June 25, 1865.
Hart, Jonathan..........	....do....	20	Aug. 16, 1862	3 yrs.	Wounded and captured June 15, 1863, in battle of Winchester, Va.; mustered out with company June 25, 1865.
Hawley, Luther C........	....do....	23	May 14, 1864	3 yrs.	Drafted; mustered out May 6, 1865, at Danville, Va., by order of War Department.
Hemp, Ephraim..........	....do....	22	Aug. 14, 1862	3 yrs.	Captured June 15, 1863, at battle of Winchester, Va.; also May 5, 1864, at battle of the Wilderness, Va.; supposed killed. No further record found.
Hemp, Josiah W	....do....	19	Aug. 14, 1862	3 yrs.	Captured June 15, 1863, at battle of Winchester, Va.; transferred to Co. C, 11th Regiment, Veteran Reserve Corps, April 17, 1864; mustered out July 29, 1865, at Providence, R. I., by order of War Department.
Hetzler, Cyrus..........	....do....	20	Aug. 8, 1862	3 yrs.	Captured June 15, 1863, at battle of Winchester, Va.; wounded July 9, 1864, in battle of Monocacy, Md.; mustered out with company June 25, 1865.
Hogan, John	....do....	19	June 8, 1864	3 yrs.	Substitute; mustered out with company June 25, 1865.
Houston, James..........	....do....	24	June 22, 1864	3 yrs.	Substitute.
James, Isaac.............	....do....	24	Aug. 17, 1862	3 yrs.	Wounded March 25, 1865, in action near Petersburg, Va.; mustered out with company June 25, 1865.
Jaqua, Horace..........	....do....	18	Sept. 22, 1864	1 yr.	Mustered out with company June 25, 1865.
Keester, Joseph..........	....do....	19	Aug. 8, 1862	3 yrs.	Died Jan. 11, 1863, at Cumberland, Md.
Kreiger, Francis..........	....do....	22	June 2, 1864	3 yrs.	Drafted; died July 12, 1864, at Frederick, Md., of wounds received July 9, 1864, in battle of Monocacy, Md.
Krouse, Eli..............	....do....	27	May 24, 1864	3 yrs.	Drafted; mustered out with company June 25, 1865.
Langdon, Sherman W...	....do....	29	May 9, 1864	3 yrs.	Drafted; discharged Sept. 27, 1865. at Washington, D. C., on Surgeon's certificate of disability.
Lawrence, Clark........	....do....	29	Aug. 10, 1862	3 yrs.	Wounded ——; captured June 15, 1863, at battle of Winchester Va.; mustered out with company June 25, 1865.
Lefler, Abraham........	....do....	23	May 16, 1864	3 yrs.	Drafted; died Sept. 22, 1864, at Winchester. Va., of wounds received Sept. 19, 1864, in battle of Opequan, Va.
Linch, Robert P..........	....do....	39	Aug. 14, 1862	3 yrs.	Captured June 15, 1863, at battle of Winchester, Va.; wounded Sept. 19, 1864, in battle of Opequan, Va.; mustered out with company June 25, 1865.
McFarland, Archibald..	....do....	22	Aug. 12, 1862	3 yrs.	Died Jan. 2, 1863, at Cumberland, Md.
McFarland, William H..	....do....	24	Aug. 10, 1862	3 yrs.	Wounded June 15, 1863, in battle of Winchester, Va.; mustered out with company June 25, 1865.
Miller, John.............	....do....	26	June 8, 1864	3 yrs.	Substitute; mustered out with company June 25, 1865.
Miller, Ramsey..........	....do....	23	Aug. 8, 1862	3 yrs.	Captured June 15, 1863, at battle of Winchester, Va.; wounded May 6, 1864, in battle of the Wilderness, Va.; mustered out with company June 25, 1865.
Murphy, George W......	....do....	23	Sept. 22, 1864	1 yr.	Drafted; mustered out with company June 25, 1865.
Murphy, William	....do....	22	June 9, 1864	3 yrs.	Substitute; wounded Sept. 19, 1864, in battle of Opequan, Va.; mustered out with company June 25, 1865.
Nelson, Benjamin........	....do....	26	June 16, 1864	3 yrs.	Substitute.
Nowlin, Francis M.......	....do....	18	Aug. 15, 1862	3 yrs.	Died Jan. 13, 1864, at Washington, D. C.
Nyswanger, Alexander..	....do....	30	Aug. 10, 1862	3 yrs.	Wounded Sept. 19, 1864, in battle of Opequan, Va.; mustered out with company June 25, 1865.
Page, John B.............	....do....	24	Aug. 5, 1862	3 yrs.	Died July 21, 1863, at Winchester, Va., of wounds received June 14, 1863, in battle of Winchester, Va.
Patterson, Samuel T....	....do....	40	Aug. 21, 1862	3 yrs.	Transferred to Veteran Reserve Corps Dec. —, 1863; mustered out Aug. 8, 1865, at Washington, D. C., by order of War Department.
Pearson, William........	....do....	26	June 20, 1864	3 yrs.	Substitute; discharged May 29, 1865, at Washington, D. C., on Surgeon's certificate of disability.

Names.	Rank.	Age.	Date of Entering the Service.	Period of Service.	Remarks.
Ray, Samuel............	Private..	18	Aug. 9, 1862	3 yrs.	Captured July 9, 1864, at battle of Monocacy, Md.; mustered out with company June 25, 1865.
Robinson, William.......	...do....	..	June 30, 1864	3 yrs.	Substitute.
Ruff, Wilson.............	...do....	43	Aug. 21, 1862	3 yrs.	Captured June 15, 1863, at battle of Winchester, Va.; transferred to Veteran Reserve Corps Dec. 29, 1863.
Rule, Thomas.............	...do....	21	Aug. 18, 1862	3 yrs.	Wounded and captured June 15, 1863, at battle of Winchester, Va.; transferred to Co. C, 14th Regiment, Veteran Reserve Corps, Dec. 19, 1864; mustered out July 24, 1865, at Washington, D. C., by order of War Department.
Schmidt, Charles.........	...do....	18	June 11, 1864	3 yrs.	Substitute; wounded July 9, 1864, in battle of Monocacy, Md.; discharged May 29, 1865, at Washington, D. C., on Surgeon's certificate of disability.
Scott, William A.........	...do....	31	Aug. 14, 1862	3 yrs.	Died Feb. 1 1863, at Winchester, Va.
Shible, George F.........	...do....	40	May 24, 1864	3 yrs.	Drafted; mustered out June 26, 1865, at Baltimore, Md., by order of War Department.
Shumaker, Daniel........	...do....	24	Aug. 15, 1862	3 yrs.	Captured June 15, 1863, at battle of Winchester, Va.; died July 10, 1863, at Winchester Va.
Shumaker, Henry........	...do....	20	Aug. 15, 1862	3 yrs.	Wounded May 12, 1864, in action; mustered out with company June 25, 1865.
Shumaker, Martin........	...do....	22	Aug. 15, 1862	3 yrs.	Died Aug. 29, 1864, at Washington, D. C.
Simpson, Thomas........	...do....	34	May 17, 1864	3 yrs.	Drafted; mustered out with company June 25, 1865.
Smith, Conrad...........	...do....	30	Aug. 10, 1862	3 yrs.	Captured Sept. 24, 1864, in action ——; died Dec. 24, 1864, in Rebel Prison at Salisbury, North Carolina.
Smith, Jeremiah.........	...do....	34	May 25, 1864	3 yrs.	Drafted; wounded and captured July 9, 1864, at battle of Monocacy, Md.; died Dec. 11, 1864, at Harper's Ferry, Va.
Smith, Thomas..........	...do....	25	May 15, 1864	3 yrs	Substitute; captured July 9, 1864, at battle of Monocacy, Md. No further record found.
Stephens, Alfred........	...do....	21	Aug. 8, 1862	3 yrs.	Discharged Feb. 27, 1863, at Columbus, O., on Surgeon's certificate of disability.
Stone, George...........	...do....	24	Sept. 15, 1864	1 yr.	Mustered out with company June 25, 1865.
Stone, Harrison.........	...do....	21	Aug. 8, 1862	3 yrs.	Captured June 15, 1863, at battle of Winchester, Va.; mustered out with company June 25, 1865.
Sweet, Joseph...........	...do....	32	Aug. 8, 1862	3 yrs.	Mustered out June 26, 1865, at Baltimore, Md., by order of War Department.
Tate, Stephen...........	...do....	18	Oct. 19, 1862	3 yrs.	Died May 7, 1864, in field hospital of wounds received May 5, 1864, in battle of the Wilderness, Va.
Thomas, Walter.........	...do....	30	Aug. 10, 1862	3 yrs.	Wounded June 3, 1864, in battle of Cold Harbor, Va.; mustered out with company June 25, 1865.
Tittle, David...........	...do....	21	Aug. 10, 1862	3 yrs.	Captured June 15, 1863, at battle of Winchester, Va.; mustered out with company June 25, 1865.
Trout, Anthony.........	...do....	24	May 16, 1864	3 yrs.	Drafted; wounded Sept. 22, 1864, in battle of Fisher's Hill, Va.; mustered out with company June 25, 1865.
Trump, William.........	...do....	20	Aug. 15, 1862	3 yrs.	Discharged June 8, 1863, at Columbus, O., on Surgeon's certificate of disability.
Ullom, Ellis.............	...do....	29	Aug. 9, 1862	3 yrs.	Captured June 15, 1863, at battle of Winchester, Va.; wounded July 9, 1864, in battle of Monocacy, Md.; mustered out May 9, 1865, at Philadelphia, Pa., by order of War Department.
Weaver, William E......	...do....	19	Aug. 10, 1862	3 yrs.	Wounded and captured June 15, 1863, in battle of Winchester, Va.; discharged to date July 12, 1864, by order of War Department.
Wenrick, Jonathan.....	...do....	20	Aug. 14, 1862	3 yrs.	Discharged April 6, 1863, at Columbus, O., on Surgeon's certificate of disability.
Wenrick, Thomas........	...do....	19	Aug. 8, 1862	3 yrs.	Died Jan. 5, 1863, at Moorefield, Va.
Whittacre, Jacob G......	...do....	18	Aug. 22, 1862	3 yrs.	Wounded May 5, 1864, in battle of the Wilderness, Va.; mustered out with company June 25, 1865.
Whittacre, Robert B.....	...do....	19	Aug. 22, 1862	3 yrs.	Captured June 15, 1863, at battle of Winchester, Va.; mustered out with company June 25, 1865.
Wiggans, Philip.........	...do....	33	Dec. 3, 1863	3 yrs.	Wounded July 9, 1864, in battle of Monocacy, Md.; mustered out with company June 25, 1865.
Wilt, Martin V..........	...do....	21	Aug. 8, 1862	3 yrs.	Mustered out with company June 25, 1865.
Wolf, Philip............	...do....	24	Aug. 8, 1862	3 yrs.	Discharged March 9, 1863, at Winchester, Va., on Surgeon's certificate of disability.
Wolf, William G.........	...do....	18	Aug. 21, 1862	3 yrs.	
Wyants, John.,..........	...do....	18	Oct. 15, 1862	3 yrs.	Captured June 15, 1863, at battle of Winchester, Va.; also missing May 5, 1864, at battle of the Wilderness, Va., supposed killed. No further record found.

COMPANY I.

Mustered in Oct. 3, 1862, at Camp Piqua, O., by Alexander E. Drake, Captain 2d Infantry, U. S. A. Mustered out June 25, 1865, near Washington, D. C., by J. C. Robinson, Brevet Major and A. C. M. 3d Division, 6th Army Corps.

Names.	Rank.	Age.	Date of Entering the Service.	Period of Service.	Remarks.
Luther Brown	Captain.	30	Sept. 10, 1862	3 yrs.	Wounded July 9, 1864, in battle of Monocacy, Md.; brevet Major July 10, 1864; detailed as Provost Marshal 3d Division, 6th Army Corps, Oct. 27, 1864; mustered out June 26, 1865, by order of War Department.
William A. Hathaway	1st Lieut.	26	July 15, 1862	3 yrs.	Promoted to Captain Co. C March 30, 1864.
Thomas J. Weakley	....do....	24	July 15, 1862	3 yrs.	Captured June 15, 1863, at battle of Winchester, Va.; promoted from 2d Lieutenant March 21, 1864; transferred to Co. D April 15, 1864; from Co. K to date Feb. 17, 1865; paroled March 1, 1865; discharged April 1, 1865. See Co. K.
Henry H. Stevens	....do....	22	Aug. 5, 1862	3 yrs.	Promoted from 1st Sergeant April 12, 1864; to Captain Co. C July 22, 1864.
Albert A. Hubbard	....do....	23	July 30, 1862	3 yrs.	Promoted to 2d Lieutenant from Sergeant Co. I July 22, 1864; 1st Lieutenant Dec. 21, 1864; brevet Captain April 2, 1865; mustered out with company June 25, 1865.
John W. Steelman	1st Sergt.	19	Sept. 22, 1862	3 yrs.	Wounded July 9, 1864, in battle of Monocacy, Md.; appointed from Sergeant Aug. 13, 1864; discharged May 30, 1865, for wounds received in action.
Joseph Deaver	....do....	37	July 28, 1862	3 yrs.	Appointed Corporal ——; 1st Sergeant June 1, 1865; mustered out with company June 25, 1865.
Erastus Layton	Sergeant.	19	Aug. 14, 1862	3 yrs.	Promoted to Hospital Steward April 20. 1864.
William T. Soward	....do....	23	Aug. 9, 1862	3 yrs.	Mustered out with company June 25, 1865.
Edward L. McGilton	....do....	20	Aug. 13, 1862	3 yrs.	Appointed from Corporal April 20, 1864; mustered out with company June 25, 1865.
Samuel Metcalf	....do....	25	Aug. 8, 1862	3 yrs.	Appointed Corporal April 27, 1864; Sergeant June 1, 1865; mustered out with company June 25, 1865.
David King	....do....	21	Aug. 2, 1862	3 yrs.	Appointed from Corporal Sept. 1, 1864; wounded March 25, 1865, in action near Petersburg, Va.; mustered out June 12, 1865, at Columbus, O., by order of War Department.
Matthew Overpack	....do....	21	Aug. 9, 1862	3 yrs.	Captured June 15, 1863, at battle of Winchester, Va.; wounded June 5, 1864, in action; appointed from Corporal July 1, 1864; died April 5, 1865, of wounds received April 2, 1865, in action near Petersburg, Va.
William Wise	....do....	21	Aug. 9, 1862	3 yrs.	Appointed Corporal Jan. 18, 1863; wounded June 3, 1864, in battle of Cold Harbor, Va.; also March 25, 1865, in action near Petersburg, Va.; appointed Sergeant April 5, 1865; discharged June 7, 1865, for wounds received in action.
Washington S. Grim	Corporal.	32	Aug. 5, 1862	3 yrs.	Discharged April 7, 1863, at Cumberland, Md., on Surgeon's certificate of disability.
Benton Moses	....do....	27	Aug. 18, 1862	3 yrs.	Died Jan. 1, 1863, at Winchester, Va.
James D. Dickerson	....do....	21	Aug. 12, 1862	3 yrs.	Discharged March 7, 1864, at Brandy Station, Va., on Surgeon's certificate of disability.
James D. Boyd	....do....	19	Aug. 5, 1862	3 yrs.	Captured June 15, 1863, at Winchester, Va., while on picket duty; appointed Corporal June 30, 1864; mustered out with company June 25, 1865.
Joshua L. Spahr	....do....	21	Aug. 29, 1862	3 yrs.	Appointed Corporal Sept. 1, 1864; wounded Sept. 19, 1864, in battle of Opequan, Va.; mustered out with company June 25, 1865.
Elias Sprowl	....do....	33	Aug. 9, 1862	3 yrs.	Appointed Corporal Sept. 1, 1864; mustered out with company June 25, 1865.
Charles H. Berry	....do....	21	Aug. 13, 1862	3 yrs.	Captured June 15, 1863, at Winchester, Va., while on picket duty; appointed Corporal April 5, 1865; mustered out with company June 25, 1865.
Philander Skillman	....do....	22	Sept. 12, 1862	3 yrs.	Captured June 14, 1863, at battle of Winchester, Va.; appointed Corporal April 10, 1865; mustered out with company June 25, 1865.
Henry Yonker	....do....	19	Aug. 13, 1862	3 yrs.	Appointed May 31, 1865; mustered out with company June 25, 1865.
Jacob M. Barr	....do....	28	Aug. 9, 1862	3 yrs.	Captured June 15, 1863, at Winchester, Va., while on picket duty; appointed Corporal June 1, 1865; mustered out with company June 25, 1865.

Names.	Rank.	Age.	Date of Entering the Service.	Period of Service.	Remarks.
Leroy B. Lowman.......	Corporal.	24	Aug. 11, 1862	3 yrs.	Wounded June 14, and captured June 15, 1863, at battle of Winchester, Va.; appointed Corporal June 30, 1864; mustered out June 19, 1865, at Baltimore, Md., by order of War Department.
Ezra C. Harris............	....do....	18	Aug. 15, 1862	3 yrs.	Captured June 15, 1863, at battle of Winchester, Va.: appointed Corporal April 20, 1864; wounded July 9, 1864, in battle of Monocacy. Md., also Sept. 19, 1864, in battle of Opequan, Va.; discharged April 5, 1865, at Columbus, O., for wounds received in action.
Ogden McCord..........	Musician	18	Sept. 22, 1862	3 yrs.	Discharged March 2, 1863, at Winchester, Va., on Surgeon's certificate of disability.
Anderson, Martin.......	Private..	20	Sept. 20, 1862	3 yrs.	Wounded Sept. 19, 1864, in battle of Opequan. Va.; discharged Feb. 9, 1865, at Columbus, O., for wounds received in action.
Aspinall, Richard........	....do....	19	Aug. 9, 1862	3 yrs.	Mustered out with company June 25, 1865.
Aspinall, Thomas B......	....do....	25	Aug. 5, 1862	3 yrs.	Mustered out with company June 25, 1865.
Baird, Robert J...........	....do....	21	Aug. 21, 1862	3 yrs.	Captured June 15, 1863, at Winchester, Va., while on picket duty; died May 6, 1864, of wounds received May 5, 1864, in battle of the Wilderness, Va.
Barr, Elias A.............	....do....	27	July 28, 1862	3 yrs.	Captured June 15, 1863, at Winchester, Va., while on picket duty; wounded April 2, 1865, in action near Petersburg, Va.; mustered out Aug. 9, 1865, at Washington, D. C., by order of War Department.
Barr, Samuel A...........	....do....	18	Aug. 13, 1862	3 yrs.	Wounded July 9, 1864, in battle of Monocacy, Md.; died Aug. 12, 1864.
Berry, Thomas S.........	....do....	19	Aug. 13, 1862	3 yrs.	Captured June 15, 1863 at Winchester, Va., while on picket duty; wounded June 3, 1864, in battle of Cold Harbor, Va.; reduced from Corporal ——; mustered out with company June 25, 1865.
Biggs, John..............	....do....	26	Aug. 11, 1862	3 yrs.	Mustered out with company June 25, 1865.
Brace, Julius R..........	....do....	18	Sept. 3, 1863	3 yrs.	Mustered out with company June 25, 1865.
Chatterton, John.........	....do....	20	Aug. 11, 1862	3 yrs.	Captured June 15, 1863, at Winchester, Va., while on picket duty; mustered out with company June 25, 1865.
Clayton, Thomas.........	....do....	23	Sept. 15, 1862	3 yrs.	Discharged March 5, 1863, at Winchester, Va., on Surgeon's certificate of disability; died May 6, 1863.
Clouse, John.............	....do....	18	Sept. 29, 1862	3 yrs.	Mustered out with company June 25, 1865.
Collins, Josiah W........	....do....	23	Oct. 20, 1863	3 yrs.	Wounded Sept. 19, 1864, in battle of Opequan, Va.; mustered out with company June 25, 1865.
Cory, Scott..............	....do....	18	Mch. 27, 1863	3 yrs.	Captured June 15, 1863, at Winchester, Va., while on picket duty; mustered out with company June 25, 1865.
Cox, John W.	....do....	21	Aug. 6, 1862	3 yrs.	Captured June 15, 1863, at Winchester, Va., while on picket duty; wounded Sept. 19, 1864, in battle of Obequan, Va.; mustered out with company June 25, 1865.
Cunningham, James....	....do....	19	Oct. 10, 1863	3 yrs.	Transferred to Veteran Reserve Corps ——; mustered out Oct. 11, 1865, at Washington, D. C., by order of War Department.
Davidson, Henry........	....do....	19	Oct. 10, 1862	3 yrs.	Died Aug. 22, 1863, at Alexandria, Va.
Donivan, William J.....	....do....	18	Sept. 29, 1863	3 yrs.	Wounded April 2, 1865, in action near Petersburg, Va.; mustered out with company June 25, 1865.
Finley, James............	....do....	39	Feb. 16, 1864	3 yrs.	Died March 18, 1864, at Brandy Station, Va.
Forbes, William..........	....do....	27	Aug. 11, 1862	3 yrs.	Captured June 15, 1863, at battle of Winchester, Va.; died Oct. 7, 1863, in Rebel Prison at Richmond, Va.
Fry, Jacob...............	....do....	22	Aug. 5, 1862	3 yrs.	Mustered out July 25, 1865, at York, Pa., by order of War Department.
Gardner, Taylor..........	....do....	18	Mch. 27, 1863	3 yrs.	Mustered out with company June 25, 1865.
Ginavan, Alexander.....	....do....	22	Aug. 7, 1862	3 yrs.	Mustered out with company June 25, 1865.
Green, Timothy G........	....do....	48	Dec. 8, 1863	3 yrs.	Mustered out with company June 25, 1865.
Griffith, Avery..........	....do....	25	Feb. 16, 1864	3 yrs.	Killed March 25, 1865, in action near Petersburg, Va.
Gummere, Reuben	....do....	19	Aug. 8, 1862	3 yrs.	Discharged March 23, 1864, at Columbus, O., on Surgeon's certificate of disability.
Honefenger, John H.....	....do....	20	Sept. 22, 1862	3 yrs.	Mustered out with company June 25, 1865.
Hooper, Zachariah.......	....do....	21	Aug. 25, 1864	1 yr.	Mustered out with company June 25, 1865.
Hubbard, Bernard S.....	....do....	19	July 30, 1862	3 yrs.	Mustered out with company June 25, 1865.
Hurst, John U...........	....do....	18	Feb. 22, 1864	3 yrs.	Wounded July 9, 1864, in battle of Monocacy, Md.; mustered out with company June 25, 1865.
Hutchinson, Henry......	....do....	28	Aug. 5, 1862	3 yrs.	Mustered out with company June 25, 1865.
Kauffman, Henry........	....do....	19	Aug. 5, 1862	3 yrs.	Captured June 14, 1863, at battle of Winchester, Va.; wounded Oct. 19, 1864, in battle of Cedar Creek, Va.; mustered out June 19, 1865, at Baltimore, Md., by order of War Department.

Names.	Rank.	Age.	Date of Entering the Service.	Period of Service.	Remarks.
Kelly, James............	Private..	23	Aug. 2, 1862	3 yrs.	Wounded June 5, 1864, in battle of Cold Harbor, Va.; mustered out with company June 25, 1865.
Kelly, Joseph.............	....do....	18	Feb. 21, 1864	3 yrs.	Mustered out with company June 25, 1865.
King, James E.............	....do....	23	Aug. 16, 1862	3 yrs.	Captured May 6, 1864, at battle of the Wilderness, Va.; paroled April 10, 1865; mustered out June 30, 1865, at Camp Chase, O., by order of War Department.
Kingore, Charles..◄......	....do....	32	July 28, 1862	3 yrs.	Discharged May 14, 1863, at Columbus, O., on Surgeon's certificate of disability.
Lamme, Edwin H........	....do....	18	Aug. 9, 1862	3 yrs.	Wounded June 14, and captured June 15, 1863, at battle of Winchester, Va.; mustered out with company June 25, 1865.
Laurence, Alexander..	....do....	18	Sept. 30, 1862	3 yrs.	Discharged Oct. 14, 1862, at Piqua, O., by civil authority.
Layton, Nile J..........	...do....	21	Sept. 12, 1863	3 yrs.	Wounded July 9, 1864, in battle of Monocacy. Md.; transferred to Co. A, 10th Regiment, Veteran Reserve Corps, March 11, 1865; mustered out July 20, 1865, at Washington, D. C., by order of War Department.
Lehman, Christian.......	....do....	18	Jan. 21, 1864	3 yrs.	Mustered out with company June 25, 1865.
Lippincott, Darius.......	....do....	35	Aug. 8, 1862	3 yrs.	Mustered out with company June 25, 1865.
Lippincott, John R.......	....do....	37	Aug. 14, 1862	3 yrs.	Captured June 14, 1863, at battle of Winchester, Va.; discharged July 2, 1864, at Columbus, O., on Surgeon's certificate of disability.
Littlejohn, George W...	....do....	19	Aug. 9, 1862	3 yrs.	Wounded June 14, 1863, in battle of Winchester, Va.; transferred to 96th Co., 2d Battalion, Veteran Reserve Corps, ——; mustered out Oct. 2, 1865, at Baltimore, Md., on expiration of term of service.
Ludy, Samuel............	....do....	19	Oct. 15, 1862	3 yrs.	Discharged March 12, 1863, at Columbus, O., on Surgeon's certificate of disability.
McAllister, Malcom.....	....do....	37	Aug. 18, 1862	3 yrs.	Captured June 15, 1863, at battle of Winchester, Va.; died Aug. 28, 1863, at Annapolis, Md.
McGilton, James F......	....do....	23	Aug. 13, 1862	3 yrs.	Mustered out with company June 25, 1865.
McManus, Joseph.........	....do....	45	Jan. 20, 1864	3 yrs.	Transferred to Co. H, 18th Regiment, Veteran Reserve Corps, ——; mustered out July 25. 1865, at Washington, D. C., by order of War Department.
Martin, Andrew J.......	....do....	35	Aug. 9, 1862	3 yrs.	Mustered out May 24, 1865, by order of War Department.
Martin, Emanuel........	...do....	17	Aug. 22, 1864	1 yr.	Mustered out with company June 25, 1865.
Maxsom, Simeon.........	....do....	24	Sept. 15, 1862	3 yrs.	Mustered out June 15, 1865, at Washington, D. C., by order of War Department.
Maxwell, Ezekiel H.....	....do....	18	Sept. 4, 1863	3 yrs.	Wounded May 5, 1864, in battle of the Wilderness, Va.; discharged May 15, 1865, at Danville, Va., for wounds received in action.
Metcalf, Swithen.........	....do....	27	Sept. 8, 1862	3 yrs.	Wounded May 6, 1864, in battle of the Wilderness, Va.; died April 3, 1865, of wounds received Oct. 19, 1864, in battle of Cedar Creek, Va.
Milford, George..........	....do....	23	Jan. 19, 1864	3 yrs.	Killed May 6, 1864, in battle of the Wilderness, Virginia.
Mott, Elias	....do....	20	Aug. 15, 1862	3 yrs.	Discharged June 13, 1863, at Cumberland, Md., on Surgeon's certificate of disability; re-enlisted Jan. 23, 1864, for three years; killed June 3, 1864, in battle of Cold Harbor, Va.
Munk, John..............	....do....	43	Aug. 22, 1862	3 yrs.	Killed June 15, 1863, in battle of Winchester, Virginia.
Overpack, George.........	....do....	22	Aug. 8, 1862	3 yrs.	Wounded June 15, 1863, in battle of Winchester, Va.; mustered out with company June 25, 1865.
Petty, John..............	....do....	41	Aug. 22, 1862	3 yrs.	Killed Oct. 19, 1864, in battle of Cedar Creek, Virginia.
Polhemus, Aaron	....do....	27	Aug. 17, 1862	3 yrs.	Wounded June 3, 1864, in battle of Cold Harbor, Va.; died Aug. 2, 1864.
Quinn, Bernard..........	....do....	26	Jan. 9, 1864	3 yrs.	Transferred to 143d Co., 2d Battalion, Veteran Reserve Corps, July 30, 1864.
Racy, William H........	....do....	23	Jan. 4, 1864	3 yrs.	Mustered out with company June 25, 1865.
Raffensperger, Peter	....do....	40	Aug. 14, 1862	3 yrs.	Transferred to Co. F., 15th Regiment, Veteran Reserve Corps, ——; mustered out Aug. 1, 1865, at Cairo, Ill., by order of War Department.
Ramy, Green P..........	....do....	18	Aug. 5, 1862	3 yrs.	Mustered out with company June 25, 1865.
Reese, Hiram C..........	....do....	18	Aug. 22, 1862	3 yrs.	Captured July 9, 1864, at battle of Monocacy, Md.; mustered out July 11, 1865, at Washington, D. C., by order of War Department.
Reese, Isaiah C..........	....do....	24	July 28, 1862	3 yrs.	Transferred to Veteran Reserve Corps ——; mustered out May 23, 1865, at Philadelphia, Pa., by order of War Department.
Robertson, William......	....do....	18	Aug. 22, 1862	3 yrs.	Wounded and captured June 14, 1863, in battle of Winchester, Va.; mustered out with company June 25, 1865.
Ruffin, Charles K........	....do....	20	Jan. 29, 1864	3 yrs.	Wounded July 9, 1864, in battle of Monocacy, Md.; discharged March 20, 1865, at Cincinnati, O., for wounds received in action.

Names.	Rank.	Age	Date of Entering the Service.	Period of Service.	Remarks.
Ruffin, Samuel N.	Private..	26	Jan. 29, 1864	3 yrs.	Mustered out with company June 25, 1865.
Sensabaugh, John	....do....	23	Aug. 5, 1862	3 yrs.	Discharged Sept. 28, 1863, at Columbus, O., on Surgeon's certificate of disability.
Shellbarger, Jonas	....do....	21	July 29, 1862	3 yrs.	Wounded July 9, 1864, in battle of Monocacy, Md.; also April 2, 1865, in front of Petersburg, Va.; mustered out with company June 25, 1865.
Shrader, Isaac	....do....	28	Aug. 9, 1862	3 yrs.	Captured June 15, 1863, at battle of Winchester, Va.; mustered out with company June 25, 1865.
Snider, Peter	....do....	19	Jan. 21, 1864	3 yrs.	Mustered out with company June 25, 1865.
Sparrow, Absalom L.	....do....	37	Jan. 29, 1864	3 yrs.	Died July 6, 1864, at City Point, Va., of wounds.
Sparrow, Richard	....do....	19	Feb. 16, 1864	3 yrs.	Wounded June 22, 1864, in action in front of Petersburg, Va.; discharged to date June 25, 1865, by order of War Department.
Stickle, Benjamin	....do....	21	Aug. 15, 1862	3 yrs.	Mustered out with company June 25, 1865.
Stickle, Henry	....do..	19	Aug. 15, 1862	3 yrs.	Mustered out with company June 25, 1865.
Sutton, Darius	....do....	18	Jan. 24, 1864	3 yrs.	Mustered out with company June 25, 1865.
Timmons, James M.	....do....	18	Mch. 2, 1863	3 yrs.	
Trout, Henry	....do....	19	Aug. 15, 1862	3 yrs.	Mustered out with company June 25, 1865.
Troxell, George W.	....do....	20	Aug. 9, 1862	3 yrs.	Died June 1, 1863, at his home in Sidney, O.
Waldron, Thomas	....do....	24	Aug. 9, 1862	3 yrs.	Captured June 15, 1863, at Winchester, Va., while on picket duty; mustered out with company June 25, 1865.
Walker, Jesse T.	....do....	19	Aug. 5, 1862	3 yrs.	Mustered out with company June 25, 1865.
Walker, William L.	....do....	26	Aug. 5, 1862	3 yrs.	Mustered out with company June 25, 1865.
Wallace, Hugh M.	....do....	26	Aug. 14, 1862	3 yrs.	Captured June 15, 1863, at battle of Winchester, Va.; mustered out with company June 25, 1865.
Ward, John H.	....do....	19	Sept. 11, 1863	3 yrs.	Mustered out with company June 25, 1865.
Warfield, Joseph	....do....	19	Aug. 12, 1862	3 yrs.	Drowned July 7, 1864, in James River, Va.
Wentz, Elder	....do....	19	Aug. 16, 1862	3 yrs.	Mustered out with company June 25, 1865.
Wentz, Samuel	....do....	22	Aug. 16, 1862	3 yrs.	Mustered out with company June 25, 1865.
Williams, Isaac W.	....do....	19	Aug. 14, 1862	3 yrs.	Mustered out with company June 25, 1865.
Wissinger, John W.	....do....	18	Sept. 30, 1862	3 yrs.	Wounded July 9, 1864, in battle of Monocacy, Md.; mustered out July 15, 1865, at Columbus, O., by order of War Department.
Yetter, Amos	....do....	37	Aug. 26, 1862	3 yrs.	Captured June 15, 1863, at battle of Winchester, Va.; wounded July 9, 1864, in battle of Monocacy, Md.; mustered out with company June 25, 1865.
Yonker, Charles	....do....	18	Aug. 14, 1862	3 yrs.	Wounded June 13, 1863, in battle of Winchester, Va.; also Sept. 19, 1864, in battle of Opequan, Va.; discharged May 14, 1865, at Gallipolis, O., for wounds received in action.
Zeigler, Moses	....do....	18	Aug. 16, 1862	3 yrs.	Killed June 1, 1864, in battle of Cold Harbor, Virginia.

COMPANY K.

This company was organized at Camp Mansfield, O., on the eighth day of December, 1862, by Lieutenant John M. Smith. Mustered out June 25, 1865, near Washington, D. C., by J. C. Robinson, Brevet Major and A. C. M. 3d Division, 6th Army Corps.

Names.	Rank.	Age	Date of Entering the Service.	Period of Service.	Remarks.
John M. Smith	Captain.	36	Nov. 5, 1862	3 yrs.	Promoted to 1st Lieutenant from 2d Lieutenant April 9, 1863; Captain March 30, 1864; died May 27, 1864, at Washington, D. C., of wounds received May 5, 1864, in battle of the Wilderness, Va.
Thomas J. Weakley	....do....	24	July 15, 1862	3 yrs.	Transferred from Co. D as 1st Lieutenant Aug. 25, 1864; to Co. I to date Feb. 17, 1865; appointed Captain April 8, 1865; mustered out with company June 25, 1865.
Henry N. Hackett	1st Lieut.	29	April 9, 1863	3 yrs.	Promoted from 2d Lieutenant March 21, 1864; captured July 9, 1864, at battle of Monocacy, Md.; mustered out with company June 25, 1865.
George W. Traub	2d Lieut.	29	Nov. 13, 1862	3 yrs.	Mustered in as private; appointed 1st Sergeant ——; wounded May 5, 1864, in battle of the Wilderness, Va.; promoted to 2d Lieutenant Sept. 8, 1864; discharged March 7, 1865.
Amos Shaul	....do....	35	Aug. 21, 1862	3 yrs.	Promoted from 1st Sergeant Co. C to date Dec. 9, 1864; to 1st Lieutenant Co. C April 8, 1865.
Milton H. Myers	1st Sergt.	21	Nov. 13, 1862	3 yrs.	Mustered in as private; appointed Sergeant ——; 1st Sergeant ——; wounded June 5, 1864, in battle of Cold Harbor, Va.; promoted to 2d Lieutenant Dec. 24, 1864, but no muster found; 1st Lieutenant Co. A May 31, 1865.

Names.	Rank.	Age.	Date of Entering the Service.	Period of Service.	Remarks.
Christian C. Roan	Sergeant.	32	Nov. 12, 1862	3 yrs.	Appointed from private Jan. 1, 1864; mustered out with company June 25, 1865.
Henry J. Jacob	...do...	19	Nov. 13, 1862	3 yrs.	Appointed from Corporal Jan. 1, 1865; mustered out with company June 25, 1865.
Joshua E. Pollock	...do...	29	Nov. 13, 1862	3 yrs.	Appointed from private ——; captured June 15, 1863, at battle of Winchester, Va.; paroled July 3, 1863; mustered out June 3, 1865, at Pittsburgh, Pa., by order of War Department.
Jacob W. Stansbury	...do...	34	Nov. 9, 1862	3 yrs.	Appointed Jan. 1, 1864; discharged Nov. 21, 1864, for wounds received Sept. 19, 1864, in battle of Opequan, Va.
Hiram D. Walker	...do...	27	May 8, 1864	3 yrs.	Drafted; appointed from private Jan. 1, 1865; wounded March 25, 1865, in action near Petersburg, Va.; discharged June 28, 1865, at Columbus, O., on Surgeon's certificate of disability.
John J. Wolf	Corporal.	19	Nov. 7, 1862	3 yrs.	Captured June 15, 1863, at battle of Winchester, Va.; appointed Jan. 1, 1865; mustered out with company June 25, 1865.
William J. Wilson	...do...	37	Nov. 11, 1862	3 yrs.	Appointed April 10, 1865; mustered out with company June 25, 1865.
John C. Taylor	...do...	44	Nov. 10, 1862	3 yrs.	Appointed ——; transferred to 42d Co., 2d Battalion, Veteran Reserve Corps, ——; mustered out June 13, 1865, at Washington, D. C.
George Cavender	...do...	30	Nov. 7, 1862	3 yrs.	Appointed ——; captured June 15, 1863, at battle of Winchester, Va.; killed May 6, 1864, in battle of the Wilderness, Va.
Jacob Cuyler	...do...	20	Nov. 12, 1862	3 yrs.	Appointed ——; captured June 15, 1863, at battle of Winchester, Va.; wounded Sept. 22, 1864, in battle of Fisher's Hill, Va.; discharged May 29, 1865, at Philadelphia, Pa., for wounds received in action.
James W. McKibben	...do...	23	May 16, 1864	3 yrs.	Drafted; appointed Sept. 1, 1864; wounded Sept. 19, 1864, in battle of Opequan, Va.; discharged May 23, 1865, at Philadelphia, Pa., for wounds received in action.
Almy, Nelson	Private.	18	June 20, 1864	3 yrs.	Substitute; mustered out with company June 25, 1865.
Barnes, Thomas	...do...	25	May 23, 1864	3 yrs.	Drafted; mustered out with company June 25, 1865.
Beard, Reuben	...do...	21	Nov. 14, 1862	1 yr.	
Blising, Adam	...do...	21	Nov. 20, 1862	1 yr.	Mustered out June 15, 1865, at Columbs, O., by order of War Department.
Bishop, Joseph L	...do...	18	Nov. 14, 1862	1 yr.	
Bowman, John	...do...	24	June 20, 1864	3 yrs.	Substitute; wounded and captured July 9, 1864, at battle of Monocacy, Md. No further record found.
Brandt, Charles	...do...	26	Nov. 22, 1862	3 yrs.	Captured June 15, 1863, at battle of Winchester, Va.; also July 9, 1864, at battle of Monocacy, Md.; paroled Oct. 17, 1864; mustered out May 16, 1865, at Philadelphia, Pa., by order of War Department.
Brannan, James	...do...	18	June 6, 1863	3 yrs.	Died May 13, 1864 of wounds received May 5, 1864, in action.
Burgess, Charles	...do...	22	June 10, 1864	3 yrs.	Substitute; mustered out with company June 25, 1865.
Burnett, John E	...do...	18	May 15, 1863	3 yrs.	Captured July 9, 1864, at battle of Monocacy, Md.; mustered out June 16, 1865, at Washington, D. C., by order of War Department.
Caplinger, Sampson	...do...	27	June 2, 1864	3 yrs.	Drafted; discharged Dec. 24, 1864, on Surgeon's certificate of disability.
Carson, David	...do...	21	Nov. 20, 1862	1 yr.	
Chaney, Charles J	...do...	27	Nov. 20, 1862	3 yrs.	Transferred to Co. ——, 125th O. V. I., but not borne on rolls of 125th O. V. I.
Cline, Joseph	...do...	42	June 2, 1864	3 yrs.	Drafted; mustered out June 13, 1865, at Washington, D. C., by order of War Department.
Colvin, Clark	...do...	19	June 14, 1864	2 yrs.	Substitute.
Cook, Frederick	...do...	42	Mch. 10, 1863	1 yr.	Mustered out Nov. 7, 1864, on expiration of term of service.
Cook, George D	...do...	37	Nov. 12, 1862	3 yrs.	Discharged Feb. 6, 1863, at Camp Chase, O., on Surgeon's certificate of disability.
Dennis, Robert	...do...	19	Nov. 25, 1862	1 yr.	Captured June 15, 1863, at battle of Winchester, Va.; discharged Dec. 24, 1863, on Surgeon's certificate of disability.
Dixson, William C	...do...	27	May 16, 1864	3 yrs.	Drafted; mustered out with company June 25, 1865.
Double, John	...do...	18	June 1, 1863	3 yrs.	
Downes, John	...do...	40	June 17, 1864	3 yrs.	Substitute.
Doyle, James	...do...	23	Nov. 18, 1862	3 yrs.	
Dusenberry, Isaac	...do...	23	June 9, 1864	3 yrs.	Drafted; wounded Oct. 19, 1864, in battle of Cedar Creek, Va. No further record found.
Englehart, Casper	...do...	..	Jan. 3, 1863	1 yr.	Discharged April 16, 1863, at Camp Chase, O., on Surgeon's certificate of disability.
Farrar, George R	...do...	21	Nov. 18, 1862	1 yr.	Discharged Dec. 24, 1863, on expiration of term of service.

Names.	Rank.	Age	Date of Entering the Service.	Period of Service.	Remarks.
Feit, Lewis..............	Private..	24	Nov. 5, 1862	3 yrs.	Killed May 5, 1864, in battle of the Wilderness, Virginia.
Fetters, Ambrose........	....do....	35	June 21, 1864	3 yrs.	Drafted; wounded Sept. 22, 1864, in battle of Fisher's Hill, Va.; mustered out May 24, 1865, at York, Pa., by order of War Department.
Fissell, Charles..........	....do....	18	June 6, 1864	3 yrs.	
Flynn, John..............	....do....	18	June 7, 1864	3 yrs.	
Forest, Michael	....do....	35	June 17, 1864	3 yrs.	Drafted; captured July 9, 1864, at battle of Monocacy, Md. No further record found.
Frank, Jacob.............	....do....	36	Nov. 20, 1862	3 yrs.	
Gardner, William........	....do....	21	June 9, 1864	3 yrs.	Drafted; mustered out June 16, 1865, at Washington, D. C., by order of War Department.
Gill, Bentley	....do....	35	Nov. 25, 1862	1 yr.	Transferred to Co. K, 11th Regiment, Veteran Reserve Corps, Sept. 12, 1863; mustered out April 8, 1864, at Washington, D. C., on expiration of term of service.
Gray, Thomas........	....do....	24	Mch. 25, 1863	1 yr.	Transferred to Veteran Reserve Corps Nov. 12, 1863.
Griffin, George..........	....do....	22	Nov. 14, 1862	1 yr.	Captured June 15, 1863, at battle of Winchester, Va.; mustered out Dec. 24, 1863, on expiration of term of service.
Hammontree, John L....	....do....	43	June 16, 1864	3 yrs.	Drafted; died Sept. 16, 1864, in Jarvis Hospital, Baltimore, Md.
Hartsock, Jonathan.....	....do....	31	June 8, 1864	3 yrs.	Drafted; mustered out with company June 25, 1865.
Haver, Jacob...........	....do....	30	Feb. 7, 1863	1 yr.	Died April 28, 1863, in hospital at Winchester, Virginia.
Heath, George W......	....do....	26	May 3, 1864	3 yrs.	Drafted; mustered out with company June 25, 1865.
Hickey, Peter	....do....	26	June 20, 1864	3 yrs.	Substitute.
Holland, Henry W......	....do....	22	Mch. 15, 1863	1 yr.	Captured June 15, 1863, at battle of Winchester, Va.; mustered out Aug. 9, 1864, on expiration of term of service.
Holland, James W	....do....	30	Mch. 15, 1863	1 yr.	Captured June 15, 1863, at battle of Winchester Va.; mustered out Aug. 9, 1864, on expiration of term of service.
Hoppes, William G......	....do....	18	Nov. 7, 1862	3 yrs.	Killed May 5, 1864, in battle of the Wilderness, Virginia.
Horner, James	....do....	31	Nov. 25, 1862	1 yr.	Transferred to Veteran Reserve Corps Sept. 12, 1863.
Hough, Nicholas S......	....do....	18	Nov. 14, 1862	3 yrs.	Died May 12, 1864, of wounds received May 5, 1864, in battle of the Wilderness, Va.
Hughes, Henry..........	....do....	18	July 1, 1863	3 yrs.	Mustered out with company June 25, 1865.
Irwin, Samuel...........	....do....	21	April 8, 1863	1 yr.	Captured June 15, 1863, at battle of Winchester, Va.; mustered out July 1, 1864, on expiration of term of service.
Johnson, James	....do....	23	Sept. 1, 1863	3 yrs.	Wounded May 5, 1864, in battle of the Wilderness, Va.
Jones, William..........	....do....	20	June 17, 1864	3 yrs.	Substitute; absent, sick in general hospital. No further record found.
Kane, Thomas	....do....	18	June 11, 1864	3 yrs.	Substitute; captured July 9, 1864, at battle of Monocacy, Md.; mustered out with company June 25, 1865.
Keach, James...........	....do....	24	June 2, 1864	3 yrs.	Drafted; mustered out with company June 25, 1865.
Kelly, John	....do....	19	June 16, 1864	3 yrs.	Substitute; wounded July 9, 1864, in battle of Monocacy, Md. No further record found.
Kelly, Patrick...........	....do....	43	June 11, 1864	3 yrs.	Substitute.
Kerr, Samuel	....do....	20	Nov. 14, 1862	1 yr.	Mustered out Dec. 24, 1863, on expiration of term of service.
Kerstetter, Mortimer....	....do....	18	Feb. 12, 1863	3 yrs.	Mustered out with company June 25, 1865.
Kimberlin, Henry J.....	....do....	40	June 7, 1864	3 yrs.	Substitute; captured July 9, 1864, at battle of Monocacy, Md.; died Nov. 15, 1864, in Rebel Prison at Danville, Va.
Livingston, Oliver......	....do....	25	Nov. 12, 1862	3 yrs.	Captured June 15, 1863, at battle of Winchester, Va.; died Sept. 15, 1864, in hospital at Annapolis, Md.
Long, Jacob	....do....	26	Nov. 17, 1862	1 yr.	Mustered out Dec. 24, 1863, on expiration of term of service.
Long, James.............	....do....	25	Nov. 14, 1862	3 yrs.	
Long, John..............	....do....	30	June 9, 1864	3 yrs.	Substitute.
McCort, Hugh...........	....do....	21	Nov. 18, 1862	1 yr.	Wounded June 13, 1863, in battle of Winchester, Va.; mustered out Dec. 24, 1863, on expiration of term of service.
McCort, William........	....do....	19	Nov. 14, 1862	1 yr.	Died Feb. 20, 1863, at Camp Chase, O.
McQueen, Andrew D....	....do....	25	Nov. 14, 1862	1 yr.	Captured June 15, 1863, at battle of Winchester, Va.; mustered out Dec. 24, 1864, on expiration of term of service.
Mahafay, Henry.........	....do....	22	June 2, 1864	3 yrs.	Substitute; mustered out with company June 25, 1865.
Mark, Joseph............	....do....	43	June 17, 1864	3 yrs.	Substitute; died April 21, 1865, of wounds received March 25, 1865, in action near Petersburg, Va.
Martin, John....	....do....	23	Nov. 20, 1862	1 yr.	

Names.	Rank.	Age	Date of Entering the Service.	Period of Service.	Remarks.
Martin, John	Private.	38	June 21, 1864	3 yrs.	Substitute; captured July 9, 1864, at battle of Monocacy, Md. No further record found.
Melvers, David	...do...	19	June 17, 1864	3 yrs.	Substitute; wounded and captured July 9, 1864, in battle of Monocacy, Md. No further record found.
Melvin, Thomas	...do...	..	June 17, 1864	3 yrs.	Substitute.
Miller, David P	...do...	29	Nov. 7, 1862	3 yrs.	Transferred to 125th O. V. I. Dec. 12, 1862, but not borne on rolls of 125th O. V. I.
Miller, Jacob F	...do...	35	Nov. 20, 1862	3 yrs.	
Miller, John D	...do...	18	Sept. 14, 1863	3 yrs.	Mustered out with company June 25, 1865.
Misinger, Daniel	...do...	23	May 16, 1864	3 yrs.	Drafted; captured July 9, 1864, at battle of Monocacy, Md.; died Jan. 20, 1865, in Rebel Prison at Danville, Va.
Moody, William F	...do...	38	May 18, 1864	3 yrs.	Drafted; died Aug. 27, 1864, at Annapolis, Md.
Moore, Harrison	...do...	21	Nov. 14, 1862	1 yr.	Captured June 15, 1863, at battle of Winchester, Va.; mustered out Dec. 24, 1863, on expiration of term of service.
Moore, James	...do...	18	June 15, 1864	3 yrs.	Substitute.
Moore, John	...do...	21	Nov. 27, 1862	3 yrs.	
Moore, Richard M	...do...	17	July 9, 1863	3 yrs.	
Neason, John	...do...	21	Nov. 8, 1862	3 yrs.	Killed April 2, 1865, in action near Petersburg, Va.
Newman, John R	...do...	25	June 2, 1864	3 yrs.	Drafted; mustered out with company June 25, 1865.
Overcashier, Frederick	...do...	18	Feb. 20, 1863	3 yrs.	Captured June 15, 1863, at battle of Winchester, Va.; transferred to Co. K, 1st Regiment, Veteran Reserve Corps, Jan. 15, 1864; mustered out June 19, 1865, at Elmira, N. Y.
Panyard, John	...do...	18	June 6, 1863	3 yrs.	Died July 10, 1863, at Camp Chase, O., of accidental wounds.
Pearch, Jacob	...do...	27	Nov. 14, 1862	1 yr.	Mustered out Dec. 24, 1863, on expiration of term of service.
Pease, Samuel	...do...	18	June 20, 1864	3 yrs.	Substitute; wounded July 9, 1864, in battle of Monocacy, Md.; mustered out June 9, 1865, at Cleveland, O., by order of War Department.
Pervines, John	...do...	44	Nov. 10, 1862	3 yrs.	Killed June 14, 1863, in battle of Winchester, Virginia.
Pool, Jeremiah	...do...	28	Mch. 10, 1863	1 yr.	Captured June 15, 1863, at battle of Winchester, Va.; died March 21, 1864, in Rebel Prison at Richmond, Va.
Porter, James	...do...	24	June 8, 1864	3 yrs.	Substitute; captured July 9, 1864, at battle of Monocacy, Md.; died Nov. 15, 1864, in Rebel Prison at Danville, Va.
Ripley, Luther	...do...	20	June 4, 1864	3 yrs.	Substitute; wounded July 9, 1864, in battle of Monocacy, Md.; transferred to Co. G, 24th Regiment, Veteran Reserve Corps, ——; mustered out July 18, 1865, at Washington, D. C. by order of War Department.
Rittgers, Tobias	...do...	32	June 8, 1864	3 yrs.	Drafted; mustered out with company June 25, 1865.
River, Henry	...do...	32	June 4, 1864	3 yrs.	Drafted; mustered out May 17, 1865, at Wilmington, Del., by order of War Department.
Robinson, Henry C	...do...	23	Nov. 7, 1862	3 yrs.	Captured June 15, 1863, at battle of Winchester, Va.; died July 25, 1864, in Rebel Prison at Andersonville, Ga.
Rummell, David C	...do...	24	June 10, 1864	3 yrs.	Substitute; captured July 9, 1864, at battle of Monocacy, Md.; mustered out June 5, 1865, at Columbus, O., by order of War Department.
Rundell, David	...do...	27	June 4, 1864	3 yrs.	Substitute.
Saylor, John E	...do...	44	June 20, 1864	3 yrs.	Substitute.
Shank, John W	...do...	19	Oct. 24, 1863	3 yrs.	Mustered out with company June 25, 1865.
Shaw, James	...do...	25	June 11, 1864	3 yrs.	Substitute.
Shilling, Harrison	...do...	25	Nov. 14, 1862	1 yr.	Transferred to Veteran Reserve Corps Jan. 15, 1864.
Shiltz, John	...do...	18	Nov. 20, 1862	1 yr.	Discharged April 11, 1863, at Camp Chase, O., on Surgeon's certificate of disability.
Shultz, George	...do...	32	June 20, 1864	3 yrs.	Substitute; mustered out with company June 25, 1865.
Slentz, Henry	...do...	..	Mch. 10, 1863	3 yrs.	
Smith, Calvin	...do...	22	Mch. 10, 1863	1 yr.	Captured June 15, 1863, at battle of Winchester, Va.; mustered out July 1, 1864, on expiration of term of service.
Smith, Charles	...do...	23	Nov. 11, 1862	3 yrs.	
Smith, James	...do...	23	Nov. 28, 1862	3 yrs.	
Smith, William	...do...	23	Nov. 24, 1862	3 yrs.	
Snow, John	...do...	33	Nov. 17, 1862	1 yr.	
Speelman, Joseph	...do...	18	Nov. 10, 1862	3 yrs.	Mustered out June 17, 1865, at Washington, D. C., by order of War Department.
Sullivan, James	...do...	35	June 2, 1864	3 yrs.	Substitute.
Thomas, William	...do...	22	Nov. 11, 1862	3 yrs.	Wounded March 25, 1865, in action near Petersburg, Va.; discharged June 26, 1865, at Chester, Pa., on Surgeon's certificate of disability.
Thompson, William	...do...	..	June 8, 1864	3 yrs.	Substitute.

Names.	Rank.	Age.	Date of Entering the Service.	Period of Service.	Remarks.
Tisdale, William........	Private..	24	June 8, 1864	3 yrs.	Drafted; mustered out with company June 25, 1865.
Toll, Jose.................	...do....	35	June 2, 1864	3 yrs.	Drafted; mustered out with company June 25, 1865.
Tombow, John............	...do....	18	Nov. 7, 1862	3 yrs.	Mustered out with company June 25, 1865.
Vanduyn, Jonathan......	...do....	20	April 8, 1863	1 yr.	Captured June 15, 1863, at battle of Winchester, Va.; mustered out Aug. 9, 1864, near Harper's Ferry, Va., on expiration of term of service.
Vinton, William H......	...do....	25	Dec. 2, 1862	3 yrs.	
Wages, Leonard..........	...do....	30	June 9, 1864	3 yrs.	Drafted; captured July 9. 1864, at battle of Monocacy, Md.; transferred to Co. K, 32d O. V. I., ——.
Walt, John................	...do....	18	Nov. 15, 1862	1 yr.	Mustered out Dec. 24, 1863, on expiration of term of service.
West, John................	...do....	27	June 21, 1864	3 yrs.	Substitute.
Weir, John I..............	...do....	28	Nov. 14, 1862	1 yr.	Captured June 15, 1863, at battle of Winchester, Va.; mustered out Dec. 24, 1863, on expiration of term of service.
Williams, Thomas L.....	...do....	41	June 2, 1864	3 yrs.	Drafted; mustered out July 5, 1865, at Columbus, O., by order of War Department.
Wilson, John..............	...do....	21	June 18, 1864	3 yrs.	Substitute; captured July 9, 1864, at battle of Monocacy, Md. No further record found.
Wilson, Thomas..........	...do....	28	Nov. 22, 1862	3 yrs.	
Wolf, Henry J...........	...do....	21	Nov. 25, 1862	1 yr.	Died March 9, 1863, at Camp Chase, O.
Wolf, Philip..............	...do....	36	June 2, 1864	3 yrs.	Drafted; mustered out with company June 25, 1865.

UNASSIGNED RECRUITS.

Names.	Rank.	Age.	Date of Entering the Service.	Period of Service.	Remarks.
Boden, John............	Private..	21	Sept. 26, 1863	3 yrs.	No record found.
Dial, Patrick.............	...do....	23	Oct. 24, 1863	3 yrs.	Sent to regiment Oct. 28, 1863. No further record found.
Hudnall, Alexander....	...do....	44	Jan. 25, 1864	3 yrs.	Discharged Feb. 27, 1864, at Columbus, O., on Surgeon's certificate of disability.
Johnson, Charles.........	...do....	23	Feb. 26, 1864	3 yrs.	
Kitchell, Charles.........	...do....	18	Feb. 3, 1864	3 yrs.	No further record found.
West, Joseph E...........	...do....	18	Oct. 19, 1863	3 yrs.	No record found.

Notes

ABBREVIATIONS

AGR State of Ohio Adjutant General Records, Ohio Historical Society, Columbus

KP J. Warren Keifer Papers, Clark County Historical Society, Springfield, Ohio

OR *The War of the Rebellion: A Compilation of the Official Records of the Union and Confederate Armies,* 128 vols. (Washington, D.C.: GPO, 1880–1901), series 1 (unless otherwise noted)

PE *Piqua (Ohio) Enquirer*

PR *Piqua (Ohio) Register*

Roster Ohio Adjutant General, *Official Roster of the Soldiers of the State of Ohio in the War of the Rebellion, 1861–1866,* 12 vols. Cincinnati: Ohio Valley Press, 1886–95.

SEN *Springfield (Ohio) Evening News*

SMN *Springfield (Ohio) Morning News*

SR *Springfield (Ohio) Republic*

TT *Troy (Ohio) Times*

XT *Xenia (Ohio) Torchlight*

1. THE UNION, NOW, HENCEFORTH, FOREVER! AMEN

1. *SMN,* Apr. 17, 18, 1861; *XT,* Apr. 24, 1861; *SMN,* Apr. 19, 20, 23, 26, 1861.

2. *SMN,* Apr. 19, 1861; *XT,* Apr. 17, 24, May 1, 1861.

3. *SEN,* July 9, 1862; James W. Geary, *We Need Men: The Union Draft in the Civil War* (DeKalb: Northern Illinois Univ. Press, 1991), 27–28.

4. *XT,* Aug. 13, 1862; *SEN,* Aug. 13, 1862.

5. *XT,* Aug. 13, 1862.

6. Dr. Thomas Beamer to W. Diviney, Aug. 29, 1862, MSS 22, William R. Moore Papers, Ohio Historical Society, Columbus.

7. *Roster,* 8:8.

8. Ibid., 8:8–15, 36–39; Josiah Hill, diary, Sept. 19, 1862, Local History Room, Troy Historical Society, Troy, Ohio; *Roster,* 8:3; *PR,* Sept. 18, 1862.

9. *SEN,* Aug. 23, 1862; *Roster,* 8:1–43.

10. *SEN,* Sept. 11–26, Nov. 5, 1862, Aug. 1, Sept. 10, 1863, Mar. 12, 1864; *SR,* Nov. 4–5, 1862, Oct. 5, 1863; Geary, *We Need Men,* 12–19.

11. Copies of laws to provide for Ohio volunteers' bounties—1862–65, AGR, Series 2929.

12. *XT,* Aug. 20, 1862; *PE,* Sept. 11, 1862; John Hoover, descriptive roll, "Descriptive Rolls of Ohio Volunteer Infantry, 1861–65," AGR, Series 1774.

13. *XT,* Dec. 3, 1862.

14. "Time Book for Recruiting Officers," AGR, Series 96; *PR,* Sept. 18, 1862; Henry Rush to William Moore, Oct. 22, 1863; and Joseph McKnight to William Moore, Dec. 17, 1863, Moore Papers; muster records, AGR, Series 168.

15. Muster records, AGR, Series 168; McKnight to Moore, Dec. 17, 1863; "Recruiting Officers of Old Regiments for the latter part of 1863," AGR, Series 100; *PE,* Sept. 24, 1862. See also various items in the William R. Moore Papers.

16. L. W. Chapman to William Moore, Dec. 28, 1863; and Dr. Thomas Beamer to W. Diviney, Aug. 22, 1862, Moore Papers; *Roster,* 8:20; muster record, AGR, Series 168.

17. William R. Moore to Sarah Moore, Dec. 5, 1862, Moore Papers.

18. Muster record, AGR, Series 168; J. Warren Keifer, *Slavery and Four Years of War,* 2 vols. (Springfield, Ohio: Republic Steam Press, 1900), 2:84; muster record, AGR, Series 168.

19. "Morning Reports of Camp Piqua," AGR, Series 2107; "Time Book for Recruiting Officers."

20. "Morning Reports of Camp Piqua."

21. Ibid.

22. "County Draft Records for 1862," AGR, Series 98.

23. Ibid.

24. Muster record, AGR, Series 168; Warren Keifer to Eliza Keifer, Nov. 12, 1862, KP.

25. John R. Rhoades to Sarah Rhoades, Dec. 12, 1862, John R. Rhoades Papers, Rutherford B. Hayes Presidential Center, Fremont, Ohio; Warren Keifer to Eliza Keifer, Dec. 14, 1862, May 23, 1863, KP.

26. Warren Keifer to Eliza Keifer, Oct. 31, 1863, Apr. 15, 1864, KP.

27. Robert Baird to Carrie Baird, Feb. 6, 1864, Baird Family Papers, Ohio Historical Society.

28. Ibid.

29. John Rhoades to Sarah Rhoades, Oct. 29, 1862, Feb. 2, 1863, Rhoades Papers.

30. Rhoades to Rhoades, Feb. 2, 1863.

31. Warren Keifer to Eliza Keifer, Dec. 7, 1863, KP; Robert Baird to Carrie Baird, Feb. 15, 1863, Baird Family Papers.

32. *PE,* June 2, 1864; Rhoades to Rhoades, Feb. 2, 1863.

33. John Rhoades to Sarah Rhoades, Feb. 21, 1865, Rhoades Papers.

2. NOW WE ARE SOLDIERS

1. Keifer, *Four Years,* vol. 2, passim; Whitelaw Reid, *Ohio in the War: Her Statesmen, Her Generals, and Soldiers,* 2 vols. (Cincinnati, Ohio: Moore, Wilstach, and Baldwin, 1868), 2:587.

2. Warren Keifer to Eliza Keifer, Nov. 12, 1863, KP.

3. John Rhoades to Sarah Rhoades, Nov. 23, 1862, John R. Rhoades Papers, Rutherford B. Hayes Presidential Center.

4. Warren Keifer to Eliza Keifer, Oct. 5, 1863, KP.

5. Robert Baird to Carrie Baird, Apr. 7, 1864, Baird Family Papers, Ohio Historical Society.

6. *OR,* vol. 27:61; James B. Casey, ed., *Libby Prison Autograph Book* (Salt Lake City: Utah Genealogical Association, 1984), 16–18; Warren Keifer to Eliza Keifer, Dec. 23, 1862, KP.

7. Warren Keifer to Eliza Keifer, Jan. 4, 1863, KP.

8. John Rhoades to Sarah Rhoades, May 2, 26, 1863, Rhoades Papers.

9. John Rhoades to Sarah Rhoades, Jan. 24, July 14, Nov. 6, 1864, Rhoades Papers.

10. John Rhoades to Sarah Rhoades, May 2, 1863, Feb. 2, 1865, Rhoades Papers; William Moore to Sarah Moore, May 18, 1863, William R. Moore Papers, Ohio Historical Society.

11. John Rhoades to Sarah Rhoades, Feb. 2, Mar. 14, 1865, Rhoades Papers; David McCordick, *The Civil War Letters (1862–1865) of Private Henry Kauffman: The Harmony Boys Are All Well* (New York: Edwin Mellen Press, 1991), 24.

12. *XT,* Apr. 13, 1864; John Rhoades to Sarah Rhoades, Apr. 1, 1864, Sept. 15, 1865, Rhoades Papers.

13. Warren Keifer to Eliza Keifer, Dec. 4, 1863, KP; Robert Baird to Carrie Baird, Dec. 6, 1863, Baird Family Papers; McCordick, *Kauffman,* 54.

14. "List of Returns and Reports to be Forwarded to Brigade Head Quarters," 110th Ohio Volunteer Infantry folder, Civil War Miscellany, Clark County Historical Society, Springfield, Ohio.

15. Reid, *Ohio in the War,* 2:587; *OR,* vol. 27, 2:780.

16. William Moore to Sarah Moore, Sept. [?], 1863, Moore Papers; Rhoades to Rhoades, Jan. 24, 1864; and miscellaneous items, Rhoades Papers.

17. John Rosser to Lucy Rosser, May 31, Aug. 24, Sept. 30, 1864, John F. Rosser

Papers, Wright State University, Dayton, Ohio; John Rhoades to Sarah Rhoades, May 31, Aug. 21, 31, 1864, Rhoades Papers.

18. John Rhoades to Sarah Rhoades, Jan. 10, 1865, Rhoades Papers.

19. John Rosser to Lucy Rosser, July 24, 1864, Rosser Papers; John Rhoades to Sarah Rhoades, Nov. 6, 1864, Rhoades Papers; McCordick, *Kauffman,* 96.

20. Warren Keifer to Eliza Keifer, Jan. 14, 23, 26, 31, Mar. 1, 14, 1864, KP.

21. *TT,* Nov., 20, 1862, Feb. 26, Apr. 9, May 14, Nov. 5, 1863, June 23, Aug. 4, Dec. 1, 1864.

22. *TT,* Apr. 23, May 14, 1863.

23. *XT,* Sept. 23, Dec. 23, 1863, Jan. 27, Mar. 2, May 4, Oct. 12, 1864.

24. *SEN,* Mar. 14, Apr. 7, 1863, Oct. 29, 1864; *SR,* Nov. 13, 1863, May 6, June 27, July 20, 1864.

25. *SEN,* May 17, 1864; *SR,* June 29, July 8, 29, 1864.

26. W. A. Lamme to Luther Brown, June 23, 1864, Luther Brown Papers, Clark County Historical Society.

27. Green Ramey, deposition, July 2, 1864; William Wise, deposition, July 3, 1864; Leroy Lowman, deposition, July 2, 1864; T. G. Green, deposition, July 2, 1864; Willard Childs, deposition, July 2, 1864; Luther Brown to W. A. Lamme, July 4, 1864, Luther Brown Papers; Edwin H. Lamme, military record, Edwin H. Lamme Papers, National Archives and Records Administration, Washington, D.C.

28. John R. Rhoades to Willy Rhoades, May 24, 1863, Jan. 11, 1864, Jan. 6, 1865, Rhoades Papers.

29. Warren Keifer to Eliza Keifer, Feb. 27, 1864, KP; J. F. McKinney to William Moore, Jan. 22, 1864; Rep. J. F. McKinney to Mrs. Moore, Feb. 23, 1864; and J. F. McKinney to Mrs. Moore, Feb. 23, 1864, Moore Papers.

30. Warren Keifer to Eliza Keifer, May 13, Nov. 17, 1863, Jan. 15, Nov. 6, 1864, KP.

31. Warren Keifer to Eliza Keifer, Apr. 25, 1864, KP.

32. John Rhoades to Sarah Rhoades, Jan. 2, 1864, Mar. 14, 1865, Rhoades Papers; McCordick, *Kauffman,* 24, 71.

33. Warren Keifer to Eliza Keifer, Jan. 5, 1863, KP; John Rhoades to Sarah Rhoades, Feb. 6, 1863, Rhoades Papers; *SR,* Nov. 20, 25, 1863; *XT,* Dec. 2, 1863, July 20, 1864; *TT,* Jan. 12, 1865.

34. John Rhoades to Sarah Rhoades, Feb. 18, May 10, 26, 1863, Rhoades Papers.

35. John Rhoades to Sarah Rhoades, Jan. 24, 31, Apr. 28, May 17, 1864, Rhoades Papers.

36. Bell Wiley, *The Life of Billy Yank* (New York: Bobbs-Merrill, 1952), 247–52; John Rhoades to Sarah Rhoades, July 23, Aug. 12, 1863, Rhoades Papers.

37. Warren Keifer to Eliza Keifer, Nov. 6, Dec. 14, 1863, Jan. 1, 1864, KP.

38. Keifer to Keifer, Jan. 5, 1863.

39. William Moore to Sarah Moore, Jan. 12, 1863, Moore Papers.

40. *PR,* Sept. 18, 1862; William Moore to Sarah Moore, May 18, Aug. 27, 1863; Moore Papers; Keifer, *Four Years,* 2:251–86; Thomas Wheeler, *Troy: The Nineteenth Century* (Troy, Ohio: Troy Historical Society, 1970), 261.

41. John Rhoades to Sarah Rhoades, Oct. 11, 12, Nov. 9, 1864, Rhoades Papers; McCordick, *Kauffman,* 89.

42. *SEN,* Mar. 14, Aug. 6, Sept. 10, 1863, Jan. 30, 1864; *PE,* Feb. 5, Sept. 24, 1863; Warren Keifer to William Moore, Mar. 29, 1863; Dr. Abbott to Capt. William Moore, Feb. 26, 1863; Dr. Thomas Beamer to Capt. William Moore, Mar. 21, 1863; Dr. Neff to Capt. William Moore, Apr. 11, 1863; and Rep. J. F. McKinney to Mrs. Moore, Feb. 23, 1864, Moore Papers; John Rosser to Lucy Rosser, Nov. 26, 1863, Mar. 10, 1864, Rosser Papers; Josiah Hill, diary, Mar. 29, 1863, Local History Room, Troy Historical Society; Warren Keifer to Eliza Keifer, Mar. 28, 1863, KP; McCordick, *Kauffman,* 23.

43. Warren Keifer to Eliza Keifer, Dec. 5, 1862, May 22, June 5, 1863, KP; William Moore to Sarah Moore, Mar. 17, 1863, Moore Papers.

44. Warren Keifer to Eliza Keifer, June 16, 26, July 4, 1863, KP.

45. *OR,* ser. 2, vol. 7:101, 763.

46. William B. Hesseltine, *Civil War Prisons* (Columbus: Ohio State Univ. Press, 1930), 74.

47. *OR,* ser. 2, vol. 5:39–40, 466; *OR,* ser. 3, vol. 3:160–61.

48. *OR,* ser. 2, vol. 5:39.

49. John Rhoades to Sarah Rhoades, July 23, Aug. 12, 1863, Rhoades Papers; *Miami Valley (Ohio) News,* Oct. 26, 1988; McCordick, *Kauffman,* 34.

50. John Rhoades to Sarah Rhoades, Apr. 19, 1864, Rhoades Papers; Warren Keifer to Eliza Keifer, Apr. 18, 1863, Feb. 28, 1864, Mar. 7, 9, 10, 1865, KP.

3. EVERYTHING DEPENDED UPON THIS EFFORT

1. *PR,* Sept. 18, 1862; Josiah Hill, diary, Aug. 22–Oct. 19, 1862, Local History Room, Troy Historical Society.

2. Hill, diary, Aug. 23, 24, 1862.

3. Ibid., Sept. 2, 21, 22, 1862.

4. Lorenzo Barnhart, reminiscences, 1, Greene County Public Library, Xenia, Ohio.

5. Hill, diary, Aug. 31, Sept. 3, 26, 27, 28, 1862.

6. Ibid., Oct. 1, 8, 1862

7. Warren Keifer to Eliza Keifer, Oct. 20, 1862, KP; Hill, diary, Oct. 19–21, 1862; Barnhart, reminiscences, 1; McCordick, *Kauffman,* 8.

8. Hill, diary, Oct. 21–Nov. 2, 1862; John Rosser to Lucy Rosser, Oct. 26, 1862, John F. Rosser Papers, Wright State University.

9. Hill, diary, Oct. 21–Nov. 2, 1862; Rosser to Rosser, Oct. 26, 1862; McCordick, *Kauffman,* 9–10; Barnhart, reminiscences, 2.

10. John Rhoades to Sarah Rhoades, Nov. 5, 1862, John R. Rhoades Papers, Rutherford B. Hayes Presidential Center; Hill, diary, Nov. 3, 1862.

11. Barnhart, reminiscences, 2; Hill, diary, Nov. 8, 1862.

12. Hill, diary, Nov. 15, 16, 1862; John Rhoades to Sarah Rhoades, Nov. 18, 1862, Rhoades Papers; Warren Keifer to Eliza Keifer, Nov. 16, 1862, KP.

13. John Rhoades to Sarah Rhoades, Nov. 23, 1862, Rhoades Papers; Warren Keifer to Eliza Keifer, Nov. 18, 1862, KP; Hill, diary, Nov. 22, 1862.

14. Warren Keifer to Eliza Keifer, Oct. 25, Nov. 8, 12, 1862, KP.

15. Warren Keifer to Eliza Keifer, Nov. 12, 17, 18, 1862, KP; Stephen Sears, *George B. McClellan: The Young Napoleon* (New York: Ticknor and Fields, 1988), 329–40; Stephen D. Engle, "Generalship on Trial: Don Carlos Buell's Campaign to Chattanooga," in *Civil War Generals in Defeat,* ed. Steven Woodworth (Lawrence: University Press of Kansas, 1999), 95–97, 116; Robert J. Chumney Jr., "Don Carlos Buell: Gentleman General" (Ph.D. diss., Rice University, 1964), 98–123.

16. Robert Johnson and Clarence Buel, *Battles and Leaders of the Civil War,* 4 vols. (Secaucus, N.J.: Book Sales, 1983), 4:767; *PR,* Sept. 18, 1862; *Roster,* 8:15; Warren Keifer to Eliza Keifer, Dec. 27, 1862, Jan. 16, 1863, KP; William Moore to Sarah Moore, Nov. 28, 1862, William R. Moore Papers, Ohio Historical Society; James McPherson, *Battle Cry of Freedom* (New York: Ballatine Books, 1988), 486–88.

17. McCordick, *Kauffman,* 17; Warren Keifer to Eliza Keifer, Apr. 11, May 14, 1863, KP.

18. Warren Keifer to Eliza Keifer, Feb. 14, May 18, 1863, KP.

19. Warren Keifer to Eliza Keifer, Dec. 12, 1862, KP; Hill, diary, Dec. 12, 1862; Barnhart, reminiscences, 2; John Rhoades to Sarah Rhoades, Dec. 12, 1862, Rhoades Papers.

20. Warren Keifer to Eliza Keifer, Dec. 13, 14, 1862, KP; Rhoades to Rhoades, Dec. 12, 1862; Barnhart, reminiscences, 2–3; Hill, diary, Dec. 12, 13, 1862.

21. John Rhoades to Sarah Rhoades, Dec. 16, 22, 1862, Rhoades Papers; Hill, diary, Dec. 15–24, 1862; Warren Keifer to Eliza Keifer, Dec. 17, 18, 24, 1862, KP; Barnhart, reminiscences, 3.

22. Hill, diary, Dec. 29, 30, 31, 1862, Jan. 1, 1863; Warren Keifer to Eliza Keifer, Dec. 30, 31, 1862, Jan. 1, 1863, KP; Barnhart, reminiscences, 3.

23. Hill, diary, Jan. 1, 2, 1863; Brandon Beck and Charles Grunden, *Three Battles of Winchester* (Berryville, Va.: Country Publishers, 1988), 17.

24. Charles H. Berry to Annie Hall, Jan. 10, 1863, Charles Berry Papers, Clark County Historical Society; Hill, diary, Apr. 1–June 13, 1863; John Rhoades to Willy Rhoades, May 24, 1863, Rhoades Papers.

25. John Rhoades to Sarah Rhoades, Jan. 19, 1863, Rhoades Papers.

26. Warren Keifer to Eliza Keifer, Mar. 24, 30, Apr. 2, 6, 7, 8, 10, May 4, June 3, 6, 9, 1863, KP.

27. Hill, diary, Jan. 3, 24, Feb. 10, Mar. 30, Apr. 28, 29, 30, May 1, 1863; John Rhoades to Sarah Rhoades, May 26, 1863, Rhoades Papers.

28. Warren Keifer to Eliza Keifer, Jan. 12, 14, 1863, KP; Hill, diary, Jan. 12, 13, 14, 1863.

29. Warren Keifer to Eliza Keifer, Jan. 18, 19, 1863, KP; Rhoades to Rhoades, Jan. 19, 1863; William Moore to Sarah Moore, Jan. 19, 1863, Moore Papers

30. Hill, diary, Apr. 12, 13, 1863; Warren Keifer to Eliza Keifer, Apr. 12, May 19, 1863, KP; McCordick, *Kauffman,* 21–25; *TT,* Apr. 23, 1863; *SR,* Apr. 22, 1863.

31. Hill, diary, May 5, 6, 7, 8, 9, 1863; Warren Keifer to Eliza Keifer, May 9, 1863, KP; John Rhoades to Sarah Rhoades, May 10, 1863, Rhoades Papers.

32. Hill, diary, May 19, 1863; Warren Keifer to Eliza Keifer, Feb. 14, Apr. 21, May 19, 28, 29, 30, 31, June 1, 2, 3, 4, 7, 8, 11, 1863, KP.

33. *OR,* vol. 27:43.

34. Beck and Grunden, *Three Battles of Winchester,* 18; *OR,* vol. 27:44–5, 57, 60; Keifer, *Four Years,* 2:7–9; Hill, diary, June 13, 1863; Barnhart, reminiscences, 4.

35. *OR,* vol. 27:46, 60–61; Hill, diary, June 13, 14, 1863; Keifer, *Four Years,* 2:10–11; Barnhart, reminiscences, 4.

36. Barnhart, reminiscences, 4.

37. *OR,* vol. 27:46, 60–61, 73–74; Hill, diary, June 13, 14, 1863; Keifer, *Four Years,* 2:10–11; Barnhart, reminiscences, 5.

38. Keifer, *Four Years,* 2:11; Barnhart, reminiscences, 5.

39. Keifer, *Four Years,* 2:11; *OR,* vol. 27:60; *Roster,* 8:15.

40. *OR,* vol. 27:47, 57, 61; Keifer, *Four Years,* 2:13; Barnhart, reminiscences, 5; Hill, diary, June 15, 1863.

41. *Roster,* 8:1, 4, 7; *OR,* vol. 27:61; Warren Keifer to Eliza Keifer, June 15, 1863, KP.

42. Beck and Grunden, *Three Battles of Winchester,* 23; Keifer to Keifer, June 15, 1863.

43. Beck and Grunden, *Three Battles of Winchester,* 23; Warren Keifer to Eliza Keifer, June 16, 1863, KP.

44. Barnhart, reminiscences, 6.

45. Warren Keifer to Eliza Keifer, June 17, 1863, KP; *OR,* vol. 27:47, 58–59, 62, 68, 73–74, 136–39; *XT,* July 1, 1863; Beck and Grunden, *Three Battles of Winchester,* 23–24; Keifer, *Four Years,* 2:14–18.

46. Hill, diary, June 29, 30, July 1, 1863; Warren Keifer to Eliza Keifer, June 21, 1863, KP; William Moore to Sarah Moore, June 28, 1863, Moore Papers.

47. Warren Keifer to Eliza Keifer, July 3, 4, 1863, KP; Hill, diary, July 2, 3, 4, 1863; Barnhart, reminiscences, 6.

48. Hill, diary, July 6, 1863; Warren Keifer to Eliza Keifer, July 6, 9, 10, 1863, KP; Keifer, *Four Years,* 2:19–20; *OR,* vol. 27:88–197; Ezra Warner, *Generals in Blue:*

Lives of the Union Commanders (Baton Rouge: Louisiana State University Press, 1964), 326.

49. John Rhoades to Sarah Rhoades, July 23, 1863, Rhoades Papers; *SEN,* Aug. 13, 1863.

50. McPherson, *Battle Cry,* 600–601, 609–11; Bruce Catton, *Never Call Retreat* (Garden City, N.Y.: Doubleday, 1965) 170–71, 214–17.

51. Hill, diary, Aug. 23–Sept. 14, 1863; Warren Keifer to Eliza Keifer, Aug. 23, 26, Sept. 14, 1863, KP; Keifer, *Four Years,* 2:37–47; *TT,* Sept. 3, 1863.

52. Hill, diary, Sept. 8, 10, 1863.

53. Ibid., Sept. 14, 1863; Keifer to Keifer, Sept. 14, 1865.

54. Hill, diary, Sept. 16, 18, 20, Oct. 10, 1863; Warren Keifer to Eliza Keifer, Sept. 22, 1863, KP; Keifer, *Four Years,* 2:48.

55. Warren Keifer to Eliza Keifer, Sept. 27, 31, Oct. 1, 1863, KP.

56. William Moore to Sarah Moore, Sept. [?], 1863, Moore Papers; Warren Keifer to Eliza Keifer, Oct. 3, 4, 1863, KP; Keifer, *Four Years,* 2:48–49.

57. Hill, diary, Oct. 10, 11, 15, 25, 1863.

58. Ibid., Oct. 12, 1863; Warren Keifer to Eliza Keifer, Oct. 13, 1863, KP; Keifer, *Four Years,* 2:49.

59. Warren Keifer to Eliza Keifer, Oct. 13, 15, 1863, KP; *OR,* vol. 29:250, 335, 428, vol. 27:335; Keifer, *Four Years,* 2:49–54.

60. Keifer, *Four Years,* 2:54–57; Hill, diary, Nov. 7, 8, 1863; Warren Keifer to Eliza Keifer, Nov. 9, 10, 1863, KP; *OR,* vol. 27:562.

61. Keifer, *Four Years,* 2:56–57.

62. Warren Keifer to Eliza Keifer, Nov. 29, 1863, KP.

63. Keifer, *Four Years,* 2:56–57; Keifer to Keifer, Nov. 9, 10, 1863; *OR,* vol. 27:562, 776–79.

64. Keifer, *Four Years,* 2:56–57; Warren Keifer to Eliza Keifer, Nov. 10, 14, 1863, KP; Hill, diary, Nov. 16, 1863; *OR,* vol. 27:562, 776–79; Robert Baird to Carrie Baird, Dec. 6, 1863, Baird Family Papers, Ohio Historical Society.

65. Warren Keifer to Eliza Keifer, Nov. 29, 1863, KP; Keifer, *Four Years,* 2:58–82; *OR,* vol. 27:682, 776–79.

66. Keifer to Keifer, Nov. 29, 1863; Keifer, *Four Years,* 2:58–82; *OR,* vol. 27:682, 776–79.

67. Keifer, *Four Years,* 2:64–65; *OR,* vol. 27:682, 776–79; Keifer to Keifer, Nov. 29, 1863.

68. Keifer, *Four Years,* 2:66–67.

69. *OR,* vol. 27:682; Keifer to Keifer, Nov. 29, 1863; Keifer, *Four Years,* 2:64–68.

70. Warren Keifer to Eliza Keifer, Dec. 23, 1863, Jan. 4, 1864, KP.

71. Warren Keifer to Eliza Keifer, Dec. 22, 26, 1863, Mar. 13, 1864, KP; Moore to Moore, Sept. [?], 1863; Barnhart, reminiscences, 6.

72. Warren Keifer to Eliza Keifer, Dec. 12, 1863, Jan. 9, Feb. 23, Mar. 13, 15, 24, 1864, KP; McCordick, *Kauffman*, 69; Hill, diary, Mar. 27, 1864; Keifer, *Four Years*, 2:71–73; John Rosser to Lucy Rosser, Mar. 13, 1864, Rosser Papers; John Rhoades to Sarah Rhoades, Apr. 1, 1864, Rhoades Papers; *OR*, vol. 27:638–39, 774–75, 1042.

73. Warren Keifer to Eliza Keifer, Apr. 8, 1864, KP; Hill, diary, Apr. 8, 1864; John Rhoades to Sarah Rhoades, Apr. 10, 1864, Rhoades Papers.

4. WELL, I AM STILL ALIVE

1. John Rosser to Lucy Rosser, Mar. 10, 15, 1864, John F. Rosser Papers, Wright State University; Warren Keifer to Eliza Keifer, Feb. 17, Apr. 18, 29, 1864, KP; John Rhoades to Sarah Rhoades, Feb. 12, Apr. 19, 28, 1864, John R. Rhoades Papers, Rutherford B. Hayes Presidential Center; Josiah Hill, diary, Feb. 1, Apr. 18, 29, 1864, Troy Historical Society.

2. Warren Keifer to Eliza Keifer, Apr. 7, 21, 1864, KP; Robert Baird to Carrie Baird, Apr. 7, 1864, Baird Family Papers, Ohio Historical Society.

3. John Rhoades to Sarah Rhoades, Apr. 12, 1864, Rhoades Papers; Warren Keifer to Eliza Keifer, Apr. 14, 15, 16, 19, 28, 1864, KP.

4. John Rhoades to Sarah Rhoades, Apr. 16, 1864, Rhoades Papers; Hill, diary, Apr. 16, 1864; Warren Keifer to Eliza Keifer, Apr. 16, 1864, KP.

5. Warren Keifer to Eliza Keifer, Mar. 29, Apr. 18, 1864, KP; Rosser to Rosser, Mar. 15, 1864, Rosser Papers; John Rhoades to Sarah Rhoades, Apr. 26, 1864, Rhoades Papers; Lorenzo Barnhart, reminiscences, 7–8, Greene County Public Library.

6. Rhoades to Rhoades, Apr. 12, 1864; Rosser to Rosser, Mar. 15, 1864; Hill, diary, May 3, 1864; Warren Keifer to Eliza Keifer, May 1, 3, 1864, KP.

7. McPherson, *Battle Cry*, 724–28; Keifer, *Four Years*, 2:74–88; Johnson and Buel, *Battles and Leaders*, 4:118–77; *OR*, vol. 36:728–32, 741–44; John Michael Priest, *Nowhere to Run: The Wilderness, May 4th and 5th, 1864* (Shippensburg, Pa.: White Mane, 1995), 13; Gordon C. Rhea, *The Battle of the Wilderness, May 5–6, 1864* (Baton Rouge: Louisiana State University Press, 1994), 131.

8. McPherson, *Battle Cry*, 724–28; Keifer, *Four Years*, 2:74–88; Johnson and Buel, *Battles and Leaders*, 4:118–77; *OR*, vol. 36:728–32, 741–44; *SR*, June 27, 1864; Priest, *Nowhere to Run*, 126–29; Rhea, *Battle of the Wilderness*, 186.

9. Keifer, *Four Years*, 2:74–88; Warren Keifer to Eliza Keifer, May 10, 1864, KP; *OR*, vol. 36:728–32, 741–44; Priest, *Nowhere to Run*, 126–29; Rhea, *Battle of the Wilderness*, 244–49.

10. Keifer, *Four Years*, 2:74–88; Keifer to Keifer, May 10, 1864; *OR*, vol. 36:728–32, 741–44; Priest, *Nowhere to Run*, 126–29; Edward Steere, *The Wilderness Campaign* (Harrisburg, Pa.: Stackpole, 1960), 253–55.

11. Keifer, *Four Years*, 2:74–88; Keifer to Keifer, May 10, 1864; *OR*, vol. 36:728–32, 741–44; Barnhart, reminiscences, 7; Rhea, *Battle of the Wilderness*, 268–69, 322–23, 410–11, 417–20; Steere, *Wilderness Campaign*, 440–43.

12. *OR*, vol. 36:742.

13. McPherson, *Battle Cry*, 724–28; Keifer, *Four Years*, 2:74–88; Johnson and Buel, *Battles and Leaders*, 4:118–77; *OR*, vol. 36:728–32, 741–44; Barnhart, reminiscences, 7–9; Gordon C. Rhea, *The Battles for Spotsylvania Court House and the Road to Yellow Tavern, May 7–12, 1864* (Baton Rouge: Louisiana State University Press, 1997), 221, 261, 291, 304.

14. *SR*, June 27, 1864.

15. McPherson, *Battle Cry*, 724–28; Keifer, *Four Years*, 2:74–88; Johnson and Buel, *Battles and Leaders*, 4:118–77; *OR*, vol. 36:728–32, 741–44; *XT*, June 1, 1864.

16. *OR*, vol. 36:741–44.

17. John Rosser to Lucy Rosser, May 31, 1864, Rosser Papers; *XT*, June 29, 1864.

18. R. Wayne Maney, *Marching to Cold Harbor* (Shippensburg, Pa.: White Mane, 1995), 99–100; McPherson, *Battle Cry*, 724–28; Keifer, *Four Years*, 2:74–88; Johnson and Buel, *Battles and Leaders*, 4:118–77; *OR*, vol. 36:728–32, 741–44; *XT*, June 1, 29, 1864.

19. Maney, *Marching to Cold Harbor*, 105–6; *OR*, vol. 36:741–44; *XT*, June 29, 1864.

20. Maney, *Marching to Cold Harbor*, 146–48; Hill, diary, June 1, 2, 3, 1864; *SR*, June 27, 1864; Keifer, *Four Years*, 2:90–93; *XT*, June 29, 1864; *OR*, vol. 36:741–44.

21. Maney, *Marching to Cold Harbor*, 148; Hill, diary, June 5, 7, 11, 1864; John Rosser to Lucy Rosser, June 8, 1864, Rosser Papers.

22. John Rhoades to Sarah Rhoades, June 10, 11, 1864, Rhoades Papers; *XT*, July 20, 1864.

23. Hill, diary, May 18, 27, 1864; John Rhoades to Sarah Rhoades, May 31, June 2, 8, 1864, Rhoades Papers; John Rosser to Lucy Rosser, June 20, 1864, Rosser Papers.

24. Maney, *Marching to Cold Harbor*, 202; Hill, diary, June 16, 1864; Rosser to Rosser, June 20, 1864; John Rhoades to Sarah Rhoades, June 17, 1864, Rhoades Papers; Noah Andre Trudeau, *The Last Citadel: Petersburg, Virginia, June 1864–April 1865* (New York: Little, Brown, 1991), 18.

25. John Rosser to Lucy Rosser, May 15, 1864, Rosser Papers; *OR*, vol. 36:127, 146, 174, 188.

5. TEARS DRAWN FROM THE DEEPEST SORROW

1. McPherson, *Battle Cry*, 737–39; Shelby Foote, *The Civil War: A Narrative*, 3 vols. (New York: Random House, 1974), 2:301–12, 445–46; *OR*, vol. 37:94–103, 492; Keifer, *Four Years*, 2:96–99; Johnson and Buel, *Battles and Leaders*, 4:494–99;

Warner, *Generals in Blue,* 61–62; Ulysses S. Grant, *Personal Memoirs of U. S. Grant,* 2 vols. (New York: Charles L. Webster, 1886), 2:478–79, 489–94.

2. *OR,* vol. 37:94–103, 492; Keifer, *Four Years,* 2:96–99; Johnson and Buel, *Battles and Leaders,* 4:494–99.

3. *OR,* vol. 37:94–103, 492; Keifer, *Four Years,* 2:96–99; Johnson and Buel, *Battles and Leaders,* 4:494–99; Josiah Hill, diary, July 6, 7, 8, 1864, Troy Historical Society; *SR,* July 18, 1864; *TT,* Dec. 1, 1864; B. Franklin Cooling, *Monocacy: The Battle That Saved Washington* (Shippensburg, Pa.: White Mane, 1997), 111.

4. *OR,* vol. 37:191–200.

5. Ibid., 191–200, 206–10; *SR,* July 18, 1864; *TT,* Dec. 1, 1864; Keifer, *Four Years,* 2:99–100; Johnson and Buel, *Battles and Leaders,* 4:492–99; Cooling, *Monocacy,* 113–17.

6. Cooling, *Monocacy,* 118–19; *OR,* vol. 37:205, 209.

7. Cooling, *Monocacy,* 140.

8. Ibid., 140–41; *OR,* vol. 37:213.

9. *TT,* Dec. 1, 1864; John Rhoades to Sarah Rhoades, July 10, 1864, John R. Rhoades Papers, Rutherford B. Hayes Presidential Center; Cooling, *Monocacy,* 142; *OR,* vol. 37:208.

10. Cooling, *Monocacy,* 143, 146–49.

11. Ibid., 149.

12. Ibid., 151; *OR,* vol. 37:209.

13. Cooling, *Monocacy,* 151–52; *SR,* July 20, 1864; *OR,* vol. 37:210; *Roster,* 8:32.

14. Cooling, *Monocacy,* 153.

15. *OR,* vol. 37:191–200, 206–10; *SR,* July 18, 1864; *TT,* Dec. 1, 1864; Keifer, *Four Years,* 2:99–100; Johnson and Buel, *Battles and Leaders,* 4:492–99; Hill, diary, July 9, 1864; Rhoades to Rhoades, July 10, 1864.

16. Charles H. Berry to Annie Hall, July 12, 1864, Charles Berry Papers, Clark County Historical Society; *OR,* vol. 37:206–10; *Roster,* 8:32; *SR,* July 12, 16, 1864. See also various items in the Luther Brown Papers, Clark County Historical Society.

17. Rhoades to Rhoades, July 10, 1864; Hill, diary, July 10–Nov. 27, 1864; *Roster,* 20; *OR,* vol. 37:206–10; *TT,* Dec. 1, 1864.

18. *OR,* vol. 37:201–2, 209–10; *SR,* July 20, 1864.

19. *OR,* vol. 37:264–70; Keifer, *Four Years,* 2:101–3.

20. *OR,* vol. 37:204–5, 270–75.

21. John Rhoades to Sarah Rhoades, July 17, 24, 25, 28, Aug. 1, 1864, Rhoades Papers; McCordick, *Kauffman,* 80–83; John Rosser to Lucy Rosser, July 21, Aug. 24, 1864, John F. Rosser Papers, Wright State University; *TT,* Aug. 4, 1864.

22. *OR,* vol. 37:709–10; Keifer, *Four Years,* 2:101–3.

23. *OR,* vol. 37:63–75, 558; Keifer, *Four Years,* 2:107–8.

24. John Rhoades to Sarah Rhoades, Aug. 27, 1864, Rhoades Papers; Warren Keifer to Eliza Keifer, Aug. 27, 1864, KP; McCordick, *Kauffman,* 85.

25. Johnson and Buel, *Battles and Leaders*, 4:500–506; Beck and Grunden, *Three Battles of Winchester*, 26–27; Keifer, *Four Years*, 2:109–10; Foote, *The Civil War*, 3:777; Philip Sheridan, *Personal Memoirs of P. H. Sheridan*, 2 vols. (New York: Charles Webster, 1888), 2:1–9; James E. Taylor, *With Sheridan up the Shenandoah Valley in 1864* (Cleveland: Western Reserve Historical Society, 1989), 348–55.

26. Beck and Grunden, *Three Battles of Winchester*, 26–28; Sheridan, *Memoirs*, 2:10–12; Keifer, *Four Years*, 2:109–10; Johnson and Buel, *Battles and Leaders*, 4:506–10, 522–24; Foote, *The Civil War*, 3:553–55; McPherson, *Battle Cry*, 777; *OR*, vol. 43:25–27, 43–51.

27. Beck and Grunden, *Three Battles of Winchester*, 26–28; Sheridan, *Memoirs*, 2:10–12; Johnson and Buel, *Battles and Leaders*, 4:506–10, 522–24.

28. Johnson and Buel, *Battles and Leaders*, 4:522–24; Beck and Grunden, *Three Battles of Winchester*, 28–30; Jeffry D. Wert, *From Winchester to Cedar Creek: The Shenandoah Campaign of 1864* (Carlisle, Pa.: South Mountain Press, 1987), 54.

29. Keifer, *Four Years*, 2:116–17; Wert, *From Winchester to Cedar Creek*, 54, 65–66; *OR*, 43:246–48, 258–60, 263, 266, 269.

30. Beck and Grunden, *Three Battles of Winchester*, 31–35; Sheridan, *Memoirs*, 2:18–27; Keifer, *Four Years*, 2:109–10; Johnson and Buel, *Battles and Leaders*, 4:500–32; *OR*, vol. 43:25–27, 43–51, 246–50, 258; Wert, *From Winchester to Cedar Creek*, 65–66; John Rhoades to Sarah Rhoades, Sept. 20, 1864, Rhoades Papers; *XT*, Oct. 12, 1864.

31. Beck and Grunden, *Three Battles of Winchester*, 31–35; Sheridan, *Memoirs*, 2:18–27; Keifer, *Four Years*, 2:109–10; Johnson and Buel, *Battles and Leaders*, 4:500–32; *OR*, vol. 43:25–27, 43–51, 246–50, 258; Warren Keifer to Eliza Keifer, Sept. 20, 1864, KP; Rhoades to Rhoades, Sept. 20, 1864.

32. Beck and Grunden, *Three Battles of Winchester*, 31–35; Sheridan, *Memoirs*, 2:18–27; Keifer, *Four Years*, 2:109–10; Johnson and Buel, *Battles and Leaders*, 4:500–32; *OR*, vol. 43:25–27, 43–51.

33. *OR*, vol. 43:113, 118; Beck and Grunden, *Three Battles of Winchester*, 35; *TT*, Jan. 12, 1865; Keifer, *Four Years*, 2:115–17; Keifer to Keifer, Sept. 20, 1864.

34. Sheridan, *Memoirs*, 2:33–43; Keifer, *Four Years*, 118–23; Warren Keifer to Eliza Keifer, Sept. 23, 1864, KP; *OR*, vol. 43:17–57, 70–75, 221–30, 246–50, 258–60; Foote, *The Civil War*, 3:556–58; Catton, *Never Call Retreat*, 390; Johnson and Buel, *Battles and Leaders*, 510–11, 524.

35. Sheridan, *Memoirs*, 2:33–43; Keifer, *Four Years*, 2:118–23; Keifer to Keifer, Sept. 23, 1864; *OR*, vol. 43:17–57, 70–75, 221–30, 246–50, 258–60; Foote, *The Civil War*, 3:556–58.

36. Sheridan, *Memoirs*, 2:33–43; Keifer, *Four Years*, 2:118–23; Keifer to Keifer, Sept. 23, 1864; *OR*, vol. 43:17–57, 70–75, 221–30, 246–50, 258–60; Catton, *Never Call Retreat*, 390; *XT*, Oct. 12, 1864; John Rhoades to Sarah Rhoades, Sept. 22, 1864, Rhoades Papers; *XT*, Oct. 12, 1864.

37. *OR,* vol. 43:124–30; Johnson and Buel, *Battles and Leaders,* 4:525.

38. Sheridan, *Memoirs,* 2:49–57; Johnson and Buel, *Battles and Leaders,* 4:511–15; Theodore Mahr, "'Another Union Victory!': The Confederate Army of the Valley at Cedar Creek, Oct. 19, 1864" (master's thesis, Wright State University, 1988), 35–61.

39. Warren Keifer to Eliza Keifer, Sept. 30, 1864, KP.

40. Sheridan, *Memoirs,* 2:49–60; Keifer, *Four Years,* 2:124–27; John Rhoades to Sarah Rhoades, Sept. 25, Oct. 3, 11, 17, 1864, Rhoades Papers; John Rosser to Lucy Rosser, Sept. 30, 1864, Rosser Papers; Warren Keifer to Eliza Keifer, Sept. 30, Oct. 8, 12, 1864, KP; Mahr, "Another Union Victory!'" 48–66; Johnson and Buel, *Battles and Leaders,* 4:511–15, 524–26; McCordick, *Kauffman,* 88; *OR,* vol. 37:300, vol. 43:52–54, 436, 443–52, 529.

41. Sheridan, *Memoirs,* 2:60–68; *OR,* vol. 43:51–53; Mahr, "Another Union Victory!'" 127.

42. Keifer, *Four Years,* 2:128–29; Sheridan, *Memoirs,* 2:63; Mahr, "Another Union Victory!'" 79–85; *OR,* vol. 43:478, 590–91.

43. Keifer, *Four Years,* 2:130–33; Sheridan, *Memoirs,* 2:61–62; Mahr, "Another Union Victory!'" 106–8, 121–27; *OR,* vol. 43:225–30, 250, 403–4; Johnson and Buel, *Battles and Leaders,* 4:516–19.

44. Mahr, "Another Union Victory!'" 103–20; Johnson and Buel, *Battles and Leaders,* 4:526; *OR,* vol. 43:580–81.

45. Mahr, "Another Union Victory!'" 138–50; Keifer, *Four Years,* 2:132; *OR,* vol. 43:403–4, 561–64; Johnson and Buel, *Battles and Leaders,* 4:516–19, 526–30, 561–65.

46. Mahr, "Another Union Victory!'" 155–68; Keifer, *Four Years,* 2:132–33; *OR,* vol. 43:225–30, 284–86, 403–4, 561–65; Johnson and Buel, *Battles and Leaders,* 4:516–19.

47. Mahr, "Another Union Victory!'" 177–90; Keifer, *Four Years,* 2:132–34; *OR,* vol. 43:284–86; Johnson and Buel, *Battles and Leaders,* 4:516–19, 526–30.

48. Mahr, "Another Union Victory!'" 196–202; Keifer, *Four Years,* 2:132–34; *OR,* vol. 43:225–30, 250–52, 258–60; Johnson and Buel, *Battles and Leaders,* 4:516–19.

49. Mahr, "Another Union Victory!'" 196–202; Keifer, *Four Years,* 2:132–34; *OR,* vol. 43:225–30, 250–52, 258–60.

50. Mahr, "Another Union Victory!'" 219–35; *OR,* vol. 43:561–65; Johnson and Buel, *Battles and Leaders,* 4:525–30.

51. Mahr, "Another Union Victory!'" 219–35; Keifer, *Four Years,* 2:132–34; *OR,* vol. 43:225–30, 250–52, 258–60; Johnson and Buel, *Battles and Leaders,* 4:516–19, 525–30.

52. Mahr, "Another Union Victory!'" 237–42; Keifer, *Four Years,* 2:134; *OR,* vol. 43:193–96, 525–30; Johnson and Buel, *Battles and Leaders,* 4:516–19, 525–30.

53. Mahr, "Another Union Victory!'" 242–55; *OR,* vol. 43:193–96; Johnson and Buel, *Battles and Leaders,* 4:516–19, 525–30.

54. Mahr, "Another Union Victory!'" 255–58; *OR,* vol. 43:561–65; Johnson and Buel, *Battles and Leaders,* 4:525–30.

55. Mahr, "Another Union Victory!'" 262–68; Keifer, *Four Years,* 2:138–39; *OR,* vol. 43:52–53; Johnson and Buel, *Battles and Leaders,* 4:516–19; Sheridan, *Memoirs,* 2:82–83.

56. Sheridan, *Memoirs,* 2:86–88; Mahr, "Another Union Victory!'" 298–99.

57. Mahr, "Another Union Victory!'" 281–84; Johnson and Buel, *Battles and Leaders,* 4:525–30; *OR,* vol. 43:561–65.

58. Sheridan, *Memoirs,* 2:88–91.

59. Mahr, "Another Union Victory!'" 315–20; Keifer, *Four Years,* 2:145–51; *OR,* vol. 43:225–30, 250–52, 258–60; Johnson and Buel, *Battles and Leaders,* 4:516–19; Warren Keifer to Eliza Keifer, Oct. 21, 1864, KP.

60. *OR,* vol. 43:228–30, 233–34, 250–52, 259–60; Keifer, *Four Years,* 2:147–50; Keifer to Keifer, Oct. 21, 1864.

61. Mahr, "Another Union Victory!'" 336–38, 348–50, 353–59; *OR,* vol. 43:561–65; Johnson and Buel, *Battles and Leaders,* 4:525–30.

62. Mahr, "Another Union Victory!'" 383; Johnson and Buel, *Battles and Leaders,* 4:532.

63. *OR,* vol. 43:132, 137; Keifer, *Four Years,* 2:154–55.

64. Keifer, *Four Years,* 2:135–36; *OR,* vol. 43:230, 252.

65. McCordick, *Kauffman,* 90–95; *SR,* Oct. 29, 1864.

66. *OR,* vol. 43:138, 259–60; *Roster,* 8:20; John Rhoades to Sarah Rhoades, Oct. 21, 1864, Rhoades Papers; Warren Keifer to Eliza Keifer, Oct., 21, 24, 1864, KP.

67. John Rosser to Lucy Rosser, Oct. 22, 1864; William L. Reed, deposition, Nov. 14, 1865; and George Sprecher, deposition, Nov. 11, 1865, John Rosser Papers; *Roster,* 8:11.

68. *OR,* vol. 37:202, vol. 43:113, 121, 132; Luther Brown to W. A. Lamme, July 4, 1864, Brown Papers; Charles Berry to Annie Hall, Nov. 24, 1864, Berry Papers.

6. THE LAND OF THE FREE

1. Josiah Hill, diary, Nov. 27, 1864; McCordick, *Kauffman,* 90–95; Warren Keifer to Eliza Keifer, Nov. 13, 1864, KP.

2. Warren Keifer to Eliza Keifer, Oct. 28, 1864, KP; John Rhoades to Sarah Rhoades, Nov. 6, 1864, John R. Rhoades Papers, Rutherford B. Hayes Presidential Center.

3. Warren Keifer to Eliza Keifer, Oct. 29, 1864, KP.

4. Warren Keifer to Eliza Keifer, Mar. 29, Dec. 7, 1864, KP.

5. Hill, diary, Dec. 19, 1864; John Rhoades to Sarah Rhoades, Jan. 26, Feb. 2, 1865, Rhoades Papers.

6. Warren Keifer to Eliza Keifer, Dec. 16, 1864, KP; John Rhoades to Sarah Rhoades, Nov. 6, 27, 1864, Jan. 4, 6, 26, Feb. 21, 27, 1865, Rhoades Papers; Hill, diary, Dec. 29, 1864, Jan. 10, 11, 13, 24, 29, 30, Feb. 5, 1865.

7. Hill, diary, Feb. 9, 13, 14, 15, 1865; Warren Keifer to Eliza Keifer, Feb. 9, 1865, KP.

8. Warren Keifer to Eliza Keifer, Dec. 16, 1864, Feb. 9, 10, 1865, KP; Keifer, *Four Years,* 2:184; McCordick, *Kauffman,* 98.

9. Keifer to Keifer, Feb. 9, 1865; Rhoades to Rhoades, Feb. 21, 27, 1865; Hill, diary, Feb. 23, Mar. 3, 1865; McCordick, *Kauffman,* 100; Francis M. McMillen, diary, Feb. 12, 22, Mar. 2, 14, 1865, U.S. Army Military History Institute, Carlisle Barracks, Carlisle, Pa.; Ella Lonn, *Desertion during the Civil War* (Boston: American Historical Association, 1928), 27–29, 38–40.

10. "List of Rebel Deserters," Luther Brown Papers, Clark County Historical Society; McMillen, diary, Mar. 2, 1865; Lonn, *Desertion,* 35.

11. Rhoades to Rhoades, Feb. 27, 1865.

12. According to my research, there exists a discrepancy regarding the identity of the condemned man. In Warren Keifer's letter to his wife dated Mar. 11, 1865, the general wrote that the young man's name was James Kelly. But on page 185 of his 1900 book, *Slavery and Four Years of War,* Keifer states that the man's name was James L. Hicks. Two orders from the War Department also listed the young man as James Hicks. Thus far, further investigation has not provided any conclusive answers. Published in 1869, Samuel Bates's *History of Pennsylvania Volunteers,* volume 2, does not list a James Kelly in the 67th Pennsylvania Volunteer Infantry's roster. On page 649, it does list a James L. Hicks of Company C. According to Bates, however, Pvt. James L. Hicks mustered out with the regiment on July 14, 1865.

13. U.S. War Department, Adjutant General's Office, Special Order No. 6, Feb. 2, 1865, Brown Papers; Lonn, *Desertion,* 169–70, 179–82.

14. Keifer, *Four Years,* 2:185; Warren Keifer to Eliza Keifer, Mar. 11, 1865, KP; U.S. War Department, Adjutant General's Office, Special Order No. 146, Mar. 25, 1865, Brown Papers; Hill, diary, Mar. 10, 11, 1865; McMillen, diary, Mar. 11, 1865; Lonn, *Desertion,* 179–82.

15. Warren Keifer to Eliza Keifer, Feb. 21, 22, Mar. 5, 7, 1865, KP; McMillen, diary, Mar. 7, 1865.

16. Warren Keifer to Eliza Keifer, Mar. 9, 10, 1865, KP.

17. Warren Keifer to Eliza Keifer, Mar. 16, 17, 18, 1865, KP; Hill, diary, Mar. 17, 20, 1865.

18. Johnson and Buel, *Battles and Leaders,* 4:579–89; Keifer, *Four Years,* 2:188–89.

19. Keifer, *Four Years,* 2:188–89; Warren Keifer to Eliza Keifer, Mar. 25, 1865,

KP; Hill, diary, Mar. 25, 1865; John Rhoades to Sarah Rhoades, Mar. 28, 1865, Rhoades Papers; McCordick, *Kauffman*, 102; *SEN*, Apr. 5, 1865; Chris Calkins, *The Appomattox Campaign* (Conshohocken, Pa.: Combined Books, 1997), 45; Noah Andre Trudeau, *Out of the Storm* (New York: Little, Brown, 1994), 53–54; Trudeau, *Last Citadel*, 352.

20. *Roster*, 8:3, 36–39; McCordick, *Kauffman*, 102; Keifer to Keifer, Mar. 25, 1865; McMillen, diary, Mar. 25, 1865.

21. Warren Keifer to Eliza Keifer, Mar. 27, 1865, KP.

22. Foote, *The Civil War*, 3:863–67.

23. Keifer, *Four Years*, 2:189–91.

24. Ibid., 184–86; Foote, *The Civil War*, 3:865; Trudeau, *Last Citadel*, 366.

25. Keifer, *Four Years*, 2:192–95; *OR*, vol. 46:901–5; Calkins, *Appomattox Campaign*, 45; Trudeau, *Last Citadel*, 367–71.

26. Keifer, *Four Years*, 2:193–97; *OR*, vol. 46:791, 992–95, 1003–4, 1259–60; Warren Keifer to Eliza Keifer, Apr. 2, 1865, KP; McMillen, diary, June 11, 1865.

27. *OR*, vol. 46:993; Foote, *The Civil War*, 3:879–80; Keifer, *Four Years*, 2:195; Calkins, *Appomattox Campaign*, 46; Trudeau, *Out of the Storm*, 55; Trudeau, *Last Citadel*, 374–75.

28. Keifer, *Four Years*, 2:196; Keifer to Keifer, Apr. 2, 1865; Calkins, *Appomattox Campaign*, 46.

29. Hill, diary, Apr. 3, 1865.

30. Foote, *The Civil War*, 3:913–18; Calkins, *Appomattox Campaign*, 74, 89.

31. Foote, *The Civil War*, 3:915–19; Chris Calkins, *Thirty-Six Hours before Appomattox: The Battles of Sayler's Creek, High Bridge, Farmville, and Cumberland Church* (Farmville, Va.: *Farmville Herald*, 1980), 5–8; Calkins, *Appomattox Campaign*, 98–100, 105; Trudeau, *Out of the Storm*, 108–9.

32. Calkins, *Thirty-Six Hours*, 8–13; Calkins, *Appomattox Campaign*, 107–8; *OR*, vol. 46:905–7; Keifer, *Four Years*, 2:206–12; Trudeau, *Out of the Storm*, 108–9.

33. Calkins, *Thirty-Six Hours*, 11; Calkins, *Appomattox Campaign*, 108; Warren Keifer to Eliza Keifer, Apr. 7, 1865, KP; Keifer, *Four Years*, 2:207, 211; *OR*, vol. 46:979–80, 997–98, 1002–4; Trudeau, *Out of the Storm*, 109–10.

34. Keifer, *Four Years*, 2:209; Calkins, *Thirty-Six Hours*, 14; Calkins, *Appomattox Campaign*, 108–12; Keifer to Keifer, Apr. 7, 1865; Trudeau, *Out of the Storm*, 111–16.

35. Keifer, *Four Years*, 2:210; Keifer to Keifer, Apr. 7, 1865.

36. *OR*, vol. 46:907–8, 999.

37. Keifer, *Four Years*, 2:228; Hill, diary, Apr. 10, 13, 1865; John Rhoades to Sarah Rhoades, Apr. 10, 1865, Rhoades Papers.

38. Warren Keifer to Eliza Keifer, Apr. 15, 1865, KP; Hill, diary, Apr. 17, 19, 1865; McCordick, *Kauffman*, 104–5; John Rhoades to Sarah Rhoades, Apr. 17, 1865, Rhoades Papers.

39. Warren Keifer to Eliza Keifer, Apr. 17, 1865, KP; Charles Berry to Annie Hall, Apr. 18, 1865, Charles Berry Papers, Clark County Historical Society.

40. John Rhoades to Sarah Rhoades, Apr. 17, 24, 27, May 2, 9, 12, 1865, Rhoades Papers; Warren Keifer to Eliza Keifer, Apr. 22, 27, 1865, KP; McCordick, *Kauffman,* 106; Calkins, *Appomattox Campaign,* 188; Hill, diary, Apr. 23–27, 1865.

41. Warren Keifer to Eliza Keifer, Apr. 27, 30, May 2, 1865, KP.

42. Hill, diary, May 15, 21, 22, 1865; Warren Keifer to Eliza Keifer, May 16, 19, 1865, KP.

43. John Rhoades to Sarah Rhoades, May 28, 1865, Rhoades Papers.

44. Warren Keifer to Eliza Keifer, June 8, 1865, KP; Hill, diary, June 8, 1865; John Rhoades to Sarah Rhoades, June 8, 1865, Rhoades Papers; *SEN,* June 9, 1865.

45. Warren Keifer to Eliza Keifer, June 2, 5, 6, 8, 10, 1865, KP.

46. Charles Berry to Annie Hall, June 22, 1865, Berry Papers.

47. Warren Keifer to Eliza Keifer, June 22, 1865, KP; Hill, diary, June 25–30, 1865.

48. Rhoades to Rhoades, Apr. 10, 1865.

Bibliography

ARCHIVAL SOURCES

Clark County Historical Society, Springfield, Ohio.
  Luther Brown Papers
  Charles Berry Papers
  Civil War Miscellany
  J. Warren Keifer Papers
Greene County Public Library, Xenia, Ohio.
  Reminiscences of Lorenzo Barnhart
Library of Congress, Washington, D.C.
  J. Warren Keifer Papers
National Archives and Records Administration, Washington, D.C.
  J. Warren Keifer Papers
  Edwin H. Lamme Papers
Ohio Historical Society, Columbus.
  Baird Family Papers
  William R. Moore Papers
  John Patterson Papers
  State of Ohio Adjutant General Records
  Joshua Whiteman Papers
Rutherford B. Hayes Presidential Center, Fremont, Ohio.
  J. Warren Keifer Papers
  John R. Rhoades Papers
Troy Historical Society, Troy, Ohio.
  Josiah Hill Diary
U.S. Army Military History Institute, Carlisle, Pennsylvania.
  Francis M. McMillen Diary
Wright State University, Dayton, Ohio.
  John F. Rosser Papers

NEWSPAPERS

The Franklin (Ohio) Chronicle
Miami Valley (Ohio) News
Piqua (Ohio) Enquirer
Piqua (Ohio) Register
Springfield (Ohio) Evening News
Springfield (Ohio) Morning News
Springfield (Ohio) Republic
Troy (Ohio) Times
Xenia (Ohio) Torchlight

BOOKS, ARTICLES, AND OTHER SOURCES

Bates, Samuel P., ed. *History of Pennsylvania Volunteers.* Harrisburg, Pa.: B. Singerly, State Printer, 1869–71.

Beck, Brandon, and Charles Grunden. *Three Battles of Winchester.* Berryville, Va.: Country Publishers, 1988.

Buel, Clarence, and Robert Johnson. *Battles and Leaders of the Civil War.* 4 vols. New York: Charles Webster, 1888.

Calkins, Chris. *The Appomattox Campaign.* Conshohocken, Pa.: Combined Books, 1997.

———. *Thirty-Six Hours before Appomattox: The Battles of Sayler's Creek, High Bridge, Farmville, and Cumberland Church.* Farmville, Va.: *Farmville Herald,* 1980.

Casey, James B., ed. *Libby Prison Autograph Book.* Salt Lake City: Utah Genealogical Association, 1984.

Catton, Bruce. *Never Call Retreat.* Garden City, N.Y.: Doubleday, 1965.

———. *Stillness at Appomattox.* Garden City, N.Y.: Doubleday, 1953.

Chumney, Robert J., Jr. "Don Carlos Buell: Gentleman General." Ph.D. diss., Rice University, 1964.

Cooling, B. Franklin. *Monocacy: The Battle That Saved Washington.* Shippensburg, Pa.: White Mane, 1997.

Directory of Xenia, Ohio, and Greene County, 1892. Xenia, Ohio, 1892.

Edmondson's Xenia City Directory for 1875 and 1876. Xenia, Ohio, 1875.

Engle, Stephen D. "Generalship on Trial: Don Carlos Buell's Campaign to Chattanooga." In *Civil War Generals in Defeat,* edited by Steven Woodworth. Lawrence: University Press of Kansas, 1999.

Foote, Shelby. *The Civil War: A Narrative.* 3 vols. New York: Random House, 1974.

Geary, James W. *We Need Men: The Union Draft in the Civil War.* DeKalb: Northern Illinois Univ. Press, 1991.

Grant, Ulysses S. *Personal Memoirs of U. S. Grant.* 2 vols. New York: Charles L. Webster, 1886.

Griffith, Paddy. *Battle Tactics of the American Civil War.* New Haven, Conn.: Yale University Press, 1989.

Hesseltine, William. *Civil War Prisons.* Columbus: Ohio State University Press, 1930.

Horn, John. *The Petersburg Campaign: June 1864–April 1865.* Mechanicsburg, Pa., 1993.

Keifer, J. Warren. *Slavery and Four Years of War.* 2 vols. Springfield, Ohio: Republic Steam Press, 1900.

Lonn, Ella. *Desertion during the Civil War.* Boston: American Historical Association, 1928.

Mahr, Theodore. "'Another Union Victory!': The Confederate Army of the Valley at Cedar Creek, October 19, 1864." Master's thesis, Wright State University, 1988.

Maney, R. Wayne. *Marching to Cold Harbor.* Shippensburg, Pa.: White Mane, 1995.

McCordick, David. *The Civil War Letters (1862–1865) of Private Henry Kauffman: The Harmony Boys Are All Well.* New York: Edwin Mellen Press, 1991.

McPherson, James M. *Battle Cry of Freedom.* New York: Oxford University Press, 1989.

Moe, Richard. *The Last Full Measure: The Life and Death of the First Minnesota Volunteers.* New York: Henry Holt, 1993.

Ohio Adjutant General. *Official Roster of the Soldiers of the State of Ohio in the War of the Rebellion, 1861–1866.* 12 vols. Cincinnati: Ohio Valley Press, 1886–95.

Pope, Thomas E. "The Weary Boys: Colonel J. Warren Keifer and the 110th Ohio Volunteer Infantry." Master's thesis, Wright State University, 1998.

Priest, John Michael. *Nowhere to Run: The Wilderness, May 4th and 5th, 1864.* Shippensburg, Pa.: White Mane, 1995.

———. *Victory without Triumph: The Wilderness, May 6th and 7th, 1864.* Shippensburg, Pa.: White Mane, 1994.

Reid, Whitelaw. *Ohio in the War: Her Statesmen, Her Generals, and Soldiers.* 2 vols. Cincinnati: Moore, Wilstach, and Baldwin, 1868.

Rhea, Gordon. *The Battle of the Wilderness, May 5–6, 1864.* Baton Rouge: Louisiana State University Press, 1994.

———. *The Battles for Spotsylvania Court House and the Road to Yellow Tavern, May 7–12, 1864.* Baton Rouge: Louisiana State University Press, 1997.

Sears, Stephen. *George B. McClellan: The Young Napoleon.* New York: Ticknor and Fields, 1988.

Sheridan, Philip. *Personal Memoirs of P. H. Sheridan.* 2 vols. New York: Charles Webster, 1888.

Steere, Edward. *The Wilderness Campaign.* Harrisburg, Pa.: Stackpole, 1960.

Taylor, James E. *With Sheridan up the Shenandoah in 1864.* Cleveland: Western Reserve Historical Society, 1989.

Thackery, David T. *A Light and Uncertain Hold.* Kent, Ohio: Kent State University Press, 1999.

Trudeau, Noah Andre. *Bloody Roads South.* New York: Little, Brown, 1989.

———. *The Last Citadel: Petersburg, Virginia, June 1864–April 1865.* New York: Little, Brown, 1991.

———. *Out of the Storm, April–June 1865.* New York: Little, Brown, 1994.

U.S. War Department. *Atlas to Accompany the Official Records of the Union and Confederate Armies.* Washington: GPO, 1891–95.

———. *The War of the Rebellion: A Compilation of the Official Records of the Union and Confederate Armies.* 128 vols. Washington: GPO, 1880–1901.

Warner, Ezra. *Generals in Blue: Lives of the Union Commanders.* Baton Rouge: Louisiana State University Press, 1964.

Wert, Jeffry D. *From Winchester to Cedar Creek: The Shenandoah Campaign of 1864.* Carlisle, Pa.: South Mountain Press, 1987.

Wheeler, Thomas. *Troy: The Nineteenth Century.* Troy, Ohio: Troy Historical Society, 1970.

Wiggins and McKillop's Directory for Greene County for 1878. Wellsville, Ohio, 1878.

Wiley, Bell I. *The Life of Billy Yank.* New York: Bobbs-Merrill, 1952.

Williams's Xenia City Directory for 1870–71. Xenia, Ohio, 1870.

Xenia City and Greene County Directory, 1881. Xenia, Ohio, 1881.

Xenia City Directory. Xenia, Ohio, 1895.

Index

The Weary Boys

was designed and composed

by Christine Brooks

in 11/14 Adobe Garamond with display type in Latin Condensed

on a Macintosh G4 using PageMaker 6.5;

printed on 55# Supple Opaque stock

by Thomson-Shore, Inc. of Dexter, Michigan;

and published by

THE KENT STATE UNIVERSITY PRESS

Kent, Ohio 44242